L. B. Blacksmith

3 JAN 1925

fourth edition

L. B. Blacksmith

3 JAN 1925

fourth edition

to my loved ones

Acknowledgements

Thanks are due to

Alan Hall
for proofread assistance
during the first edition

Mary Goodwin
for proofreading the update
of the following editions

ISBN 978-0-9935417-4-2

Index

Prologue..5
The Westroyd Park..7

The Bible and the Satanic Verses....................9
Galileo was not Italian 41
Jason...61
The Transcript of the video [A10]...................77

Aisling...93
The Education Act 99
The French Revolution 125
The Headingley Literary Festival 151

Appendix..178

Overtime...249
From the Second Edition: Foreword....................249
From the Second Edition: Farewell......................250
Foreword to the third edition................................251
Cambridge's deception and Giulio Regeni............253

List of Images in Appendix...............................264
Index of names..265
Bibliography and further reading....................267

Prologue

English rendering of the leaflet posted in Italy after WWII (img 40). Original Italian leaflet (img 39) pag 247. From Wikipedia [W71].

CURIA OF THE BISHOP OF PIACENZA

AFTER THE DECREE OF THE HOLY OFFICE

NOTICE

IT IS SEVERE SIN TO:

1. Register as member of the Communist Party
2. Support in any way or to Vote for the Communist Party
3. Read Communist Publications
4. Distribute Communist Publications

Therefore one cannot receive absolution without repentance and firm disposition not to repeat

●

Whoever, registered or not to the Communist Party, who acknowledges the Marxist doctrine, Atheist and anti-Christian and propaganda such ideals, is

APOSTATES OF THE FAITH AND EXCOMMUNICATED

and can be absolved only by the Holy See

●

What said for the Communist Party is extended to the other parties making common cause with it

May God enlighten and have mercy of those sinners about so serious matter, because the eternal life is at risk

PIACENZA - 1949

The Westroyd Park

The Westroyd Park is a well-maintained public garden along the lane where I live. Random benches hide behind trees and bushes, and the singing of the birds stands above the roaring of the suburb around. I used to go there with my dog, like most of the people living nearby.

One of the familiar users of the park I used to see was an Irish woman, of about my age, with a small dog always on the move. Her name is Aisling, meaning, "dream" or "vision" in Irish, and from the time I came to know her I knew the solution for all my investigation was just clear crystal in her eye.

We loved chatting of Art and Humanities, Freedoms and Philosophies, but at the end we both knew our daily goal was to survive the rain, like the trees and the bushes in the park.

Not far from the bench where we used to sit, inside the Park is a prominent House with the Coats of Arms, and sometime we played pretending Charles Darwin or Isaac Newton was living there, fuelling mysteries in life and evolution, chemistry and astronomy.

Than, one day she came out with the idea of writing a book, something to remind us of our educated conversations. "We can name it 'The Catholic Satanic Verses'. I know you are after it! Came on!" she said, and since that day we have been searching for uncharted thoughts in education, assembling a map from the controversies that made our history since the ancient past, and the contradictions emerging from the textbooks.

Day-by-day, it was a point-to-point analysis, cleaning our education from false myths and parasites making their life out of our blood and our freedoms, and day-by-day meeting with Aisling become a part of my daily life.

Aisling was living a few minutes walk from the Park, with her dog Webster, and her love for him was unconditional; probably the only way she could be loved. This is the early impression I had.

Most of the time she was dressed in rough clothes, very cheap, almost to shield her beauty and sensitivity behind a misleading appearance, and that contrast was so attractive and disarming, so innocent, if the furrows of sorrow like scars and clouds were not to suggest a very different story.

"I know we have something in common, I feel it, but what is it?" I asked myself so many times but I never knew what was behind her tramp-like appearance. May be she was just a tramp, laughing at misery, or simply she was fickle and inconstant but for sure, I cannot doubt it, for a moment I felt her soul, coming close to me, and staying with me for a little while, companion.

The Bible and the Satanic Verses

That morning I made my way to the park earlier than usual but even so Aisling was already there, reading a magazine on the bench. Also the sun in the clear blue sky was promising a beautiful day, and my delight couldn't find any resistance.

"Hi" I said, "What a nice day for a walk in the Park, isn't it?"

"Oh, here you are. I have been waiting for you" she said, closing the magazine and looking up in my direction. "Do you remember the Satanic Verses [A1] of Salman Rushdie?' she asked, with a thoughtful expression. "Would that be possible to do the same controversy about the Bible?"

One of the gardeners was moving the soil around the flowers, and a delicate wind was carrying the perfumes all around, suggesting that our roots may also need some oxygen and attention.

"Sure it is possible," I said, "But already there exist several different versions of the Bible, also stating the opposite of each other, and this is the reason why the Bible is the most controversial book of all. Already there exist several different interpretations of the same text, and also there exist Bibles made of completely different text and meaning. There is no Version of the Bible absolutely true to pick on, like Rushdie did, but really there is a collection of different Bibles contradicting each other, and in this scenario what are Heresies and Blasphemies to some Christians, are Values and Holy Words to other Christians, and they would die for them."

"And what about the Satanic Verses of the Bible? Would that be possible?" she asked again, revealing some impatience and disappointment.

"Sure it is, but it is not exactly the same. For Rushdie it was possible to quote the Quran, but for the Bible [W1] [W7][W37] what version would you quote? I never heard of the Satanic Verses of the Bible but I am sure someone heard of it, even before the New Testament was ever assembled. For clarity, what would you take into consideration? The Old Testament is not an original Christian writing, and was made long before the arrival of Jesus, long before Christianity ever existed."

"I know this. I know the Old Testament resemble the Tanakh, the Bible of the Jew. No, I don't mean the Genesis, or the Old Testament" she said, "I mean the true original Christian Bible, which is the New Testament with the Gospels of the Apostles."

"Yes but, even if we admitted that Jesus really existed, and was the Son of God, even with this concession if you consider 8 Apostles out of 12 have been wiped out of the New Testament, how could you take into consideration the authenticity of it? Each of the Apostles was a messenger divulging the life of Jesus, this is what the Apostles were all about, advocates and teachers of the new Christian Religion. Each of the Apostles has been narrating and divulged the life of Jesus, and passed on his memories in writing, by himself, or by witnesses or disciples. Each of them had records in writing of their direct memories, with the personal experience and the episodes of the life of Jesus they have witnessed. I believe each of the Apostles had his own Gospel, one way or another, like also Judas and Mary Magdalene had their own, but many more were made. So? How is it now, that there are only 4 Gospels in the New Testament of the Bible? In reality, most of the original Christian experience has been wiped out from the New Testament, and from what is left over it will be difficult to find any Satanic Verses never pointed out before. Unless..."

"Right, I got it" she said, taking over. "There is no comparison with the Satanic Verses, but the controversial points are charted within the several different versions and interpretations of the Bible. And what about listing these differences? Would that make sense in terms of the Satanic Verses?" she asked.

"Perhaps, but the essence of the Satanic Verses of the

Bible concerns Philosophy more than Religion, and will go far beyond the interpretation of a few words of the Bible. The meaning of the Satanic Verses of the Bible is not to be found in any version of the Bible, because the matter is not one of Religion but of Philosophy, pushing the intellectual limits of human conscience and comprehension far beyond the limits of the blind belief of Religion. The true heresies don't concern Religion, however we interpret the Bible or the New Testament, but rather concern philosophical doubts and the freedom of having a personal opinion, the freedom of thought, the freedom for curiosity and knowledge, and never mean the Bible or Religion. Eventually one may dispute the arrogance of some intolerant Religious authority pretending to be infallible [W2] and to talk in the name of God, but also in this case the heresies don't concern the Bible but what people do in the name of their Religion.

If you are after the backbone of Christianity, and require an intellectual compass to find secure directions concerning the essence and disputes over the New Testament, you should ask yourself what the Catholic Heresies are, and how the Catholic Heresies could become Catholic Legacy?"

"What?" she asked, with a look of surprise. "What are the Catholic Heresies? And why? The original Christian Legacy is in the New Testament, I can understand that, but I meant the Christian Satanic Verses, not just the Catholic ones. Why the Catholic Heresies now? What is it? Witches and magic?" she asked again, not sure about my answer.

"Because the different Christian Cults have different Values, and the values for one person may be heresies and blasphemies for someone else: Christianity doesn't share the same values. On the other hand the Catholic Heresies are essential to see how the Christian Cults unfolded along the centuries. The Roman Catholic Church has the list of all the heresies they have persecuted throughout history, and from that list it would be easier to see the differences and the Moral Values in discussion, with Saint Peter or Martin Luther perhaps. Forget the strictly religious and theological matters like the nature of God and the Trinity; there are much more important issues to disclose, important to all and not to the believers only."

"What is it?" she asked confused. "What may be more important than God, in religious matters?"

"Actually there are a few things, like freedom of thought and Justice perhaps, but also Science, Philosophy and the Arts. Over time Religion has become a cultural filter, an instrument of Cultural and Social Control, and this is exactly what happened with Constantine and the Nicaea Council."

"You are complicating things," she warned, "I understand from the Catholic perspective the Catholic Heresies are Satanic Verses, but this is a Catholic matter. How does it affect the others?" she asked.

"Take this case for example, where does the Morality of Justice come from? Is it from the codes of the law, or from the Bible? Who is to decide what Justice is, and who is to administer Justice? The men on earth with the codes of the law, or is it rather God in the afterlife? Is it tolerable for someone to pretend to have High Moral Values above the law? Can we expect some Human Justice on earth, or do we necessarily have to wait for God because his disciples pretend the Law of Man is not the true law to obey and rather live outside the law, like a bunch of mobsters and gangsters. Also the Racial Laws of Mussolini had the blessing of the Pope, in writing, justified by the Moral Leadership of the Pope. In other words, is God an excuse to justify and get away with abuses, crimes, genocides and intellectual cleansing? Do you see? Religion is interfering with the Civic values of Equality, with Morality and the social Justice to which all people have the same rights, freedoms and obligations despite their belief or Religion."

"Oh, yes" she said, "Of course I can see. The Divine Justice of God is far above the human laws and justice. It is a dispute concerning the relative value of man, compared to the absolute value of God. But it is also a dispute undermining the value of the law and equality, and breaking society apart."

"Yes, exactly. The magnitude of the Cultural devastation that came with Christianity was immense, from Philosophy to the Sciences and the Arts, for millennia until today. Justice is not the only problem, but only one of the aspects. Put the case of Eratosthenes, calculating the circumference of earth 300 years before Jesus was born, 1800 years before the birth of Copernicus. Imagine if you looked in the school textbooks and found no mention of Eratosthenes, but only the modern heroes Copernicus and Galileo. Imagine that the schoolbooks represent the Nicaea Council as a milestone in shaping our current culture and values, while in reality it could only represent the beginning of the dark ages, the foundation of the Catholic Inquisition forewarning the incoming censorship and revisionism we witness in our current schoolbooks.

How could you or anybody explain how the Catholic Heresies became Catholic Legacy? And, if not Philosophy, or Justice or Science, what about the revisionism of the New Testament, vanishing 8 out of 12 Apostles? What is the magnitude of the devastation, and the intellectual cleansing behind all of this? Imagine that the School Programs disregard the Catholic Heresies as marginal aspects of History. Who may be the mastermind behind this System of Values?

No, the Catholic Heresies don't concern witches and magic, and still today are important even more then we could imagine. We start from the prejudice and preconceptions we learn as mandatory part of the school syllabus. What matter if we glorify Copernicus, or Galileo, if Eratosthenes was erased from history and we cannot even ask the reasons why he was cancelled, like he was a Devil? So I wonder how the Catholic Heresies became Catholic Legacy, including Justice, Philosophy, Science, and the Arts. But above all I wonder about the probability, the likelihood nobody ever asked such simple questions. I wonder, who is to pass the exams? I wonder if the best students, the most inquisitive, have a chance to pass the exams. Is it possible nobody ever asked, and nobody ever noticed such inconsistencies?"

"I understand what you mean. Yes, it is very sad" she agreed, looking at the notes. "This is a version of the truth from the school books; but we know the disciples were not 4, and this is also the reason for the notes we are collecting, pointing out some reflections concerning our expensive education, isn't it?"

"Yes. In my perspective I wish we had a kind of anti-virus or a debugging tool for our school textbooks; a documented reflection to scan and counterbalance the monotony and the contradictions of our education. On the other hand it must be educational, it has to be reasonable and invite reflection; it cannot be just a mockery of the misery of the best education we could buy. It must be substantiated with evidence beyond doubt.

Take this case, this is not in the schoolbooks either. When the early Christians arrived in Rome, Rome was a polytheistic town with its own Gods, and more Gods arrived from all over the provinces. The religious tradition of Rome was polytheism, the Gods were coexisting peacefully, and one God more or less did not make any difference until the Christians arrived, with the pretence that the law of Rome was not the true law to obey but there would be another law to obey above it. The Christians were pretending to have higher moral values, above the law, as if morality and Justice were not to be found in the law but in the Gospels. So, the Christians were in the Coliseum with the lions, not because of religious intolerance but because of their pretence that the law of Rome was not the true law to obey. The religious persecution of the Christians is fiction. Rome was a polytheistic town and didn't have any problem with the Christian God. It was the disrespectful habit of the Christians causing social disorders, undermining of the Law and offending other Cults and Cultures. We can also see today, that this habit has not changed throughout history."

"I see. But, for what reason was Jesus crucified?" she asked.

"Pretty much for this very same reason. Because in the

words of Jesus the law of Rome was not the true law to obey, but there would be another law to obey above it. Nevertheless, in ancient Rome, the pre-Christian Gods from all over the provinces were coexisting peacefully and sharing their powers for the public good. Until the Christians arrived, with Monotheism and their Moral Supremacy."

"Moral Supremacy? What is that?" she asked.

"It is a long story concerning the Supremacy of the Pope, the Bishop of Rome [W60], among the other bishops. It concerns the Moral and Cultural Leadership of the Roman Tradition of Christianity. The foundation of this Primacy, or Supremacy, may be found in Matthew, when Jesus said, "You are Peter, and upon this rock I will build my Church" (Matthew 16:17-19) [B1]. It was Jesus himself who appointed Peter, and for this reason Saint Peter's Square was made in the Vatican, just in front of the Basilica of Saint Peter. For this reason the Roman Church claims a kind of supremacy, because Saint Peter was in Rome and started it. On the other hand the Primacy, or Supremacy, of Rome was also one of the causes of the schism with the Orthodox tradition, which was unwilling to respect absolute obedience to Rome in matters of Religion; it was another problem dividing more and more the eastern part of the Roman Empire. More recently this very same Moral Supremacy was also adopted by Mussolini to justify the Cultural Supremacy and the Racial Laws he enacted to persecute Apostates and Heretics."

"The Racial Laws of Mussolini." she said repeating.

"It was a cultural regime, with its foundation in the Moral pre-eminence of the religious tradition. It was the Church to prepare and provide the Syllabus, and Mussolini simply embraced the Catholic Tradition. He signed the Lateran Treaty with the Vatican, and then, to enforce the Catholic Culture and Tradition against the new political parties demanding no more High Moral Values above the Law, he endorsed the Catholic Education and enacted the Racial Laws, all with the blessing of the Pope [W3]. But primarily the Racial Laws were Cultural Laws, against democrats, liberals, socialists, against every political party supporting the secular values of democracy.

It was a proper intellectual cleansing, a holy war against the values of democracy and the freedom of information.

The 3rd January 1925 [A34][W73] Mussolini made a speech for the murder of the member of parliament Giacomo Matteotti [W74] and with that speech he said that the democratic values had to be found within the Catholic tradition. Then the same day he dismissed the parliament, the freedom of press, the political parties, and persecuted the oppositions as apostates of the faith and enemies of the state.

But no fascist was ever able to state one of these democratic values that would be of Catholic legacy, in fact the democratic values like the freedom of choice and the secular value of justice are the result of the emancipation from the absolute power of the church [W42], and have never been Catholic values but Catholic heresies, and have been persecuted throughout history and continue to this day.

In 1860 the Italian Unification and the Monarchy ended the despotic tyranny of the Absolute Power of the Church. In 1929 Mussolini reinstated the Vatican City [A35][W3], and the alternative system of values transforming the perjury of public officers into acts of devotion and career opportunities.

Still today the students of the bishops can have recommendations for diplomas and degrees they never had, and manage to feel honest with it even after the scam is public knowledge. On the other hand, legitimate students cannot have confirmation of their true academic careers from Italian state universities and their lawsuits are swept into the afterlife. The Minister for Justice reported a backlog of over 9.000.000 legal cases and the reason for this systematic disruption of people rights is to be found in the alternative system of values and the tradition of bribery and blackmail, administrative horrors, perjury and defamation they organise as institutions.

The ancient pre-Christian Romans used to nick name

the Catholic as barbarians and sociopaths because of their pretence to be above the law and to undermine other people's rights. Several hundred years later they put this privilege in the Bible, and tried to find followers for their system of abuses, and made Peter and the apostles talk concerning the law of man saying, «But Peter and the Apostles answered, 'We must obey God rather than man'» [B3].

The problem is not only the hundreds and thousands of sexual abuses they perpetrate, but the millions of students they indoctrinate into their double-standard and alternative system of values.

Like Cecile Kyenge and Giulio Regeni we know from the news, and the many thousands they represent, Ministers and consultants of the govern concerning sensitive matter like the democratic values and people rights.

Cecile Kyenge [A15][A16][W48] admitted during a television interview she knew she had no rights for the documents she was asking, that means she had the perception of wrong doing, but nothing compared to the greed and complicity with the democratic mission of the bishop helping whatever idiot was willing to feel comfortable with the recommendations for diplomas and degrees he never had.

Similarly, the mother of Giulio Regeni [A30][W64] is seeking the secular Justice she undermined from the start, with the recommendations of the bishop for diplomas and degrees Giulio actually never had. Giulio in Italy only completed the compulsory education at 13 years of age and then, after 2 years of college in the oratory of the bishop in New Mexico he was at Oxford and then Cambridge consulting the Think Tank and the Oxford Analytica. He was on a holy mission, like Tony Blair and Cambridge Analytica, and the mastermind they represent so well with their actions.

In the end the crucifix in the courtrooms will transform the perjuries and abuses into acts of devotions and career opportunities, in the name of the alternative system of value they impose above the law and people rights.

The 3rd January 1925 [A34][W73] Mussolini said that the democratic values had to be found within the Catholic tradition, and still today almost 100 years later the parliament, the universities, the news, are all doing exactly the same and for the same reasons. There are plenty of 'good' Catholics from all over the world willing to feel honest with the recommendations of the bishop for diplomas and degrees they never had, and willing to return any favour for it.

But Mussolini didn't need to invent any 'Roman Supremacy', it was already there, but at the time of Saint Peter, when the New Testament of the Bible didn't exist at all, the Moral Supremacy was just word of mouth of St Matthew, he put in writing.

Also a few centuries later, at the time of Constantine and the Nicaea Council, Christianity was still completely undefined and inconsistent; it was literally a word of mouth Religion. From the start, early Christianity was a chaotic proliferation of prophets, different Gospels, different stories about Jesus, and different ways to pray. Then, all these differences become roots for different Religious Cults, turning differences into divisions. So, the need to define how to pray and what to pray, the need to define the liturgy, the theology and the doctrine of the new Cult was increasingly important in order to maintain unity inside the new Cult, but also inside the Roman Empire. In fact the Christian pretence to be above the law and above the other Cults fuelled social disorders, and was undermining the authority of the law. So Constantine took the decision to help the process of definition of the new Cult, he set up the Nicaea Council in 325 AD, and in 331 AD he commissioned Eusebius of Caesarea to prepare 50 copies of The Bible from the original writings available at his time." [W5] [W6] [W7]

"So, there was a Bible at the time of Constantine" she said, expectantly.

"Well, Constantine probably wanted to read the Holy Scriptures, but there was no Bible available; nobody before thought to make a Bible out of the Holy Scripture, to preserve them, and today the Bible of Eusebius is not available because all 50 copies are lost. Now it is impossible to know how many books more were available in terms of Gospels and original writings that have been vanished later on, all together with the Bibles of Eusebius."

"It is hard to believe, but somehow I am not surprised. The most adored book of all, to vanish in thin air. I was actually expecting something like this from the time you said the Catholic Cult was undefined, and the Bible was a pile of different versions and interpretations of something so actually we can say it never existed" she said again, with a baffling smile.

"Well, I am not inventing anything. I am just reporting some contradictions, evidence the schoolbooks partially introduce but never unveil or disclose properly. Anyway, sometime after Constantine the Cult probably changed again because the old Canons didn't fit the new needs anymore. With time, some books become more important than others, some become inappropriate and have been judged heretical and purged from the Bible as have most of those by the Apostles.

Play this game. One of the points in discussion at the Nicaea Council [W39] was the syllabus, the duration and the program of the catechism in preparation for the sacrament of the Baptism. Clearly the course had a few prerequisites, like students being able to learn and reply in conscience to some easy questions, but nowadays children are baptized at a few weeks of age, and clearly the Act of Choice is not necessary anymore. So, what do you believe may have happened to the Gospels demanding the Act of Choice as a prerequisite for the Baptism? What do you think about the missing Gospels? Bit by bit, from the personal and spiritual experience it once was, Christianity has become the pile of impositions it is now, enforced by Canon Laws [W8], the laws made by the Church, in the name of God. Will they ever understand that the Law of the Church is not the true law to obey, and that there is another law to obey above it?

After the Nicaea Council in 325 A.D. the disputes

between the Bishops of the East and West parts of the Roman Empire went on and on, concerning who to pray, and how to pray. Several more Councils have been organized, changing roles and Canons until Christianity become what it is today. But despite several Councils having been organized, the problem concerning true Christianity was never resolved because freedom of conscience has never been tolerated, and the points of the disputes become new Canons, new Laws and new Dogmas, absolute impositions of the Bishop of Rome pretending to have a better understanding of God. Later on, in 1276 A.D., after ages of controversies and disputes, Gregory X [W9] set up the procedure of the 'Conclave' for the election of the Roman Pope because the bishops everywhere were self-electing and self-proclaiming Popes, probably to wind up the Roman pretence of being the only Pope accredited in heaven. Obviously the coexistence of bishops and Popes excommunicating each other was causing even more divisions and schisms within Christianity, so the necessity to structure and discipline the new Cult was really a major problem not only for Constantine but even more for his successors. This situation lasted for a long time, and the Pope John Paul II [W10] in 2001 made the last update to the 'Annuario Pontificio', the Pontifical yearbook with Official List of the Popes of the Roman Catholic Church, adding almost 200 corrections. This is nowadays, isn't it?"

"Wow. I see what you mean about word of mouth and High Moral Values above the law," she said enlightened.

"Just imagine the First Vatican Council was organized in 1869 [W2], at the time of Italian unification, and on that occasion the Pope proclaimed himself infallible. Just consider the arrogance of this moralist above the law. But the point I was to discuss was that, with Constantine and after him, the new Roman Christian Cult gained more and more power and privileges until it was imposed in all provinces as the official Christian Religion of the Empire."

"And what about the early Roman Christian Religion, when Saint Peter and Paul were in Rome? Was it really different from now?" she asked.

"There are several differences, and sure I cannot list them all. First I would say that Rome was a polytheistic town, and the Gods from all over the Empire were coexisting peacefully and sharing their power. But obviously this is not the case of the God of Saint Peter, which was rather challenging for the exclusive worship and seeding the high moral values of the holy war we witness today.

Another very important difference concerns the lost Gospels; in fact more than 50 Gospels [W12][W13] of the Gnostic Tradition have been rejected by the Catholic Church, but many more have been rejected and vanished, besides those of Saint Peter, Mary Magdalene and Judas.

Don't you wonder why in the New Testament there are only 4 Gospels? And what happened to the others? The Gospel of Peter was condemned as heretical by 200 A.D., and probably the reasons all these Gospels went missing are to be found in the list of the Catholic Heresies, the Index of the Roman Catholic Inquisition, the only Book we can rely on in order to understand the History and the values of Christianity along with the History of the Catholic Church. Keep in mind these are the very same reasons we have a number of Bibles today, stating the opposite of each other."

"Are you sure about the Gospel of Saint Peter" she asked, with an expression of disbelief.

"I wouldn't tell you, if I were not sure. I believe you can find this also in Wikipedia" [W14] I said again reassuring.

"Right. I understand how the Catholic Heresies may help tracking the Satanic Verses of the Bible; I mean the New Testament. The Values and Morality through the different Christian Cults are not the same and have changed throughout history. Yes, the Catholic Heresies well represent a big part of the Satanic Verses of the Bible, and the different versions of the Bible we have today well represent the moral dissent, the moral rebellion against the Roman Church. That pile of different Bibles really stands like a pile of complaints to the Roman Morality, isn't it?"

she asked.

"Yes it is. That pile of Bibles is standing exactly like a pile of complaints" I repeated returning the smile, "That happened because Christianity at its origin was a spiritual experience, was a private experience, was a personal matter of conscience but during the time it become more and more materialistic, ruled by more and more legal procedures and Canon Laws until it become the instrument of Cultural and Social Control it is today.

But at the time of Saint Peter the relationship between God and Men was a personal direct relationship, a personal matter of conscience, and the prayers didn't need a middleman like a priest to intercede to God on their behalf. Saint Peter himself would have perceived the imposition of uncritical obedience a monstrosity, annihilating the personal Act of Choice and Will of the worshipper, and would have condemn the suffocating of personal feelings, precluding the possibility to express and share the inner personal beliefs.

Take the case of Arius and the Arian controversy concerning the nature of the relationship between God and Jesus, the Father and the Son. The controversy found its conclusion during the First Ecumenical Council of Nicaea, when Arius was put to the stake because of his personal belief. Arius was sharing his sincere feelings, but the main reasons to organize the Nicaea Council was not to dispute any controversy, but to stop the Religious disputes all together and for consequence Arius was sacrificed to the Catholic God of Obedience. In other words, it was not the Trinity to be upset by the miscomprehensions of Arius, but the expectations of the Roman Catholic priests demanding absolute obedience.

The Nicaea Council was just about Control and Obedience, and no personal feelings or understanding were needed anymore. So, by the time of the first Nicaea Council in 325 AD the original spirituality of Christianity was already downgraded to Heresy, a blasphemy to be persecuted and eradicated from Christian History, like most of the Gospels.

The execution of Arius is maybe the first execution at the stake of the Inquisition, but Arius is not the first in the list of the heretics because a few happened before. About 150 years before Nicaea, Saint Peter was already dead but his Gospel was accused of Heresy, for similar reasons to Arius. But Saint Peter was appointed by Jesus to be the First Stone of his Church, and for this reason it is truly Saint Peter who deserves the honour of being the Father of all the Heretics. The execution of Arius was to set the standard for the next centuries and millennia until today, but concerning the honour of launching the long tradition of heresies, that is for Saint Peter himself, the Apostle chosen by Jesus to build his Church.

I worry about being unclear; does it emerge that the Roman Catholic Church has a serious issue with the freedom of conscience of the prayers? Especially the act of being conscious of having a personal opinion is particularly perceived as rebellion against their will and insubordination. But freedom of conscience is part of Human nature, it is built in the nature of mankind, and the pretence of eradicating the freedom of conscience from the human nature is really undermining the Divine Nature of the Creation they pray for. They don't respect the laws of the Creation of their God, they don't respect the Human Nature for what it is, and they don't respect the laws they made and then change at will to better suit them. From wherever you start, Justice, Philosophy, the Science or the Arts, it always turn up the same censorship and revisionism, a pile of nonsense, contradictions, abuses and intellectual cleansing of biblical proportions, with the stamps of the infallibility of the Pope on it [W2].

Definitively, the Roman Catholic Cult is not concerned about the personal spiritual experience of the faithful, but Obedience and Cultural control. That was the reason for Constantine, to keep the Empire Culturally United, and for the same reason after Constantine the Roman Religion has gained more and more power within the Imperial offices, it was levelled and made equal to the Imperial administration, and finally the administration of the Priests took over the offices of the Roman Empire itself, which probably collapsed suffocated by the high moral values above the Laws and Culture of Rome."

"I understand, it is clear that freedom of thought is truly part of Human nature, not like the Roman Catholic Cult. The freedom of conscience is built in, but Religion is not, and different people have different ideas and the same freedom to believe it" she said again.

"Sure, a human friendly Religion should respect the freedom of conscience, and if we frame the Christianity of Saint Peter [W15], also for the founder of the Catholic tradition was inadmissible, unacceptable to baptize a child unable to understand and to choose with a Free Act of Choice and Will. On the other hand we know that at the time of the Nicaea Council the Gospel of Saint Peter was already condemned as heretical, because of docetism [W16] a heresy concerning the true nature of Jesus, similar to Arius, and later also the few remaining fragments have been rejected as apocryphal. Today only a few words survive of the Gospel of Peter, and we cannot read it anymore.

Also from the minutes of the Nicaea Council we see one of the points in discussion was the catechism, the course in preparation for the Baptism. It is implicit students of the course had to be capable of some understanding, and were not a few weeks old like children baptized today. We know for sure Saint Peter was practicing a different Christianity, and like Arius, Saint Peter would also have been condemned by the Nicaea Council to the stake of the inquisition, maybe because of Heresy but overall because Peter was appointed by Jesus, but not by the Romans.

It is obvious. After Saint Peter the Roman Christian Cult was changed, and after Constantine and the Nicaea Council it was changed again and again, and never in favour of individual spirituality, or the personal experience of the faithful. With time, Roman Christianity became an instrument of social and cultural control, and the pretence of being above the law become a reason of state and was never resolved, like the issue with freedom of conscience was never resolved, despite this freedom being prearranged and built in by the book of nature.

At the time of the Pre-Christian Romans the Gods didn't challenge each other for exclusive worship but rather coexisted peacefully and shared their powers for the public good. The provinces of the Roman Empire used to trade with Rome and maintain their local cultures and deities, but when the imposition of the Roman Catholic Cult arrived, that made it all different, leading to the quick dissolution and collapse of the Empire. The monotheism transformed the Empire into a collection of Barbarians, pagans and heretics to be converted or scrapped."

"Are you saying that Christianity is the cause of the collapse of the Roman Empire?" she asked, with an expression like she couldn't believe it.

"Several reasons are listed by historians. Maybe we can check if any Christian ever listed Christianity within the causes of the fall of the Roman Empire. Nevertheless, with the arrival of Christianity, Roman Culture was changed, the meaning of Justice also changed, the administration changed, freedom in Science, Philosophy, also the meaning of Religion was changed, introducing cultural intolerance and the Holy War of monotheism. Clearly the imposition of Christianity has transformed the Roman Provinces into a collection of heathens and heretics to be converted, but I am sure this is nothing to do with the fall of the Roman Empire, which is still living today through the Christian tradition, or at least this is the opinion of some distinguished historians, very devoted and accredited in the most prestigious Universities. Despite it is apparent they confuse the Catholic Heresies as Catholic Legacy.

Concerning historians and archaeologists we can quote 'Forbidden Archaeology', by Michael Cremo and Richard Thompson [A3][W17]. In their book Cremo and Thompson investigate the mysteries hiding in the underground of the museums, of human fossils hundreds of thousand years old. They also discuss the Knowledge Filter, the method and the process the scientists use to investigate, interpret, and finally confirm the Archaeological findings. Well, apparently, several Archaeological discoveries are stocked in the underground of museums, inaccessible to visitors, because these findings don't support or cannot be explained within the paradigm of the predominant theory, and as consequence are disregarded and abandoned simply because they cannot be explained from the perspective of our culture and our knowledge. Apparently our scientists are only after reassuring confirmations. Do you remember we spoke before about this book, a few days ago?"

"Yes" she said, "We have also seen a documentary on YouTube, and I remember Cremo saying that the «Archaeologists and anthropologists have covered up as much evidences as they dug up, literally» [A4.1]. Thompson was complaining about the existence of a «Knowledge Filter» [A4.2], and made the example of a «colander» for knowledge, but at the same time he said, «It is not a deliberate conspiracy in the sense of some people getting together in a smoky room and saying, we are going to deceive people» [A4.3]. And then? Are we supposed to believe this Knowledge Filter is random, or casual, and happens by chance, without nobody actually doing it?"

"Cremo and Thompson said the cause of this Knowledge Filter is to be found in the confirmation bias, the mechanism of confirmation and agreement of scientists within the scientific community. But this is really funny because this bias originates from the schoolbooks. It is the writers of the schoolbooks who confirm each other and vanish the findings not substantiating the high moral values of their education. It is the cultural and knowledge backgrounds interfering with the process of interpreting and understanding new information, in this case the new findings, attributing inappropriate meanings and values. Like in the case of the Nicaea Councils, if you ask them, they will tell you that it was nothing to do with Roman Censorship but the beginning of our contemporary western civilization. Nevertheless the Knowledge Filters are made by the law, are enforced by the law, and the schoolbooks and the Nicaea Councils are just examples of this process. The Nicaea Councils represent the early Acts of Moral Supremacy of the new Roman Christian Religion, imposing the pre-eminence of Religion above the Morality of the Law of Man."

"Do you believe in God?" she asked.

"Claiming, or pretending to have some comprehension or certainty of the existence of God, I would perceive myself very arrogant. If God ever existed, He would be far beyond our imagination. I'm feeling agnostic, and believe that God is just another temptation from the unknown around us. The universe is so precise compared to the Bible it is hard to believe both are from the same artist. My Bible is the Cosmos, the outer space of gasses and galaxies. Concerning the Bible of the missing Gospels I am not sure, but concerning God, if He ever existed, if He really made us, why did He give us the freedom of thought, if we didn't need it?"

"You said God is a temptation. I like temptations. Good luck God made them!" she said smiling. "Temptations are essentials, and also the Satanic Verses are temptations, aren't they?"

"Yes they are, but even the best temptations of God were powerless without a woman. In the Bible, also the snake and the apple were unconvincing and unable to seduce without a woman, and Eve is portrayed like a tempting redhead, like you."

"I was," she said smiling, "but now I am going white, you see?"

"It makes your eyes stand out even more. This is not a compliment; I really like your eyes so much I cannot explain."

"What is wrong with my eyes?" she asked.

"Your eyes are a beautiful gift; there is nothing wrong with your eyes, but 'Complete Heterochromia' is a masterpiece of the Book of Nature. Your eyes challenge the unfeasible, and make it real. I like your eyes for what they represent, an instance of the impossible made real by the book of nature. I have never met a person with the eyes of two different colours, one blue eye, and the other eye green. It is a case of complete heterochromia but it doesn't matter. This is nature, claiming her freedom of speech. How could I believe the Bible more than the beauty of nature? Your eyes make a mockery of the impossible, and make the least of chances factual and real. This is what I see in your eyes, the impossible chance made real by the book of Nature."

"Maybe, but I know you can do better than flattery" she said. "Do you know what? Probably we should talk more about temptations; it would be more interesting also for the students. In the end, also temptations are part of Creation, aren't they? It is probably the most interesting part of life, and students may like it more than the tricky nonsense of the school programs."

"Yes, you are right, but temptations are not missing from the Bible, not like the freedom of choice, and most of the Apostles. But you are right; we cannot forget temptations, and especially your eyes. And you? What is tempting you most?"

"Oh, I live day by day. I don't know my temptations of tomorrow, but I know I have been tempted by your stories. Knowledge is tempting, and curiosity is probably the heart of all the temptations. We should talk more about taboos. What's wrong with physical pleasure, and Hedonism? And what's wrong with sex? How could possibly sex be a sin? What would Humanity be without sex? On the other hand, isn't it clear that creation supposes incest from the start? Furthermore, in accord with the early versions of the Genesis, Adam and Eve had only three male sons; what monstrosity is this? What am I supposed to believe, we descend from the mystery of the homosexual conception? How could humanity exist without women, and without sex from the start? And what about 'Free Love' to separate the State from sexual matters? Why do men have a harem, and women don't? Why cannot we have a group marriage, with a few men and women all married together? And what about female priests? What High Moral Values may a man have more than a woman? And what about the Magdalene laundries [W49]? What about the nuns and the sexual abuses of the priests? What about the freedom of choice for abortion? Why women are paid less than men, for the same job of a man? What is this, Magdalene laundries legacy? Now you tell me, who really is on the cross, a man or a woman?" she asked in a rush, with the understanding she was not to have an answer, not different from the abuses and violence she was listing. "Who is on the cross, a man or a woman?" she asked again, repeating, but I was already buried in my thoughts. For a long time I was considering writing the Catholic Satanic Verses, but during all this time I have never questioned myself about the feminine part of it. The female part of the Catholic Satanic Verses was missing, and maybe this is the reason I was unsure, and never moved any further from the notes I was collecting since long before Aisling arrived.

She was right, despite my attempt to put myself in her shoes, I could have never imagined what she could have wanted, needed, felt or said. The freedom of choice was lurking through her eyes now, the eyes of her freedom, and the essence of her was fading away, inaccessible, something I could have never reached or comprehended. She became a figment incarcerated in the confines of my imagination, but could I be a gaoler? I asked myself, until I saw her freedom coming to me through her freedom, sitting next to me on the bench, so I could see her view, and she reappeared again as the only actor on the stage, the only flower in the Park I loved to listen to.

"Yes the Church and the female gender is another issue of biblical proportions" I said, back in this world, "Probably to be consistent on the cross there should have been a woman from the start" I said smiling, but she didn't reply to my teasing.

"If there is any Knowledge or Cultural Filter, and we know it is, Religion plays a major role in building it. We should list a few more examples of Knowledge Filter, shaping the national system of values and its meritocracy, the values in which society is educated. This is a set up for guinea pigs!"

"Definitely. Starting from the freedom of conscience of having a personal opinion, in philosophy, cosmology, science and arts. I already have a few questions to ask, you know. There is no doubt, in education religion is more influential than the State, and Justice is not to be found in the Laws of the Sate but in the afterlife."

"Yes, so how do we do this?" she queried.

"Well, concerning the Cultural and Knowledge filter we can quote the Forbidden Archaeology, listing the waste of Archaeological findings, but I doubt we will ever find any quote explaining how the Catholic Heresies become Catholic Legacy. Eventually we can quote a few pages from the Wikipedia, to introduce a few Historical figures like Eratosthenes, Constantine or the Bible of Eusebius of Caesarea."

"Yes but the most of Wikipedia is made by students copying the schoolbooks on the Internet. Furthermore, it is not really possible to quote Wikipedia because the text is unstable, and the Universities don't accept it as a reliable source. What help may be from Wikipedia?"

"If someone likes more documentation, Wikipedia offers a bibliography and someone may continue his exploration, but the most of our writing should be put into a few simple self-explanatory questions. We should make easy questions, and then, if the readers cannot find an answer, not from Wikipedia, and not from the reliable sources of the Universities, then they have to think with their own head, and with that we made our point. What could we do more than this? We are not responsible for all of this; we are just snooping around for uncharted thoughts in Education, don't you remember?" I asked smiling.

"What questions have you in mind?" she asked rolling the pen on the notebook.

"I would like to ask how the Catholic Heresies become Catholic Legacy" I replied promptly. "Because for the students to understand this question they have to think with their own head, and this is important. They have to experience the contradictions of their textbooks; they have to learn to use their own heads, and not just be obedient, and repeat like parrots everything they are told."

"Yes but this question needs an explanation because the schoolbooks don't even mention what the Catholic Heresies are, and Wikipedia is no different."

"We said something about, introducing the Catholic Heresies; it shouldn't take more than what we already said. The point is not in listing the heresies analytically one by one, but to highlight a few examples, a few contradictions, and reflect on them, to explore the connections, consequences and implications."

"And then, what is there more to say?" she asked again.

"There is evidence of millennia of abuses, and we can only scratch the surface. We can list a few inconsistencies from our schoolbooks, showing that the cultural revisionism of the Nicaea Council is still ruling the society of today, but the list of the abuses perpetrated by the Catholic Church in history is immense and we cannot pretend to do a complete list. One man's entire lifetime wouldn't be enough to catalogue all the devastation, the cultural and intellectual revisionism that came with Christianity; we can only introduce a few characters like Eratosthenes, Aristarchus of Samos, or Hypatia, and then the Nicaea Council flattening the Earth for millennia. But freedom of thought, curiosity and temptations are built in the book of nature, and no Church will ever be able to prevent nature from its course, whatever Bible they may have. Freedom of thought is in the big scheme from the start, and was unavoidable more people after Eratosthenes travelled through again similar observations and intuitions of the repetitive movements of the cosmos, like the Astronomers of the Middle East did, publishing doubts on Ptolemy Theory and improving substantially the accuracy of their experimental observations, not only with the leap year. In 850, al-Farghani wrote a compendium of the science of stars [W61], and by the year 1030 the Ptolemaic System [W4] was openly criticized by Astronomers from Middle East, long before Copernicus and Galileo arrived with their observations. How far from truth would it be, if Copernicus or Galileo knew about the ancient Greek Heliocentric theories, or the Islamic improvements in Astronomy? On the other hand we know the real fear of Copernicus is well represented by his decision to publish his book only after death. And sometime later, when Galileo decided to prove Copernicus Heliocentric Theory was real, Galileo turned up demonstrating Copernicus' fear of the Inquisition was even more real. Astronomical knowledge was available since long before Jesus arrived, but His Church flattened the skies; no wonder the Vatican made crusades to stop the Astronomical revolution during the Islamic Golden Age, pointing out the Catholic Heresies shining in the night sky!

Another case I love from the schoolbooks concerns the Renaissance Culture, becoming intellectual legacy of the persecutors of the Renaissance Culture. The schoolbooks pretend that Italy is the flagship of the Renaissance Culture, with Galileo, Michelangelo and many more historical figures, but in evidence the Renaissance Culture was made up of Catholic Heresies, and cannot be Catholic Legacy. The Renaissance was made of Catholic blasphemies, and in Italy, at the time of the Renaissance, the Inquisition and the Counter-Reformation strove exactly against the heresies of the Renaissance Culture, the heresies of Copernicus and Luther perhaps, but also against the heresies of Galileo and Michelangelo.

The Renaissance was blooming with different versions of the Bible, and even more curiosities for natural sciences; it was the rediscovering, the rebirth of the ancient Greek Pre-Christian Philosophy the Nicaea Council was unable to vanish from history, and even less from human nature. The Renaissance was the resurrection of the freedom of conscience, which is part of the human being and as such cannot be dismissed or erased. This is a solid statement of the book of nature, and not a disputable quote from the Bible."

"And concerning the characters? Did you think about this?" she asked, recalling the literary perspective of the writing we were discussing sometime before.

"We are only expected to conform and obey, and to forget our individual differences and personal curiosities which are not accepted. We are expected to conform to the schoolbooks and to the selected words of Jesus, but if I cancel our individualities I only see our ghosts, lifeless and unreal. As a consequence our characters should be like ghosts, artificial characters, straw men, deprived of individuality and personality, just like puppets following a script; like Galileo did in his dialogue [W18]. But really there is something I am tempted to say."

"Something about what?"

"Something about your eyes."

"You could tell my name, it would be the same."

"I like your eyes for what they represent, an instance of the impossible made real by the book of nature."

"Whatever."

"Thank you."

"What about you? Will you say anything about the vanishing of your passport and your degree? Would you talk about that?" she asked changing the subject.

"The story of my personal documents may be perceived as a personal matter and I wouldn't confuse public and private matters. On the other hand I see it could be an example, a case I know from my personal experience, something I am sure and have no doubt about. Maybe I say something, but just to explain what it means having rights we cannot really claim, not even the most basic rights, and also our name may be taken from us.

After complaining about the vanishing of archaeological findings, I rather wonder how the Professors Cremo and Thompson would comment on the disappearance of University Degrees from the offices of Universities, and the vanishing of Legal Suits from the Courts of Justice. Because all these disappearances are not random but have the same High Moral Values in common."

"Maybe we should ask the European Union; if the E.U. was as serious as it pretends to be, your personal documents shouldn't be a problem. Why don't you send them the transcript of your video, when you were arrested and you taped the policeman informing you about the false accusations of anonymous informants? Tell them you would like to know about your personal documents. Tell them you are paperless like an illegal immigrant, in that civilized place of Europe. Ask them how long it may take to find your passport?"

"They already know all of this; years ago the European Office OLAF sent a copy of my legal claim to the Court of Justice in Milan, and the prosecutor Corrado Carnevali swept that legal claim under the carpet on behalf of his God, the puppeteer. Definitely the meaning of Justice in Italy is 'special', and for the same reason also the Nuremberg trials [W63] had different results for the Fascists, compared to the Nazis, despite both being responsible for the same crimes, and despite the fact that it was not the Nazis who invented 'The Holocaust'. The Jewish ghetto in Rome was made with the remains left over from the building of the Basilica of Saint Peter, and that made the difference also in Nuremberg, almost 2000 years later.

Why should I be surprised if still today the same High Moral Values of the Fascists are tolerated and promoted in Europe, above the Law? Why should I be surprised if the European Union needs this 'Moral Supremacy' in order to exist?

Why should I be surprised if step by step the Catholic Heresies have become slogans for the Catholic Propaganda, and the System of Corruption of the Roman Supremacy is taught and imposed as Values and Virtues of Democracy? As matter of facts, the Catholic Church has persecuted the Catholic Heresies throughout history, but these Values, the pompous "Catholic Heresies" in discussion are nothing more than the Freedom of Choice and the Secular Value of Justice, individual and personal Values the Church has always refused to respect.

In fact the Church is a Theocracy, a totalitarian absolute regime demanding to rule Earth like God would, or at least this is their sincere intention; it was within this framework of Culture and Tradition of Absolute Power that Mussolini religiously persecuted the dissenter demanding the Secular Values of Democracy and Justice, and deserter and recusant as Apostates of the faith. Mussolini did not persecute the Jew as infidels, but persecuted the Democrats, the Liberals and the Socialist as infidels, and the intellectual cleansing he enforced. The inquisition he revamped was demonstrating the millenary extent of the Catholic tradition of Democracy.

After the march on Rome in 1922, after the fraudulent elections in 1924, the 3 January 1925 during the speech for the murder of the member of parliament Giacomo Matteotti [W74] Mussolini said that - the democratic values have to be found in the Catholic tradition - and after he said that, the very same day he dismissed the parliament, dissolved the political parties, suspended the freedom of press and religiously persecuted the oppositions, as apostates of the faith and enemies of the state, anticipating the future words of the Excommunication of the democratic values, and providing further privileges he granted to the Vatican. A few years later in 1929 Mussolini signed the Concordat with the Vatican [W3], reinstating the Vatican City after the Italian Unification, endorsing the Cultural Supremacy of the Roman Catholic Tradition as the only Religion of State, and completing the cultural foundation of the Fascist Regime and the Racial Laws he enacted all the way to promote and privilege the Catholic Tradition.

The parliament was already dismissed for 14 years when on the 11 November 1938 Mussolini promulgated the Racial laws [W52] concerning the senator for life Liliana Segre [W74] but for the democrats the holocaust was started 14 years before, and to this day has not ended.

In fact in 1949, after WWII, after the Nuremberg Trials absolved the Racial Laws of Mussolini as Culture and Tradition, the Vatican repeated the Anathema against the Democratic Values with the Holy Decree against Communism [W71]. But the problem was not concerning the Communist party but with the Freedom of Choice and the Secular Value of Justice; the Democratic Values historically persecuted as Heresies of rebels and conspirators plotting against the Absolute Power of the Church.

Sometime after the dark ages, after Saint Peter was declared Heretic and most of the gospels were lost, after all the copies of the Bible of Eusebius ordered by Constantine were lost, sometime later in the history you can read in the Bible concerning the law of man << But Peter and the Apostles answered, 'We must obey God rather than man' >> [B3].

At the time of Mussolini the Church was opposing the democratic movements meant to limit the despotic tyranny and abuses of the Absolute Power of the Church, and for the occasion the Church was addressing the rebels as communists, in order to maintain their privilege and pretence to be above the common laws. In fact the clergy never consider themselves as commoners, never liked to be subject to the common laws, and to respect this tradition they made it that the common laws would not apply to them.

Similarly at the time of the French revolution the church was addressing the chartist movements as anarchists, people not respecting the authority, but in reality it was the Church that was the real anarchist that never respected any law or authority, not even their own, and prefers to interpret God's will case by case, conforming and confirming the ancient Romans nickname of barbarians and sociopaths for their pretence to be above the law and disregard other people's rights.

Today the moral leadership of the Catholic Church is out for every kind of abuse they can exploit, and along with the sexual abuses scandals, the abuses in education should be of equal concern. In fact the Church likes to recruit students internationally with the lure of education, and than makes them believe they are intelligent students that have to fight for their rights and for democracy.

I am not sure such students are aware that the democratic values are the result of the emancipation from the absolute power of the church, and the bishop will never be able to tell one democratic value that has ever been a Catholic value in history, and the lawsuit stack up to the millions of cases and are swept into the afterlife for Justice.

Also the reformation of the Churches was more about rights and freedoms than religion, and the propaganda pretending the democratic values are Catholic legacy is just a slogan Mussolini invented for the 3 Jan 1925 when he dismissed the parliament.

Recently in Italy the Minister of Justice reported over a 9.000.000 legal case backlog; does this happen by chance or is there a plan to organize this disruption? The Judge Luigi Tosti [A33] was disbarred as a Judge and Lawyer after suggesting the removal of the crucifix from the Courts of Justice, as if the rights of people had to be found in the Bible rather than the Codes of the Law. But the best is the evidence that since the time of the Decree against Communism nobody ever asked how the Democratic Value have become Catholic Legacy. As if the Freedom of Choice and the Secular Value of Justice could have possibly ever been Catholic Values.

The Fascist Regime is still there the same as it was, and the end of WWII in Italy has never arrived. Nuremberg in Italy never brought Justice but the confirmation and consolidation of the Racist Regime as good values of the Italian Culture and Tradition. No matter the Racial Laws, the intellectual cleansing and the persecution of the democrats as Apostates of the faith and enemies of the state since the 3 January 1925. Today the Senator for Life Ms Liliana Segre [W74] feels impelled to tell about the racial laws promulgated from 1938 until the end of the war, but for the democrats the holocaust started 14 years prior, and has not ended yet. In fact after WWII the Pope repeated the racial laws with the excommunication of the communists and those making common cause with the democratic values, the freedom of choice and the secular values of justice. Giacomo Matteotti was murdered for expressing the human sense of Justice against this tyranny of corruption and deception pretending to be above the law for divine reasons of Roman Supremacy.

After WWII Italy never had any re-education program concerning the Holy Racial Laws, and the fascist tormentors have continued their Culture and Tradition of abuses with the blessing of the Pope as before, against the democrats and those demanding the secular value of justice.

Since the end of WWII the Public Administration in Italy blackmails people for personal documents, intentionally makes people paperless, vanishes lawsuits from the Courts of Justice and prints fake Passports and University Degrees for good Catholic people like Kyenge, Regeni and the thousands they represent from the schools of the bishops. They can have recommendations for diplomas and degrees they never had, meanwhile others cannot have confirmation of their legitimate academic careers from State Universities and their lawsuit are swept under the carpets as living offers to the crucifix of Jesus.

For a long time after Nicaea these High Moral Values have been above the law in Europe, until the end of the Dark Ages, and we shouldn't be surprise if the European Union of today looks like a revival of the Dark Ages, when Europe was all united under the Moral Leadership of the Pope. Until the Renaissance arrived, shattering the Catholic hegemony into pieces, with the Catholic Heresies once again fuelling that revolt.

So, it may be worth remembering that Galileo and Michelangelo were just repeating the reasons of the rebels fuelling the Renaissance, and also Mussolini was not the mastermind of the racial laws he enacted in the name of such High Moral Values he embraced with the Concordat, with the mentoring and blessing of the Pope. It should be worth remembering that the Holocaust didn't concern the Jews only, but it was a Cultural matter more then racial, against the democrats, the liberals and socialists persecuted by Mussolini because of their Political Ideal of Justice, incompatible with the Catholic Holy scripture. In fact, the democrats were expecting Justice from the law of man, rather than postponing it to the afterlife, in accord with the tradition and the blessing of the Pope.

Why be surprised if still today, in the name of these High Moral Values, legal claims are swept under the carpets, and our rights for Justice are postponed to the afterlife? Still today I know for sure people's degrees and passports vanish into thin air, in the office, and we cannot ask Justice for the millenary tradition of forgeries and intellectual cleansing because the European Union tolerates and acts as an accomplice to all of this, since the time of the Nuremberg trial, the European Union needs this morality above the laws to exist, and since then is sweeping more and more people under the carpets.

But it is comical to see, in Germany in the last few years two Ministers have been stripped of their University Degrees because they have plagiarized some parts or paragraphs of their Theses. In Italy Ministers and Members of Parliament have been found with totally fake degrees; I mean they have never been to University at all, and despite faking legal documents they have never been prosecuted.

In Italy the Public Administration vanishes people and documents all together, and the Courts of Justice vanish the legal claims even if the European Union issued these claims, concerning my European Passport and my Degree perhaps, vanished into Italian thin air. Definitely the EU is not helping the enforcement of the law, or fighting the Italian Mafia and System of Corruption.

In evidence the Italian territory of Europe is much more tolerant than the German territory concerning the law of man, isn't it? In Italy counterfeiting is an industry since the time of Saint Peter, in Germany counterfeiters get fired, and in England the victims complaining of their rights against the mob are locked up in high security prisons as terrorists.

Tell me, what to expect from Europe? There are reasons if the Nuremberg trial prosecuted the Nazis, but not the fascists; and if in England the victims of such System of Corruption are isolated and made paperless like illegal immigrants, it is not by the law but in accord with the System of Corruption of the Catholic Tradition.

Since the time the Fathers of the Church arrived in Rome pretending the law of Rome was not the true law to obey; is it clear, the origin of this tradition of High Moral

Values above the law, where are they from?"

"Those were High Moral Values" she said, once more dismayed.

"These may be High Moral Values to someone, but not to me" I whispered standing up, and then we took our way home, though we could still discern the residual shadows of the daylight beams from behind the horizon.

Galileo was not Italian

(The Renaissance Culture)

I was recalling images and words of the recent conversations with Aisling, snooping around for uncharted thoughts in Education, when she arrived from the shortcut behind the bushes, fluttering a magazine in the air.

"Look, Italy, the flagship of the Renaissance culture. You must be so proud of Italian Culture and Tradition! Look, Galileo! Michelangelo! Have you ever seen the Sistine Chapel for real? It must be magnificent, fabulous!" she said again firmly, finding a place at my side. "This is something to talk about, isn't it?"

The sun was bright and no clouds could have dared to cross the sky without being spotted. Over the hedge, on the other side of the Park someone was playing football and the whistling and shouts of the players were reverberating and permeating the air all over.

"Concerning the Sistine Chapel a dispute was ignited while Michelangelo was still painting the vault, because the frescoes of Michelangelo were representing all the Deities and Saints naked and some bishops didn't like the idea. Nowadays there are no naked Deities or Saints in the Sistine Chapel; none of the characters of the frescoes are portrayed the same as it was by Michelangelo."

"What do you mean?" she queried surprised.

"Michelangelo, in the original version of the frescoes, has represented all the Deities naked, God included, but now none of the Saints portrayed in the vault are naked anymore. The naked version of God by Michelangelo was not accepted; same as the Gospel of Saint Peter, same as our freedom of thought we had from the most authoritative God of Nature. It is obvious something has happened during the time, to amend these things, and rather than admiring our contemporary frescoes resulting from layers of millenary censorship I rather wonder what was in the original project of Michelangelo, the reasons why Michelangelo did it his way, and why later the original frescoes have been changed, in the essence, and censored."

"This magazine doesn't say a word about censored frescoes. Are you sure of what you are saying?" she asked, testing my confidence.

"Sure I am sure, indisputable. If you like you may Google the Bishop Carafa and Daniele da Volterra [W19] [W20], or the fig leaf [W21] movement. I am not inventing anything. The bishop Carafa put pressure on Pope Julius II in order to cancel the nudity from the Sistine Chapel, and Daniele da Volterra, alias Braghettone, is the actual author of the final version of the Sistine Chapel people pay the ticket for. If you like, we may try to search on the Internet later; now I like to tell you something about the difference between the Dark Ages and the Renaissance time.

During the dark ages God was at the center of human life. It was God who decided Human destiny, and the people were just like puppets, deprived of the possibility to change the Design of God. But with the arrival of the Renaissance all of this was to change. At the time of Michelangelo there was a Cultural Revolution going on, and the ancient disputes concerning Free Will and Freedom of Choice were re-emerging from the abyss of the Dark Ages. After the Nicaea Councils, after millennia of cultural revisionism and intellectual censorship, the people were to rediscover the ancient value of freedom of choice, and the personal responsibility for the actions people choose to do. God was not the puppeteer anymore, deciding people's life and destiny but people themselves were deciding, with their free will and their actions. It is in this regard, during the Renaissance, people are at the center of their lives, because of the rediscover of the freedom of choice and the consequent personal responsibilities for one's own actions.

In this scenario Michelangelo was a man of his time, was a man of the Renaissance, and he depicted a summary of these heresies in his frescoes. It was not just a matter of nudity but Philosophy, Astronomy, Science, human destiny and God's will. How would you consider yourself baptised if you were unconscious when it happened, and you didn't choose it in conscience, with a Free Act of Will and Choice? The sacrament of Baptism was originally a matter of Will and Choice, and during the Renaissance people wanted that freedom back, the freedom to choose, eventually dissent, and be personally responsible for their individual choices. Martin Luther represented very well his moral dissent in the 95 Theses [W22] he posted on the entrance of the Cathedral in Wittenberg, but he was not the only one to feel embarrassed by the Roman Morality selling tickets to heaven to murderers, torturers and tormentors.

So, after the dark ages the Renaissance was a new age, demanding intellectual emancipation from the Moral Supremacy of the Catholic Tradition ruling Europe since the time of the Nicaea Council. The Renaissance shattered the European Catholic hegemony into pieces, and the Catholic Heresies well represent the reasons fuelling the revolt.

The Renaissance was not a point in time, or a place on earth, but was a matter of meanings, freedom of choice and personal responsibilities for one's own actions. If you didn't choose to be baptised, you were not really baptised, and this is the reason why several Reformers rejected the baptism of infants. On the other hand, with freedom of choice also comes the moral obligation to express personal dissent, which had never been an option since the time of the Nicaea Council.

Luther was not the first person to be excommunicated, and was not to be the last. In the big picture many more historical figures emerge, in all the branches of human knowledge. So, to continue, the Renaissance was a movement for the cultural and intellectual emancipation from the Catholic Tradition; it was a rebellion against the Cultural Regime, against the System and Corruption, the System of Indulgences [W23], simony [W24] and Saints above the law ruling Europe.

The Renaissance was the end of the Dark Ages, but on the other hand also nowadays I can clearly see some people are pretending Michelangelo made the frescoes of the Sistine Chapel, and the same people are selling the tickets to admire the masterpieces. But the original frescoes have been censored; have been changed in order to cancel Michelangelo's original meanings, and today there is no trace of Michelangelo left there. The funny part is that the Vatican knows all of this, but to them it doesn't look like plagiarism, or fraud, and they have no reasons to feel like con-artists.

I also understand some people express their freedom of choice claiming that Italy is the flagship of the Renaissance Culture, but who do you believe may make that claim? Galileo, or Michelangelo? Italy is the most Catholic place on earth, and the Renaissance in Italy never took place, but the inquisition did. At the time of the Renaissance in Italy there was the Inquisition and the Counter-Reformation, working against the Heresies of the Renaissance Culture. There is no way the Catholic legacy may represent the Renaissance Culture, it is impossible; the Catholic Heresies have nothing in common with the Catholic Legacy, only the stake of the inquisition, and there is no possible confusion."

"Eventually you may ask how the Renaissance Culture became intellectual legacy of the persecutors of the Renaissance Culture. It should help to highlight the Freedom of choice on one side, and absolute obedience on the other" she said continuing her last thoughts.

"Yes. But Luther was simply criticising the morality of the system of Indulgences and Corruption of the Catholic Tradition; he was commenting on the practice of the Church selling redemption from sins and crimes. The Church was selling tickets to heaven to everybody who could afford it, and was taking advantage of the fears of the poor people. In this scenario Luther was complaining about the exploitation of the most inner human feelings, about the system of corruption, indulgence and simony, and today we could file the very same complaints for the very same reasons. But did you ever wonder why Michelangelo represented God in the image of man, a naked man with all the details?" I asked.

"No. Not really, no" she said.

"Traditionally, from the Bible, we know that 'God made mankind in his own image' [B2; Genesis, 1:27]. So, Michelangelo in the frescoes of the Sistine Chapel in accord with the Bible represented God in the image of man, completely naked with all details, but soon the frescoes were censored, while Michelangelo was still alive. Apparently the problem was with the sexuality of God, but Michelangelo went further than that, expressing God as a Human projection. Michelangelo made apparent the Human origin of God, representing God in the image of man, surrounded by a crowd of Saints of well-known human origins, all looking the same as God. A crowd of man-made Saints, naked, staring from all over the Ceiling of the Sistine Chapel, this is what Michelangelo depicted, to remind the priests of their pretence playing God, and their human actions. Michelangelo represented God in the image of man, as a human projection. This is what he really did; with Michelangelo it wasn't God creating Man in his image, but Men creating Gods in their image. This is the magnitude of the revolution of the Renaissance Culture; humans are not puppets anymore but create their Gods, and are Free to Act in accord with their Freedom of Choice. The rediscovery of the ancient value of the freedom of choice became the only way leading to heaven, not the blessing or the indulgence fees of the Pope, but people's real actions, and the nude figures were only symbolic of the human condition; it was not a matter of nudity but philosophical meanings concerning the nature of Man and God.

In his art works Michelangelo represented the Renaissance Culture that he was living in, and truly the Sistine Chapel of Michelangelo was representing the Revolution of the Renaissance Culture clashing with the ancient walls of the Vatican. So, Michelangelo represented God in the image of man, like a projection of man; a man that represents himself as God. It is like saying that God is man made, like all the Deities and Saints around Him, but it also suggests that the man pretending to be God only fools himself. The Renaissance was a Cultural Revolution, and Michelangelo depicted the inner meanings of that revolution all over the ceiling. This is the reason why the Sistine Chapel was censored, and nobody ever saw the original frescoes of Michelangelo."

"Ok. This is a different scenario. I like this perspective of man inventing God" she said with a smile, like after a nice surprise. "But what about this magazine? What about the Italian leadership of the Renaissance Culture?" she asked.

"The Magazine is beautiful, the paper is exquisite and the photographs are great; I wouldn't go any further than that. At the time of the Renaissance Italy didn't even exist, and neither Michelangelo nor Galileo ever claimed to be Italian, because they couldn't, because they never knew of a town or a country named Italy, but if they were alive today they would make exactly the same complaints, for exactly the same reasons."

"What do you mean, Italy didn't exist?"

"Pretending Galileo was Italian would be like pretending Julius Caesar was Italian" I said smiling. "I am sure he never said that, and for the same reasons as Julius Caesar neither did Michelangelo, 15 hundreds years later. At the time of Michelangelo, in the territory where actually Italy is, were a number of independent states, always fighting each other. There never existed a union, a league, or a flag to unify the states of the Italian Peninsula, never before the XIX century. That was ages after Galileo and Michelangelo died".

"This is funny, yes. I don't remember anybody saying that Julius Caesar was Italian, but a number of people pretend Galileo was, like also Christopher Columbus and many more" she said.

"To make this clear, the Austrian diplomat Klemens von Metternich, an influential diplomat at the Congress of Vienna in 1814 [A31][W25][W26], concerning the Italian situation said that 'Italy is only a geographic expression', like Asia, or Africa. In fact, after the dissolution of the Roman Empire, the territory of the Italian peninsula was divided into a number of independent states, traditionally fighting each other, and there has never existed a league, a flag or an alliance to represent the united peninsula. Apparently the word, the term 'Italy', originated from an ancient Greek nickname [W27], but these are legends, like the Capitoline wolf [W59]. The Pre-Christian Romans made the Roman Empire, and never called themselves 'Italians', and before the movements for the Italian Unification in XIX century there never existed a flag or an alliance to represent the united peninsula; this is the evidence we can see from history. Anyway, despite the anachronism of pretending Galileo was Italian, I am feeling confident Galileo today would be disappointed exactly the same as he was, and exactly for the same reasons."

"Here it is. Galileo, from Wikipedia" she said, showing her smart phone and introducing the reading."

> Quote from Wikipedia [W28]
> «Galileo Galilei (15 February 1564 – 8 January 1642) was an Italian physicist, mathematician, engineer, astronomer, and philosopher who played a major role in the scientific revolution. His achievements include improvements to the telescope and consequent astronomical observations and support for Copernicanism. Galileo has been called the 'father of modern observational astronomy', the 'father of modern physics', the 'father of science', and 'the Father of Modern Science'.» [End Quote]

"I don't agree completely but I've read something similar before, from the schoolbooks. Concerning the Wikipedia claim that Galileo was Italian, for consistency, this claim would make sense only if Julius Caesar also was said to be Italian. Concerning Galileo 'Father of Modern Science', there is more to say, and more interesting characters could be introduced in these terms, like Eratosthenes, Aristarchus of Samos, or Hypatia, living more than a thousand years before Galileo. Don't get me wrong, Galileo understood that not all celestial bodies were stars;

he understood the existence of other planets, and from the phases of Venus understood that earth is orbiting around the sun. He is to be admired, but some other people did it before him and their knowledge has been vandalized by the same censors of Galileo, ages before him.

Anyway, further down the page it should mention that Galileo was on trial for heresy, for a matter of planets and orbits; don't believe it! It was not the stars of the sky who were offended, but the stars living on this planet."

"Yes, here it is" she pointed out.

> Quote from Wikipedia [W28]
> «In September 1632, Galileo was ordered to come to Rome to stand trial. He finally arrived in February 1633 and was brought before inquisitor Vincenzo Maculani to be charged. Throughout his trial Galileo steadfastly maintained that since 1616 he had faithfully kept his promise not to hold any of the condemned opinions, and initially he denied even defending them.
> However, he was eventually persuaded to admit that, contrary to his true intention, a reader of his *Dialogue* could well have obtained the impression that it was intended to be a defence of Copernicanism.» [End Quote]

"And further down it continues" she said, scrolling the text.

> Quote from Wikipedia [W28]
> «Galileo was found "vehemently suspect of heresy", namely of having held the opinions that the Sun lies motionless at the centre of the universe, that the Earth is not at its centre and moves, and that one may hold and defend an opinion as probable after it has been declared contrary to Holy Scripture. He was required to 'abjure, curse and detest' those opinions.
> He was sentenced to formal imprisonment at the pleasure of the Inquisition. On the following day this

was commuted to house arrest, which he remained under for the rest of his life. His offending *Dialogue* was banned; and in an action not announced at the trial, publication of any of his works was forbidden, including any he might write in the future.» [End Quote]

"Scary. So, Galileo was on the list of the prohibited books" she said, commenting on the reading with a smile.

"Yes he was, and if he were still alive he would probably ask how the Catholic Heresies became Catholic Legacy, starting from the freedom of conscience of having a personal opinion, in philosophy, cosmology, science and the arts.

There is no way Galileo knew about Italy, and the only Roman Culture he knew was the Roman Catholic he had experienced with the Inquisition. The Inquisition represents the Catholic Renaissance much better then Galileo or Michelangelo ever did. Still today in Italy there is no salvation except the Catholic option, and this is the reason why today Galileo would be disappointed exactly the same as he was then.

Maybe it's my fault, and I shouldn't be surprised if some accredited journalists re-publish their schoolbooks as magazines, pretending that Italy is the flagship of the Renaissance Culture. After the education people paid for, what are they supposed to do? Criticize themselves for the prejudice and preconceptions they have learned from their expensive education? Probably I shouldn't be surprised if, after all of this indoctrination, this is the selected intellectual class we've got, ready to convert and renovate the Catholic Heresies as Catholic Legacy, exactly the same as Mussolini did. We have a ridiculous intellectual class, haven't you noticed that?" I asked.

"So, Galileo was not Italian" she said smiling, writing in her notebook.

"Well, the Catholic Heresies have never been Catholic Legacy, and if someone today has the courage to pretend on the side of the Renaissance of Michelangelo was also a

Catholic Renaissance, we should underline that the Inquisition was representing the Catholic Renaissance very well" I repeated smirking with confidence. "Try again. In the presentation Wikipedia said Galileo was titled in several ways, like father of modern science, astronomer and more".

"Yes, I remember that" she said with a nod.

"Well. Galileo was not the first to imagine the spheroid shape of earth. Long before Copernicus arrived, more then 200 years before the birth of Jesus, a man in the ancient pre-Christian Greece did measure the circumference of earth, with surprising precision. I mean he measured the circumference of earth with empirical calculations. He was named Eratosthenes [W29], and lived 18 hundred years before Galileo arrived, long before the Nicaea Council flattened the Earth. In the same period of time also lived Aristarchus of Samos [W35], who is actually known as the first person who placed the sun at the center of the universe, with the earth orbiting around it. Then 600 years later the Nicaea Councils arrived, with the Inquisition and the dark ages, and all of this knowledge was lost, destroyed, devastated and persecuted. This is what happened to the science and knowledge not conforming to the Holy Scriptures, and this is the archaeological field we are supposed to dig; the trace of millenary ashes leading to how the Catholic Heresies became Catholic Legacy. Is it possible nobody ever asked? What is responsible for this confusion, the arrogance of someone or the weakness of others?

I wonder about the arrogance, claiming Galileo as the father of modern science, when at most he was only one of several victims of Modern Censorship. Furthermore Galileo abjured, he didn't pay the highest price like many others. He didn't have the courage of his own words, he didn't stand for his freedom of conscience, and because of renouncing his freedom he was rewarded with his life. On the other hand, Giordano Bruno [W31] was burnt at the stake because of his consistency in sincerely expressing his feelings and his personal opinion. But again, we can't forget that Copernicus didn't have the courage to publish his book before his own death, because of fear of the Inquisition, despite the fact that he was a priest.

Definitively, the freedom of conscience of having a personal opinion is the most controversial heresy of all time, the most persecuted, but the same heresy was also the most precious Value for several other people. In this scenario of intellectual inquisition and repression, Galileo was playing chicken, like a coward, abjuring. Maybe this is why, now, he is portrayed like a hero of modern science, because he gave up, became renegade and betrayed himself. But probably Galileo is just one out of many, scared to death, like they did to me. You should know something by now; I told you what they did to me, and I have shown you evidence of indisputable facts above any reasonable doubt. I will tell you more sometime, if you like; but concerning Galileo, isn't it clear the Censorship he had to face is the same Censorship we have today, the same quality and brand since the time of the Nicaea Council?"

"Definitively Galileo was not the first person to be threatened with the stake of the Inquisition, and was not the last either" she argued, before reading a few words from the Wikipedia page of Eratosthenes.

> Quote from Wikipedia [W29]
> «Eratosthenes of Cyrene was a Greek mathematician, geographer, poet, astronomer, and music theorist. He was a man of learning, becoming the chief librarian at the Library of Alexandria. He invented the discipline of geography, including the terminology used today. He is best known for being the first person to calculate the circumference of the Earth».
>
> ...
>
> «His calculation was remarkably accurate. He was also the first to calculate the tilt of the Earth's axis (again with remarkable accuracy). Additionally, he may have accurately calculated the distance from the Earth to the Sun and invented the leap day. He

> created the first map of the world incorporating parallels and meridians, based on the available geographical knowledge of the era.»
> ...
> «Eratosthenes was one of the most pre-eminent scholarly figures of his time, and produced works covering a vast area of knowledge before and during his time at the Library. He wrote on many topics, geography, mathematics, philosophy, chronology, literary criticism, grammar, poetry, and even old comedies.»
> ...
> «Unfortunately, there are only fragments left of his works after the destruction of the Library of Alexandria.» [End Quote]

"Eratosthenes... His work is mostly lost. Devastated during the destruction of the library of Alexandria" she said, repeating the Wikipedia. "This is the destruction of the Idols, at the time of the Nicaea Council, isn't it? The early Catholic Inquisition we said some time ago?"

"Yes it is. The library of Alexandria was devastated and set on fire a few times, but thanks to some brave librarians from the Middle East some copies of the original pre-Christian Greek books have been saved, and a few centuries later the discovery of these books was to re-birth the Philosophies at the origin of the Catholic Heresies. Also consider the improvements in Astronomy developed in the Middle East during the Western Dark Ages, and the critique to the Ptolemaic System coming from there [W61] [W4]. So, after ages of intellectual repression and Holy Wars, the heresies persecuted by the Inquisition in Philosophy and Astronomy were to bloom again, propelling the Renaissance culture with new values and new meanings of life, rooted in the ancient pre-Christian freedom of conscience, the most inner feeling of self. After ages of darkness, the Catholic Heresies were shining once again in the sky; definitively, the Renaissance Culture is a pile of Catholic Heresies from the deepest roots."

"And what about the Renaissance in Italy? What about the revolution of Michelangelo and Galileo?" she asked. "Look at this picture in the magazine, the Sistine Chapel!"

"Well. We said something about Michelangelo, and you did right coming with the magazine. It is a good example, like the school textbooks. I only wonder why our best schoolbooks never mention the bishop Carafa and Monsignor Sernini [W19] who organised the protest against the immorality of Michelangelo, depicting naked man-made Saints all over the ceilings. But Michelangelo was simply expressing the values of the Renaissance Culture, in which humans are free actors of their lives, and there is no God's destiny to decide for them but only their freedom of choice and their actions.

The Renaissance, when Michelangelo was alive, was rediscovering the ancient values of the freedom of choice and freedom of will, the values of one's own actions, and his frescoes have been censored because God in the image of man was unacceptable, because the viewers would have think being Gods, free to choose and decide. So Michelangelo represented God completely naked in all details, as a projection of man, in order to emphasize the human origin of God. Beside that, he also portrayed the mysteries no man will ever know, like the mystery of death, and the human desires to control also the afterlife. He symbolized the human condition, it's limits, and that crowd of Deities only represent the human desire of omnipotence: humans pretending to be above everything, above the laws of God made nature, and above God Himself.

It was the Bishop Carafa who led the opposition to the Sistine Chapel, when Michelangelo was still painting the ceiling; then the Council of Trent [W32][W20] condemned the representation of nudities in Religious Art Works, and Braghettone took over and covered up the frescoes of Michelangelo, while Michelangelo was mysteriously sick in the bed where he died soon after. Like if he was poisoned"

"Are you suggesting he was murdered?"

"I don't know if Michelangelo was murdered or not, but I wouldn't be surprised if he were; he wouldn't be the first.

But the point I am trying to make is that if I were to exhibit a fake Michelangelo pretending it was original, I would be prosecuted for fraud, but they are not prosecuted. What am I supposed to believe, nobody knows? It is clear the Sistine Chapel is a scam, but it is justified, by High Moral Values above the law; same as the magazine and the schoolbooks.

Back to the point, concerning the magazine we only have two options. Option one, this magazine is simply Catholic propaganda and plagiarism, like the tickets to pay to see the masterpiece Michelangelo did in the Sistine Chapel. In this case it could still makes sense, otherwise, option two, it doesn't make sense at all. But these pictures are beautiful I agree. I only hope you didn't spend too much on it."

"Don't worry. I had a coffee with a friend, a hairdresser. She has plenty of magazines and I borrowed this one. By the way, there is a travel agent at the end of the article, and maybe this is the sponsor."

"Concerning the Italian Renaissance, I really wonder how the Renaissance Culture become Catholic Legacy. Is it possible nobody ever asked? How did the Renaissance Culture become intellectual legacy of the persecutors of the Renaissance Culture? Because I only see the reign of terror established by the Catholic Inquisition. Just look at what happened to Galileo and Michelangelo, or Giordano Bruno. The real revolution feeding the Renaissance is not to be found in Italy but in the discovery of the ancient Greek books of philosophy, the philosophical foundation of the Catholic Heresies. Copernicus, and Luther are the heroes of the Renaissance, with their freedom of choice and scientific curiosities, but they came ages after Eratosthenes, Aristarchus, and Hypatia of Alexandria."

"Hypatia. Who was she?" she asked, typing on the invisible keyboard of the smartphone.

"Both Eratosthenes and Hypatia [W33] lived in Alexandria, but Eratosthenes was preceding 500 years; Hypatia was contemporaneous with the first Nicaea Council. She was professor of mathematics, philosophy and astronomy; she understood the elliptic orbit of earth, which is not a perfect circle as described in the Ptolemaic System, and was killed inside the library of Alexandria, during one of the devastations of the library."

"I believe I have seen a movie with a similar story, is it possible?"

"It is very possible, because there is a beautiful movie about her, entitled 'Agora' [A21], the director was Alejandro Amenábar".

"So, what about Italy, and Galileo?" she asked puzzled.

"Galileo was under house arrest for life, in accordance with the Italian Renaissance of the Catholic Inquisition; and concerning Italy, there is no salvation from the Catholic option" I said smiling.

"Are you trying to scare me again?" she asked.

"I am serious. The Nicaea Council was the first time the Catholic Moral Supremacy was enforced by the law. After Nicaea, it was just the destruction of everything; art, science, philosophy, astronomy, culture and traditions, starting from the judicial system, it was a total destruction. They have flattened the planet, for thousands of years, and in this scenario it is obvious Galileo is Italian, father of Modern Science; same as Columbus discovered the Americas, Michelangelo made the Sistine Chapel, and the Catholic Heresies are Catholic Legacy.

I only wonder who that may be, the mastermind of this well organized confusion? Who is the mastermind behind this knowledge filter and confirmation bias the professors Cremo and Thompson discuss in the Forbidden Archaeology [W17]?"

"I see your point, but I believe Galileo did the right thing" she said.

"Sure he did" I replied promptly, sharing the point "But concerning the freedom of conscience as a legitimate human right, stated by the law, is still has a long way to go.

Galileo was perceptive enough to have a personal opinion but he had no right to express it, and Freedom of opinion will became political matter and a personal right only after Lafayette and the French Revolution outlined and proclaimed for the first time Human Civil Rights [W34]."

"Sure, there was no freedom of conscience at the time of Galileo, just obedience and the death penalty. Probably some people consider Galileo as Italian, because he followed the Catholic Tradition" she said.

"Maybe, but it was not his choice. Maybe it is because of the education they had, but they don't really know what it means to be responsible for one's own action. They vanish people, and then pretend it was an Act of God, despite of their signature on it.

But today I don't like to talk about them. I will tell you more some other time, about the honourable Ambassadors and Consuls of Italy, faking documents in the legal offices of the Consulates. Like Paolo Galli and Pasquale Aragona, the Ambassadors when my passport and my degree went missing. At that time also the legal suits went missing, in the Courts of Justice, sacrificed to the High Moral Values of the Italian institutions. They fake documents in public offices. They are counterfeiters, mobsters and scumbags; just look at their moral leader, pretending to sell Braghettone with the signature of Michelangelo. Street scammers, I wish they could be responsible for their actions, and this is what also the Police said, they should be prosecuted, but how? Bribery and Corruption in Italy are values, custom and tradition; consequences are not prosecuted, and people are blackmailed for documents they have rights for. This is why also the European Union sent a copy of my Legal Suit concerning the vanishing of my degree and Passport, and the Prosecutor Corrado Carnevali in Milan swept the claim under the carpet, because in his understanding it was an Act of God. So I could be without a passport for a bit longer."

"Really, when you try to be rude, you are just funny. Seriously, don't hold back because I like it" she said smiling, almost inviting me to continue.

"I noticed you enjoyed my acting. Next time I will remember to play a few minutes for you, to cheer you up. Promise." I said, returning the smirk.

"Now I tell you what happened this morning, this is also funny. Do you remember yesterday we discussed the characters, how to represent and to describe them, and what style to use for the dialogues? This morning I was searching Google for suggestions when I found a book, with the title so close to the one we are doing. Believe me, I was really shocked. I was having my breakfast when I found the 'Dialogue Concerning Heresies' by Thomas More. It ruined my coffee. Because I couldn't recall any Thomas More, and the description was promoting the book like «The best English style ever», «The best dialogues ever». I read more, with growing fear, but I couldn't recall any Thomas More. Then I found out it was a mirage, or better, a man-made mirage, a marketing illusion, a booby trap. Because Thomas More is not a contemporary novelist, but the same Jesuit I studied at the University under the name of Saint Thomas. I wish Mr Thomas More, alias Saint Thomas, could put his nose in this and comment concerning Hypatia, Eratosthenes and so on. But he could truly say, in conscience, he never knew. Anyway, Saint Thomas was portrayed as an English Renaissance writer, but the name of the author on the book should have been Saint Thomas, and not Thomas More. I had to re-heat my breakfast because of that confusion between Catholic Heresies and Catholic Legacy. The only Renaissance Saint Thomas may represent, is the Renaissance of the Inquisition. As I said before, may be he was alive at the time of the Renaissance, but he was living in the dark ages of the Nicaea Council. Thomas More, alias Saint Thomas, was a very obedient man, very obedient to the will of the Roman Tradition. He could never be a man of the Renaissance, like my favourite Henry the VIII."

"Oh no!" she said, stifling a scream. "Henry VIII was a murderer, he was awful!"

"Yes, I know this version of the story. But I prefer to believe he loved his wife, more then he loved his Pope. The Pope was clear, Henry could have killed his wife but he loved her, and he made a war against God for her. It was not because Henry killed his wife he got all the trouble, but because he didn't, and showed his dissent to the Pope, and this is what the storytellers should say. He changed the Country forever, for her; but it is also possible Henry VIII asked himself who was really ruling the Country, if he, the King, was not allowed to make laws in his Kingdom. I completely agree with the Act of Supremacy of Henry the VIII, stating that Civil Laws are above the laws of the Church [W35] [W36].

Forget the Renaissance of Saint Thomas 'The Roman'. There is no Renaissance in Saint Thomas, but eventually the revival of the millenary tradition of the Inquisition. Nevertheless it is important to remind ourselves of the origin of our System of Values, and the Moral Supremacy of the Church above the laws. It helps to remember that concerning the Bible the point in discussion is not the Bible itself, but the meaning of Morality and Justice that come with it, including the System of Corruption and Indulgence.

We have no Justice by the law, and the values of Justice are not to be found in the laws; there is a market of Indulgence and Simony wide open in the churchyard, exactly the same as it was at the time of Martin Luther. It is exactly the same system of corruption, the same racket of mobsters, the same brotherhood ruling society from behind the scene with favours and blackmails. Nothing has changed since the time of Martin Luther, ages ago."

"Corruption, let me check my notes" she said turning a few pages. "Corruption. There are fees to pay to the Pope. Indulgence [W23] is buying forgiveness and a way to heaven, while simony [W24] is buying a job, titles and privileges here on earth. Is that correct?" she asked.

"Yes, it is a system selling all possible papers people may need, but historically kings and nobility could have been dethrone, deposed and excommunicated if not conforming to the High Moral Values of such System of Values, made of corruption, indulgence and blackmails.

Now, after you spent thousands and thousands of pounds for your education, imagine you would like to know what morality may pretend to transform the Catholic

Heresies into Catholic Legacy, or Thomas More into an English Renaissance Humanist?

Can you see the bias from these High Moral Values above the law is influencing the life of people, concerning the value of the Law and Justice, but also personal freedoms, knowledge, and all aspects of life? I wonder if you could see this education is indoctrination and brainwashing, flattening the Earth and the people on it. Can you see it is intentional, and we are manipulated like puppets in the name of these High Moral Value above the law?"

"Well," she paused for a smile, "I am here, trying to help. I agree, the education we had was not the education we needed, or rather, the education we had is not for this world" she said, adding something to the notes. "Our education is not of this world" she said again with a smile "It is not there. It is foolish!"

"Yes, it is inconsistent. A few days ago on the Internet I found a funny page concerning the Renaissance. You know Renaissance means re-birth, the re-discovery of the ancient Greek Pre-Christian Philosophy and Culture. On Wikipedia there is someone claiming his freedom of conscience distinguishes the northern and southern Renaissance, like it could be a matter of geography."

"You know, Wikipedia is for children; it is very popular, but is made out of schoolbooks. It is not really possible to quote Wikipedia, because the text is unstable, and the Universities don't accept it as a reliable source. It is obvious the Roman Catholic persecuted the Renaissance Culture; and it is obvious the Catholic Heresies, as heresies, have nothing in common with the Catholic Church. For us, it is important to underline that the Catholic Heresies will never be eradicated, because they are part of human nature. Freedom of thought and freedom of choice are part of human nature, the essential part of self, the inner nature of the human being. This is why we are all different from each other, and we have different opinions. We have to emphasise this" she said decisively.

"Sure, this is from the book of nature. This is the human

condition no one is above. But concerning the quotes for our writing, if the Universities accept only themselves as sources, and the Catholic Heresies have never been part of the School programmes, where are we to find our sources?

We will never find any quote from the reliable texts of the Universities. What can we do to organize bibliographic references on how the Catholic Heresies have become Catholic Legacy?" I asked, expressing my concern.

"The contradictions are so many and so evident, in philosophy, science, art. Everything is screaming out asking how the Catholic Heresies became Catholic Legacy. From the Courts of Justice, to the telescope to admire the sky. Wherever you turn, there you find the Catholic Heresies shining in the sky" she said reassuringly. "It is all self-explained, clear evidence with no explanation needed. But if you still need evidence, try exploring the many different versions of the Bible and ask yourself about Eratosthenes or Galileo. He would be disappointed exactly the same as he was, the same as you, and exactly for the same reasons" she said, repeating my words and waving the leash in the air, just before she walked away.

Jason

From the long shadows of the trees crossing the meadow I knew she was not to be seen in the park that day. Nevertheless, nothing was important anymore, not the time, not the place, not if she was to cross the gate. Another day was coming to its conclusion, and another day of my life was gone. I closed the eyes, pretending to be dead on the bench, until I felt someone was nearby.

"Hi. Have you got a light?"

"Yes, I think so" I answered, opening my eyes and checking in my pockets.

"Recently I have seen you often in the Park, with Aisling. My name is Jason".

"Hi Jason, how do you do?"

"Fine thanks, but I forgot my lighter at home."

"This is not a big problem, here is one" I said, remembering him walking in the Park.

"Thanks" he acknowledged, before lighting the cigarette;

"Do you mind if I take a seat?" he asked.

"Please do" I answered, moving the book I left open on the bench.

"What about your reading? Am I disturbing you?"

"Don't worry, I was chewing over it; it's a history book I borrowed from the library" I replied, turning the cover.

"England against the Papacy" he said reading the title, "By C.T. McIntire" [A2]. I never heard of it; it sounds like an Anti-Catholic book" he remarked.

"Yes, from the title I had the same impression, but it isn't. It's about the ending of the Absolute Power, and the English Diplomacy at the time of the making of the Kingdom of Italy, in 1860."

"Politics; I hope you are paid to read that" he said with a scornful expression.

"It's not that bad; it's like a thriller with the Great Grandpa of the Godfather." I said encouraging and adapting the story to more recent characters. "Today in the

European Parliament we can find the Catholic Democrats Alliance, the Catholic Liberals Alliance, and also the Catholic Socialists Alliance, like if the Secular Values could possibly have ever been Catholic Legacy. In 1860 a scenario like this would have never been possible, and this book helps to emerge this shift; how did the Secular Values become Catholic Legacy?"

"I can see this; but how did it happen?" he asked surprised for the unexpected turn.

"It's really not a popular subject but after World War II the Iron Curtain and the War on Communism have erased the Secular Values also from the Ideals of our Political Parties, and also from our school books, plunging Europe back in the dark ages. Like if Martin Luther, Henry VIII and Voltaire never existed. Bit by bit, the Secular Values have been erased from the schoolbooks, this is how it happened; one step at a time, and now people don't even know what the Secular Values are."

"This is twisted; so how was it before" he asked again.

"At that time, in 1860, the Democratic Movements were growing all over in Europe, establishing Constitutional Monarchies, demolishing the Absolute Power, and the traditional authority of the Pope was not enough to crown a King anymore, but the 'Will of People' was also necessary. On the other hand the Pope was still excommunicating the masses, like in the dark ages, and pretending to be above the Law, causing recurrent turmoil. During this process of emancipation from the Papacy, the Pope was also deposed and overthrown a few times from ruling the 'State of Caesar', but every time the European Catholic Monarchies challenged each other dispatching the best military contingents to restore the Papacy back, and legitimate their throne."

"I see; I wonder if a priest would read or recommend a book like this" he commented smiling.

"Maybe, but this is a history book. It reports facts, and this controversy concerning Caesar and God is also in the Bible. In the Gospels of Mark, Luke and Matthew it says to 'Render unto Caesar what is Caesar's', but in the Acts of the Apostles the Bible instead recommends 'We must obey God rather than Man' [B4] [B5][B6][W65].

Mainly the issue concerns Justice, to be administered in this side of the grave; it is about now and then, these cannot be confused with each other. Nevertheless our rights for Justice in accord to Caesar have been shifted more and more and postponed into the afterlife, and after the pretence of being above the law there is no evidence the followers of God have ever respected any law, not even the laws they made. Maybe the Bible is contradictory about this, but if you look at what they do you will see the unmasked reality of a bunch of mobsters and gangsters pretending to be above the law."

"Exactly what I meant; the kind of book a priest would never recommend" he said repeating and smiling again.

"Maybe, but this is exactly the point; would that be possible for a priest to respect a Secular System of Values in which there is no absolute power and nobody is above the law?" I asked, trying to find common ground.

"I see, it's not really Religion but Politics, Jurisprudence, Philosophy; it is complicated, isn't it?" he asked as if he wanted to acknowledge he was still listening.

"Yes, it is articulated, but it is exactly about Religion and the way Religion affects our world, including Politics, Justice, and the rights we have for our lives. There is no Philosophy that could dilute the Secular Values into Catholic Legacy, and if the followers of God cannot respect any Secular Value, how could they teach it in the Secular Schools?" I asked unveiling my concern. "What about the schoolbooks?"

"I see, you are about the schoolbooks" he said, leaking some dissatisfaction.

"Religion is influencing the secular schoolbooks more than the Civil Values do and really it's not a matter of schoolbooks. It's matter of life on this side of the grave, and not in the afterlife."

He looked at me like thoughtfully.

"I don't understand from your accent, where are you from?" he asked.

"Unfortunately" I said, commenting with my usual answer to that question.

"What do you mean by unfortunately?"

"Originally I am from Italy" I tried to explain.

"Oh; now I can understand your readings" he said. "And what about AC Milan?" he asked again.

"I was living in Milan".

"So, how are things over there? I believe you didn't come over just to read this book of McIntire for me, did you?"

"Who knows? During that time the reasons have changed from the original plan".

"I hope it has changed for the better. There are a few Italians living around here, do you know any of them?" he asked.

"No, you know more than I do" I said. "I don't know many people, especially Italians; did you ever wonder why there are so many Italian emigrants around?"

"Italy is a country of travellers and sailors, like Christopher Columbus, isn't it?" he suggested, smiling.

"I heard these words before, from some Italians. Ask them again, if they are travellers or emigrants" I said with some dissent. "The number of people leaving the country speaks for itself."

"I am curious about Italy; the Football, the Pope. Who really is the Godfather? Does he really exist? Tell me a story about it."

"I could tell you all kinds of stories, but I prefer the mysteries which reveal themselves through asking the right questions."

"Yes, like Aisling?" he said with a smile.

"No. Aisling is alright, and she is not something I am curious about" I replied to his humorous remark.

"So what is it? I am still curious. Recently I have seen you quite often here in the Park, with Aisling, talking and writing. Don't tell me it is nothing to do with her." He said, with an expression like he knew something, and was expecting from me some explanation.

"You are right, she is helping me in English; I am

writing a book and maybe we write it together."

"Oh, nice, and what is it about?"

"To outline in few words, it is about education and real life. It is a catalogue of evidence and thoughts about schoolbooks, culture and knowledge, but also deception and intentional misinformation."

"Ok, I choose real life rather than education."

"And you would be right. It would be more consistent with the world we are living in, but without education it would be more difficult to understand the world around us repeating itself. Anyway, the main reason I am here is because I had a PhD offer a few years ago, at Leeds University."

"Oh, nice. A PhD in what?"

"In visual perception" I said.

"Oh, nice. Anything to do with the Arts?"

"Not really, I am not an artist at all; and by the way I never had the chance to register for the PhD because the professors in the photograph of my degree ceremony did not confirm the degree they have issued, with their signature on it, and made me into an impostor, a counterfeiter."

"Sorry, I didn't get that. What happened?"

"The professors from Verona University where I have completed my degree did not confirm the degree they issued with their signature on it, and made me gave the impression that I was an impostor, a counterfeiter."

"I don't believe this. How is it possible they didn't confirm your degree?"

"I know it sounds odd, but you should ask the Italian Administration, not me. There is no answer to justify why the Administration of Verona University didn't confirm its own documents, with their signature on it, and questioning why it happened is misleading, like there could be a reason to justify the vanishing of degrees from the archives. It was their job, their responsibility; but they are far above all of this. They simply didn't confirm the documents they have issued, with their signature, stamps and photographs, and made me gave the impression that I was an impostor;

simple as that."

"This is really odd. Did they get fired for this?"

"Forget it. In Italy Ministers and consultants of the Government have been found declaring they have a degree they actually never had [A19], and also professors at the University have been found faking their degree and nothing ever happened, despite the fact that a Degree has a Legal Value and faking it is like faking money.

Concerning the vanishing of my degree, a few years ago I sent a Legal Claim to the OLAF Office of the European Union, concerning my rights for travelling in Europe and to fulfil my PhD opportunities, and they sent that Claim to the Court of justice in Milan but the Prosecutor swept the Claim under the carpet. In Italy, you may go to the University for years, pass your exams with the best marks, and then it may happen that the professors in the photograph of your Degree Ceremony will not confirm the degree they have issued, and rather blackmail you for documents you have rights to. This is the Italian tradition!" I said, shaking the book of McIntire in my hands.

"That was extortion, wasn't it?" he asked.

"That was well organized negligence, hiding traditional bribery and methodical blackmails. That was the tradition of favours and blackmail, the very same system of corruption also Martin Luther was complaining about ages ago.

Fortunately, the Italian Public Administration can always rely on the established beliefs that Italians are dodgy and counterfeiters; who else could be the dodgy one between the Public Office and me?

At that time I also called the office of the University in Verona, on the telephone, and I know they were aware of the situation; they also sent me an email informing me that they were aware of the request of Leeds University, but they never confirmed my degree. What they have done was intentional; it was a blackmail to get some money out of me, as if I had to pay a ransom for my personal documents. It is simply like that; and blackmail or not, this is what happened.

Furthermore they are people, but the papers they sign become words of the Institution, and offices don't blackmail people for documents people have rights to. They hide behind the respectability of these offices, and if I never had confirmation of my degree it could only be me being untruthful, and not them blackmailing honest people."

"This is quite a story; but, if the students are blackmailed and have to pay black money for their documents, why didn't you do the same?" he asked.

"Well, does it make sense to you, if I had rights for these documents?"

"Yes, of course it does, but apparently having the right is not enough" he replied.

"I was at the University, for real, and have no intention of being blackmailed by a bunch of mobsters. These people should have been prosecuted, for transforming the Public Offices into a warehouse for scammers and con artists. I have no intention of acting as an accomplice to a gang of mobsters and counterfeiters, but I want eventually to press charges, and to expose all of them. This is the worst possible mafia of all, the mafia of Public Administration, and I have no intention of being a partner in their crimes. They are the true enemy of the State, transforming the Institutions into a cover-up for counterfeiters hiding behind the respectability of Public Office."

"This is really weird. I Hope the situation will resolve itself" he said, but I knew the reality was to be quite different.

"Well, now it is too late. When my degree was vanished I was also cancelled from the population list. I have no passport, no personal ID, like I have never existed, or I were dead."

"This is unimaginable; but how is this possible?" he asked, "Don't you have someone in Italy to go to the authorities to resolve this problems?"

"I don't really like people to get involved with this; I believe I have to do it on my own. My mother sometime ago was concerned, and wanted to try but she only wasted her time. On the other hand, if the authorities, the Institution, don't confirm the document they have issued shortly before, with their signature on it, and state that you don't have a degree, what do you believe you can do? They are the reliable sources, and if the Professors in the Photograph of my Degree Ceremony did not confirm the degree they have issued, with their signature on it, all I could do was to press charges and expose them and make public my Legal Claim, because the Court would sweep it under the carpet."

"And how long has this situation been going on?"

"I had my PhD offer more then 10 years ago."

"And since then you cannot travel, and basically you are trapped here."

"Yes, exactly like that. I have been complaining for 10 years" I said.

"Unbelievable; and you can prove all of this."

"Well, I applied for my documents, and you see the results. I would really like someone to take me to Court for pretending to be Luca Benatti, with degree from Verona University. I would like to see how they could change these facts" I said, but to me was already clear also the Catholic Heresies were transformed into Catholic Legacy, and there was nothing we could have really relied on, not even our name, or the Principle of Identity.

"Anyway, the story was not finished like that. First the Italian Offices made me into an impostor, paperless like an illegal immigrant, and then, when it became clear I was just the victim of the Italian offices, some anonymous informants had the courage to suggest I could have had good reasons to organize revenge, or to become a terrorist, and I was isolated in order to protect them from their fears, for what they have done. So, I was forced into silence, in the confine of their lies, to make real their pretence I was not Luca, was not Degree at Verona University, and never had any reason or rights to claim. They can make your documents vanish, and then pretend the problem is you, not conforming to their will, the will of the Institutions; they can design you like a character from a novel, and you will never be able to complain. It is so obvious the authorities don't lie, and if they say you don't have a degree, that is the truth, and you will be forced to conform to the fiction they made real, despite whatever evidence you may provide.

This is my true and sincere experience; the photographic picture I have got from the democracy we are living in. There are people doing private business in Pubic Offices, fabricating documents, and the Courts of Justice refuse cases exposing the administrative horrors, misadministration and corruption of such Officers. It is like they had Absolute Power, and the Institutions would rather sweep under the carpet the cases they cannot stand, waiting for things to cool down and cancel as much as possible of what they have done. They are concerned for preserving the honour and the High Moral Values of the institutions, in the name of the best interest of society, and they are not concerned at all about the law, about Justice, about the victims, or the Public Order and Safety they definitively put at risk.

There are no laws or rights we can really rely on. I can assure you, also our name may be taken from us."

"How is it possible all of this, turning people into paperless impostors? It cannot be legal make people vanish like that" he said with an expression of surprise, like he couldn't believe it.

These are just papers. There are cases like Cecile Kyenge and Giulio Regeni perhaps, they also admitted with their voices the scam of dodgy documents they had, and after all, still pretend to be honest. You don't really need to master a degree to have one; they're just papers. The recent titles in the news concerned the cases of Kyenge and Regeni but these are just two cases, the most recent. Every day there are new cases, and many more could have been found as Kyenge and Regeni were not alone in their classrooms."

"I don't know; I never heard of them" he said, as he couldn't understand my point.

"The case of Cecile Kyenge [A15][A16][W48] was in the

news all over Europe" I replied promptly, "And Giulio Regeni was a PhD Student at Cambridge University." [A30] [W64]

"Oh, I didn't know. What happened?" he asked, inviting me to explain.

"Cecile Kyenge admitted with her own voice during a television interview that without the help of the Bishop and his network of friends in the Public Offices, she would have never had the documents she needed to fulfill her plan."

"What was it?"

"She is originally from Congo and needed visa, passport and funding for her University Degree. During the interview she also admitted that she knew it was illegal what she was doing but the Bishop is a master concerning morality, and if he couldn't see anything wrong, why should she? Definitely the bishop was not feeling deceitful or fraudulent but compassionate and helpful. Later Ms Kyenge also became a Member of Parliament and then Minister for Integration, which was part of the Ministry for Equal Opportunities. In fact in Italy also forgers and counterfeiters have the rights for equal opportunities, and obviously her confession was only further evidence that she is honest."

"This is crazy" he said smiling. "Is this true?" he asked as a remark looking for reassurance I was not kidding.

"Yes it's real" I said encouraging him to believe the information. "The interview is still available from YouTube and also from the website of the Italian National Television channel RAI3 [A15], in addition through Google [A16] you may find the newspapers, also in English. Not long ago this story was in the news all over Europe, because she actually is Member of the European Parliament and the people complaining the morality of the Bishop have been accused of being racist because of Kyenge's origin and her somatic traits. In reality she is very well integrated, especially with the Italian Catholic Mafia manipulating documents in the Public Offices, and this is nothing to do with the colour of the skin or racism, just Mafia.

On the other hand, in similar circumstances Italians do things differently, perhaps like Giulio Regeni did. In fact

Wikipedia [W64] doesn't say this but Giulio has been able to register at Oxford without having any real diploma or degree that would have enabled him to register at any University. In the early articles I have read from the News [A30] it clearly emerged that Giulio only had the Italian GCSE, which he finished at 13 years of age as everyone. With that diploma he couldn't register for any University except for the United World College in New Mexico [A46], where he spent two years, and from there he had the papers to register at Oxford. The United World College is the only school he could have registered with, and from there he found recommendations for diplomas and degrees he never had; two years in New Mexico with the priests was all he needed to register at Oxford and then Cambridge. But later he was murdered in Cairo doing research about Trade Union in Egypt."

"Wow, that is sad" he commented.

"Yes, it is, and even sadder was his family calling for Justice. But I have to repeat myself; I wouldn't want to give the wrong impression. The problem is not these two cases I have introduced or the many they stand for; the problem is the tradition of bribery and blackmail, in fact they print fake passports and degrees for friends they can control, while blackmailing honest people for the documents they have rights to. The problem are the true degrees and the lawsuits that vanish into thin air, in the Courtrooms, the perjury of public officers and the lives of honest people tormented by this brotherhood of gangsters pretending to be above the law for moral reasons."

"I can see, it's all about God and Caesar, but try to imagine for a moment Regeni's mother, what she may feel".

"After undermining the Law and pretending to be above it, calling for the Secular Ideals of Justice doesn't sound right, does it? I wonder was she praying to God or the priests? She was so proud when that dodgy College in New Mexico chose Giulio for the Baccalaureate Course, and helped him with the shortcut to Oxford. Now, try to imagine if Giulio or Ms Kyenge were asked for a favour, after such favours they received. Do you believe they could refuse to help the brotherhood back, by helping someone else like them, with some more dodgy documents from the Public Offices? Do you believe they could refuse, or would be blackmailed and forced into it? Do you believe they would be loyal to the law of Caesar, or to the brotherhood?"

"I can see this, yes" he said with a nod.

"Now the family of Giulio may be told that Giulio didn't have the prerequisite to join any University but only favours from priests and recommendations for diplomas and degrees he never had. But she could also be told that Giulio was just another good fascist, pretending to transform the Secular Ideals into Catholic Legacy. In fact, a Catholic College would never disclose any Secular Value in their lectures and it would be a profanity, especially concerning the Secular Values of Justice; nonetheless in his mind he was doing Trade Unions studies, as if Trade Unions and Secular Justice could have possibly ever been Catholic Legacy.

But, as you said, it's all about God and Caesar" I said shaking the book of McIntire in my hand once again.

"I understand what you're saying" he said with a nod.

"Ok. Play this game. Put yourself in the shoes of someone working in the office at the University; I filled the forms claiming I have a Degree at Verona University, but later the professors from Verona did not confirm the documents I gave you, with their signature on it, what would you do? Would you believe them or me?

Put the case I told you that I am Luca, but also the Consulate was not to confirm any of the legal documents they have issued shortly before, would you believe them or me?"

"I understand what you are saying, they are the authorities, but this is not supposed to happen. This is intolerable, unacceptable; how was it possible for someone to do all of this and get away with it?"

"Well, it is possible that they make the documents, and then reject your complaint. It is possible because they write it, with the stamps of the State, and then they will force you to conform like a puppet to whatever they wrote, and if you resist, if you don't comply, you are resisting to Public Officers. They can reinvent you on paper, like a character of a novel, and prosecute you for the story they wrote. Because they don't lie; they are reliable Institutions, and if they didn't confirm your degree it is only because you don't have one, and if you don't stop pretending to have Justice and Rights that you don't have, you may also be arrested.

The Italian Offices made my degree vanish into thin air, they made me into an impostor, and then, after years, when it came out I was not a liar but a victim, I was accused of having good reasons to organize revenge, retaliation, and could have taken Justice into my hands and plot terrorist attacks. But I was just claiming my rights, and the only people to gain something from these false accusations were the same people who vanished my papers in the first place.

I have asked a number of times if they could have taken me to Court, to see if I had rights to my personal documents, and to see if at any point they ever had any right to do anything of what they were doing; but they rather prefer to isolate and suspend all the Legal Rights of their victims, overcoming all boundaries for abuses and defamation. I have been vilified, tormented and tortured in the name of such High Moral Values above the law, just to cover up a bunch of gangsters, and actually I have no intention to forget what they have done.

It is obvious, all of this is possible only because Legal Suits are swept under the carpet, and the victims of the Institutions are systematically prevented from Justice, in the name of which kind of respectability and High Moral Value above the law common people cannot have, but Institutions can.

This is the Public Administration, and if they don't confirm that you have a degree you had better vanish before they make you vanish altogether with the papers. They can force you to live in a nightmare, in which you are not Luca anymore, and you will never have the chance to claim your rights because they act in the name of the Public Order and Safety and have Reason of State on their side. Do you believe Dr David Kelly was as unreliable as Tony Blair [W68] was pretending? Do you remember Dr David Kelly [W55], the weapon expert?" I asked, trying to express the violence of the false accusations and slander Dr Kelly had to suffer while defending his opinion under his personal responsibility.

"I do remember; it was at the time of the war in Iraq and the Hutton Inquiry [W70][A32], wasn't it?"

"Dr Kelly was just trying to be responsible for his own opinion as a consultant, but Tony Blair was demanding a different response, legitimating the invasion, so that he could have blamed Kelly if no weapons of mass destruction were found later.

The domesticated consulting Tony Blair was expecting from Kelly, Tony had to find from the NHS, in order to legally certify that Dr. Kelly was insane and suicidal, and his report unreliable.

Now, knowing of the well-organized racket behind Kyenge, Regeni and the many more friends they have in the offices, do you believe any of them receiving favours could refuse to help the brotherhood in return, or would they rather be blackmailed and forced into it?

"Yes; I can see that happening" he commented dismayed.

"In a similar way they said I was inventing stories, and that I was suicidal, as a threat, while forcing me into a paperless situation that was never resolved. I have been deprived of my civil rights and they made it impossible for me to hire a lawyer. In fact I was told that because I didn't have a passport I couldn't hire a lawyer either.

I would really like to ask Mr Tony Blair if he was concerned about Civil Rights in Europe or the Law of Man when my papers went missing, or was he rather motivated to cover up his friends in the public offices, faking documents in the name of his Moral Leader above the law. In fact I am definitely sure that my name is Luca, but they can fake your name and charge you as if you were the impostor; there is no control and no way to complain.

But it has to be clear, they do this to protect society from dangerous criminals, and with this motivation they justify whatever they do, and for instance in my case they had to deal with someone pretending to be Luca, against their will, and the will of God. They can make you paperless, and force you to live as a paperless, within the confines of their lies, the true lies of the Institutions.

Maybe it sounds like a story of the Godfather, but this is worse. Yes, this story is exposing a millenary system of Corruption pretending to blackmail people for documents they have rights to, but this is not the only way corruption works. Corruption is not just money for favours or papers; if someone gives you documents you have no rights for, later you will be blackmailed, and forced to obey the brotherhood, whatever they will ask you, forever. This is all they want from you; to control you like a puppet, forever."

"I can see this, yes; and your family? I believe you have a family, couldn't they help you with this? He asked again.

"I am not sure I want my family getting involved with this. Years ago my mother called the office in Milan about the passport, but she was told to go there personally because the office couldn't provide information on the telephone. So, she took 3 hours by train to go to the office and once there she was told to tell me to go there, because they couldn't provide her any information and basically she wasted her time. I have to do this myself.

After a while my mother suggested that I should forget what had happened, but if I were to forget it, she would have to forget she had a son, because I am pretty sure I was at the University of Verona, and I have passed all my exams."

"This is awful to hear" he commented.

"You are right, but if I had to take that advice, I couldn't take only the part she liked. If I am not Luca, degree at the Verona University, in evidence I cannot be her son either, because I know I was at the Verona University and her son was not.

About the degree the story was in the Verona daily

newspaper, L'Arena di Verona, long before they made a paperless and a terrorist out of me, but what did it matter? The Prosecutor in Verona Mr Guido Papalia after more than one year dismissed the case because the vanishing of my degree was an Act of God, like my degree was in the hands of God and not in those of the Godfather, the guardian of the Archives. Also the European Office OLAF didn't believe it was an Act of God, and sent my Legal Claim to the Court of Justice in Milan but also the Prosecutor Corrado Carnevali flushed the legal suit down the loo, like his colleague the prosecutor in Verona did sometime before."

"This is really a nightmare. I understand why you prefer to leave your family out of this, but what are you doing then?"

"Now I do videos on YouTube, repeating on the Internet the Legal Claims the prosecutors caused to vanish from the Courts of Justice. Recently I have made a video to expose once again this system of corruption, and the Italian Government has banned it. It is so obvious some Moral Authority must have seen the video in order to ban it; I wonder how they could ban the video, without watching it, and without investigating the claim in it.

The video was addressed to the new nominated Head of the Police Alessandro Pansa [A28], with the hope he could find the Legal Claims hiding under the carpets. The video was showing the Minister for Justice Paola Severino [A18] reporting a backlog of 9 millions Legal Claims, stocked in the archives of the Courts of Justice; a number equal to 15% of the entire population. Plus you have to add the best cases, lurking under the carpets, to make sense of the morality of the Judicial System.

I also tried with defamation of character, to be sued for insulting the people involved in the happenings, but also this approach didn't get the expected result; probably because I am simply telling the truth, and this is not defamation but certified reality, nobody ever took the trouble to resolve this mess. It is a legally certified mess with the signature of the most honourable professors and reliable institutions, but nobody could ever find the time of day to look into it, for the sake of respect for the law, or Justice.

In conclusion, they cover up each other the same as gangsters do, but if I say that the Prosecutor Corrado Carnevali is a mobster, and a liar, like all the other people involved, nobody will complain to the Court for defamation because what I am saying is true.

I don't see many options. Either the European Union imposes Justice by the code of the law of man, also to mobsters and to counterfeiters with high moral values above the law, or Europe exposes itself as an accomplice of this mafia, demonstrating the kind of civilized place Europe is, able to offer refuge to any refugee but unable to guarantee personal documents to the European citizens.

"In what language do you do your videos, in English or Italian?" he asked.

"I have some in Italian, and some in English."

"I would like to watch some" he said, picking the smartphone out of his pocket. "Can you find it?" he asked.

"I have a few channels on YouTube. Let me see. This may be a bit harsh, but it well represents the situation I had to face" I said, and then I clicked to start the video.

"Is this Aisling talking?" he asked.

"Yes, she helped me out with this video. We made a kind of interview" I said, and I restarted the video.

The Transcript of the video [A10]

Aisling: Hi Luca why did you come to England?

Me: I had a PhD offer from Leeds University

Aisling: And what happened then?

Me: Shortly after I arrived in England I had my passport stolen. I did go immediately to the Italian consulate and paid to start the procedure for a new passport but after almost one year I was informed I was not to have a new passport because I was cancelled from the population list

Aisling: Have you had a passport since then?

Me: No

Aisling: And what happened with the PhD offer?

Me: To register for the PhD offer I had to go again to the Italian consulate, this time to the legal office for the legal translation of my degree, with more stamps certified with the apostille. But later the professors in the picture of my degree ceremony, the professors Emilio Tiberi and Bianca De Bernardi, of the University of Verona, did not confirm to Leeds University the degree they have issued with signature stamps and photograph and made me into an impression, a counterfeiter

Aisling: Did you report this situation to the Italian consulate?

Me: Yes I did, but the Consulate refused to send the report to the relevant offices in Italy. They are not responsible for the documents they issue, with their signature on it

Aisling: What about travelling in the EU without a passport?

Me: The European commission OLAF later sent a report to the Court of Justice in Milan, exactly concerning my rights for travelling since I was clearly prevented from doing so without a passport, and also concerning my rights to have confirmation of my degree and fulfil the PhD opportunity I was offered. But the Prosecutor Corrado Carnevali has swept the report in the bin in order to preserve such high moral values above the law, the best of the Italian national tradition and culture

Aisling: So what happened then?

Me: If I told you that I am Luca Benatti, and the consul was to tell you that there is no such person as Luca Benatti, would you believe me or the consul? And if I told you that I have a degree from Verona University, but the professors from Verona did not confirm the degree they have issued, would you believe them or me? I am telling you, they fake documents in public offices, intentionally and systematically. In Italy the true degree becomes fake, and the fake become true, like acts of God, with the only difference that these are not by chance. They made me paperless like an illegal immigrant, and they did it with their signatures and stamps. And after redesigning my life with a new identity as a paperless person, they also had the courage to inform the police, and to pretend their victims should conform with their will, or they should be isolated, defamed, vilified tormented and tortured, as they did to me.

The screen of the smartphone turned black, and a creepy music started.

"The conversation with Aisling is ended" I said speaking over the video still running. "Now there is the recording of the conversation with Dissanayaka. This is what the authorities do to make their living, they cover up each other" I said trying to explain.

"I have seen it is changing; let me hear it" he said, asking for silence.

The music ended with a fading tolling bell, introducing the voice of Dissanayaka speaking.

Nuwan Dissanayaka: What we tried to do is establish what we think about the things we were told at the beginning. You are no different, I agree with you. But what we were told at the beginning ...

Me: (what??)

Nuwan Dissanayaka: All of this things, from the beginning we were told that you have mental illness, we are told that you are very risky, we were told all of these things.

Margaret: Yes, all of these things.

Nuwan Dissanayaka: And since that time what we have done, we have seen you on a regular basis, you have been kind enough to agree even if you didn't see the merit of doing so at the beginning, to see if there was anything we could see in term of illness, but also to try to support you with the things that you wanted to do, to get a bit more established and to be generally a bit happier with the way things are, not that... I know it won't make you happier, is not even whether. It Is not, you know, it is a different thing isn't it?

Now, throughout the time we have seen you, my honest

opinion of what I think, I believe in being honest, is that I don't see that you have an illness. What I see is that you had very difficult circumstances to have to deal with.

In terms of what we do, you know, we have a lack of illness going on. If we are not doing any psychological interventions that is relevant to any of these things, if we are not doing anything else than what are we doing?

Me: What are we dealing with?

Nuwan Dissanayaka: (over my voice) If you say, If you say that we, that you are the same person that you were before.

Me: I have never changed.

Nuwan Dissanayaka: But our response to you has changed, and the reason has changed is because we needed to establish ourselves

Me: What I find very funny is that nobody of you ever asked himself how could a person live in this situation, with no passport, with degree cancelled, job opportunity cancelled

Nuwan Dissanayaka: (over my voice) how do you know? How do you know that nobody asked themselves these questions? I asked myself these questions. I think it is an intolerable way to have to live…

I think, it is an intolerable way to have to live.

I think, it is an intolerable way to have to live.

I think, it is an intolerable way to have to live.

[End of the Video]

The video ended repeating the last sentence of Dissanayaka, fading in the silence of the park.

"Who is this man, with whom you had this conversation?" Jason asked, after a few moments.

"That was the recording I made with my mp3 player, after the anti-terror Police arrived and I was arrested. Did you hear what he said? That was Dissanayaka, the Psychiatrist for the Forensic Assessment, informing me that someone was accusing me of being a risk to society, and not the opposite way around. He never mentioned the name of the people accusing me of having a mental illness and being a terrorist plotting revenge and massacres. This is my true and documented experience; one day I received a PhD offer, and the next day I was paperless like an illegal immigrant, with a bunch of mobsters making up a story just to cover up their crimes. It was not by chance these honest informants never said a word concerning the vanishing of my personal documents, but only defamed and slandered me, just to cover up the situation I was reporting since the start a few years before. Definitely the Police should have paid more attention distinguishing the victims from the offenders. It wasn't me who was the criminal, but these anonymous informants, fabricating documents in public office and then accusing their victims with false accusations. This is what happened, and then the Police cover them up, because everything truly happened with the best intentions, and their worries were well justified by the evidence I was paperless. Like making people paperless, or false accusations, could possibly be legal" I said, still with a bitter taste in my mouth. "They made me paperless, and then victimized and tormented me, trying to make me to conform to their will. In fact, despite the evidence, the Public Administration doesn't cause documents to vanish in the offices, and if my personal documents couldn't find confirmation the only possible reason could be me, being an impostor. Isn't it? Because Italians are dodgy!"

"This is awful, a nightmare. When did it happen, all of this?" he asked again.

"About 10 years ago."

"And then, what happened with the Police? What did they do?"

"The police were not concerned about the illegalities I was victim of. To them it didn't matter I was paperless and targeted with false accusations; their only concern was to impose all these illegalities on me, as it could possibly be legal. I was arrested, and then you heard from his voice what Dissanayaka said, «There is a lack of illness going on, what are we doing here?» It was so obvious both the Police and the Psychiatrist were completely unaware of the target of their mission, which was to isolate, vilify, torment and torture the victims of their honest and reliable colleagues, anonymous informants tampering documents in the offices."

"Do you know who did this to you?" he asked

"A bunch of Anonymous Informants with High Moral Values above the law, good enough to mislead the Police into pursuing the victims rather than the offenders. I would bet the same people responsible for my documents were also the same responsible for the false accusations; they made me into an impostor, and nobody ever asked them to prove their accusations, or to be responsible for their actions."

"What you are saying is ruthless, and then what happened? Did you get your passport in the end?"

"No" I said smiling. "When it became clear I had no weapons of mass destruction, but I was rather the victim of false and unsubstantiated accusations, the Police gave up and didn't take any action, leaving the scene of the investigation as they found it.

But you imagine from the start I had to go to the Consulate for the Legal translation of my Degree, and then the Professors in the photograph of the degree ceremony didn't confirm the documents they have issued. They knew the photographer was taking pictures in front of a number of people and friends, but what did it matter? The offices are far above all of this; they can make you vanish, with their signatures, and then pretend it was an Act of God and blame you for being the problem. Could you imagine this? Imagine it happened to you, what would you do? Imagine someone comes to you and tells you that you are not Jason, and you are pretending to be Jason, and you may be a risk to society, and they have to take care of you. You imagine being there for real, taking notes and taping them because, despite the fact that it is in front of you and you are living it, you cannot believe it yourself what is going on. Try to put yourself into these shoes."

"I can see what you are saying. The offices supposed to help you in the situation and provide your personal documents, in reality made you paperless, and you had no place to go to claim your rights. In your shoes probably I would have done the same as you did, and I would have had to pass through a very difficult time; also that man in the video said exactly these same words. It was really outrageous and unbelievable you had to pass through this."

"I agree it was outrageous, especially because what was intolerable for Dissanayaka could be imposed on me as a normal situation to be accepted. What the fuck is this shit? Where is it, the moral integrity of these kind of people, never responsible for what they do and pretending to judge concerning being responsible and distinguish good from bad? What about this side of reality, when the intolerable may be imposed on the victims of abuses and crimes perpetrated in the name of what? Was that the law of man they enforced, or the High Moral Values of the System of Corruption blackmailing people for documents people had rights to?"

"That was a mess; really hard to believe" he said. "You did it right to record the conversation and make a video with it; all of this, is really hard to believe. Yes, that man to help you should have informed the Police; but you said the Police came just before him, and were not bothered about your personal documents. Also the Italian Consulate should have helped you, but how?"

"Well, after my personal documents were vanished into thin air, definitely it was not the Italian Consulate going to defend my rights; it was the Consulate that made me paperless, and the others just covered up of the situation, slandering and vilifying the victims.

Also a few years before, when I contacted the Citizen Advice Bureau for advice, they also found it difficult to believe I was still waiting for the replacement of my passport after almost two years, and suggested I talk to a solicitor. So I did, and later the solicitor with a letter informed me that the Italian Consulate would have been pleased to provide the passport for which I already paid in advance, but despite what the solicitor said in writing I never received the passport anyway, or any temporary replacement.

So, after a few months, as a last resort I went to the emergency department of the hospital, asking what I was supposed to do because I was paperless and the situation was deeply detrimental and preventing also the possibility to travel back home. I asked for a witness to see the unacceptable situation I was forced into, but the doctor in the emergency department believed I was inventing something. «Italy is a Civilized place» she said, and I was arrested because the reality I was reporting was not as socially acceptable as her imagination, and as an immediate consequence of that belief, in a matter of minutes I had to repeat the story all over again to Dr. Buller, the Psychiatrist on duty I had to explain again that I had no passport and the situation was causing several problems. I explained the Citizen Advice Bureau invited me to contact the Solicitor Hyams, but I only had the renewal of old promises rather then the new ID I had to pay for in advance to the Consulate in 2002, immediately after the theft. And last, I had to explain the integrity of the professors in the photograph of my degree ceremony not confirming the degree they have issued with their signatures, stamps and photographs, and turning me into an impostor.

The next day Dr Buller verified the situation, also contacting the University, and when the interpreter arrived and confirmed the documents from the Consulate exactly as I was reporting, Dr Buller stated it was his opinion and the opinion of the clinical team that I didn't have any psychological or psychiatric issue to justify me being there, and I was dismissed. This is what Dr Buller stated in June 2004, 2 years after I was paperless. But in conclusion, when the socially unacceptable situation became a true reality, that situation was imposed on me as a normal situation to be accepted."

"I can see what you mean; the Psychiatrist should have called the Police from the start, at least to inform them of your struggle. How long could you wait for your documents?"

"This is what I was after. The emergency service have a duty to report to the Police the crimes they become aware, and my intention was to report the situation as intolerable as it was; so intolerable they also couldn't believe it from the start. In fact being paperless is a breach of Human Rights, because it reduces people to slavery; because it impedes normal life, like registering for the PhD I was offered, or even going back home. Nevertheless I was dismissed, like the intolerable situation I was forced into, could be legally imposed on me. Also the solicitor Hyams was useless; what was I supposed to do?

The following year, in July 2005, the European Office OLAF sent my complaint to the Court of Justice in Milan reporting the situation of my personal documents and my freedom to fulfill the opportunity I was offered, but the Prosecutor Corrado Carnevali swept the case under the carpet, because it had never happened, and eventually it was nothing like corruption or blackmail but an Act of God, absolutely out of his jurisdiction. Then, in October 2006 I decided to write to the MP for High Education Bill Rammell, inviting to report the situation to the European Offices, and find a solution."

"And what happened?" he asked curious, like if I said something he also would have tried.

"The reply said there was nothing he could have done, and suggested to contact a solicitor in Italy. Then, a few days later I was arrested, because someone had the insolence to pretend I could have been deluded and organized revenge, and turn into a terrorist, and plot mass murders as consequence of the situation I was reporting and complaining as unjust and illegal. Since then, they went on and on with false accusations until they reported me to the Anti Terror Police and Dissanayaka arrived for his Forensic Assessment.

You heard what he said, did you? «We are told that you are risky» and then, «There is a lack of illness going on, what are we doing here?» I told him from the start about the High Moral Values of these false and anonymous accusations he took into so much consideration. I also asked him «What are we dealing with?» to recall the system of mafia and corruption and blackmails I was complaining, against the evidence of my rights to my personal documents.

During that meeting we have just listened to he didn't say the name of the mysterious informants, but what if they were not anonymous at all. I well remember Claire Flannigan providing her professional advices and informing Dissanayaka personally. There was also a Policeman present at that meeting, but obviously they preferred to resolve the situation in accordance with their notion of good and evil, and as consequence of such morality I was handed over to Dissanayaka in high security as a potential terrorist.

Do you see? It is only old style witch-hunting. They don't need to prove their accusations, and you may be held responsible for what you may do, but not them, for the crimes in evidence they have perpetrated. They vanish people into thin air, in the office, and then pretend the victims are the problem, and should be isolated. This is what they do, and whatever paranoia they have, it will become a real threat to your own life, despite the only evidence is their own fear, motivated by the abuses, illegalities and crimes they know they have perpetrated, intentionally. They know the violence, lies and cover-up they are responsible for, and in this perspective Flannigan never had to sign anything; she always made someone else do the job for her, like Dissanayaka for instance also did."

"And after all of this, you still have no passport" he asked, expressing his concern.

"Yes, still today I have no passport" I replied.

"Let me say, it is really intolerable; they really gave you a hard time" he said repeating again. "I am concerned; and this is disturbing. Because this problem you had, it was all about personal documents, but it is so obvious you exist. I mean, how could someone be paperless? It must be an impostor, but in all cases it would be an infringement of the law. Why didn't the Police do anything?" he asked again.

"Don't ask me, I am only the victim. From my perspective the best part was Dissanayaka saying that the situation was intolerable, but after all, the intolerable could be imposed on me as a standard, like it could possibly be a normal situation to be accepted. It is also illegal! Tell me they are not criminals and are not aware of what they do.

Anyway, after all of this I still have no passport, I cannot travel, and the people responsible for these documents and false accusations never had a problem about what they have done. It was as if they had a right to do it; as if they could be above the law and make people vanish. Do you believe I am free to travel without my passport? And what about accusing the victims, just to pervert the course of Justice? I have been tortured while these mobsters continue blackmailing their victims, exactly in the same way, in the name of the same High Moral Values above the law. Is this absolute power, or what?" I asked, shaking the book of McIntire in the air.

"Good luck the European Union is committed to guaranteeing Civil Rights, Passports and Freedom to travel to the European Citizens; I wonder if it works for everybody or only for people like Kyenge, Regeni and their friends."

"It won't be easy to expose all of this, and probably the Government itself would stop your Claim for Justice, as they did before."

"If we don't have rights to our personal documents, what rights do we really have? Try to imagine someone makes you vanish, and you have to live like a paperless person just to make real their dream of omnipotence or whatever paranoia they may have. Imagine being acknowledged that the situation is intolerable but it is also too much to cope with. So leave as it is; carry on sweeping people under the carpet."

"I understand what you are saying" he said smiling. "It is a catch-22. There is no way out. They make you paperless, and then pretend the problem is you."

"Yes, and how to take this mafia to Court, if the Courts vanish the Legal Claims into thin air, or under the carpets?

The European Union itself has sent my Legal Claim to the Court in Milan, and the Court dismissed the case, like it never happened, or worst, like God was the only one responsible for the vanishing of my documents.

At this time, looking at Kyenge, Regeni and their friends, I am to believe this mafia is promoted in Europe as Culture and Tradition, like a revival of the dark ages, when Europe was all united.

The European Union! What a shame! Sometime ago I wrote to the European Union; I should write again and ask if this is the case, but I had reply only from Jean Kutten."

"Who is Jean Kutten?" he asked.

"At the time he was member of the staff of the European Green Party. After one year I was waiting I contacted the European Parliament, and concerning the problems I was having with my personal documents Jean forwarded my email to two Italian members of the Parliament, Andrea Vettori and Monica Frassoni."

"That was good of him, and then what happened?"

"Nothing happened. The Italian EUMPs never replied to the email. Probably the Italian EUMPs didn't like to be involved with friends of friends, faking documents in Public Offices. They could be blackmailed as well, and get into trouble. I told you, sometime ago I made a video on YouTube repeating the legal claim the OLAF office sent to the Court in Milan, and later the Italian Government has banned the video."

"You mean YouTube has banned the video."

"No. The Italian Government banned the video; it is banned in Italy only. YouTube never had any reason to ban it, because there are no copyrights infringements. It is only in Italy people cannot watch it, and the problem is the Italian Censorship, sweeping from the Internet the complaints repeating the legal claims swept under the carpets in the Courts of Justice."

"Thank Goodness there is YouTube then, but what you are saying is outrageous; and after all of this, you still have the same problem. For how long?"

"By now, more then 10 years. My passport was stolen in

2002."

"It was a good part of your life. Sure this story has changed your life; I can see why you like this book of McIntire" he said, but on the spot I couldn't answer.

"I don't know about refugees and illegal immigrants, but for sure people made paperless in Europe by European Countries don't have any rights at all, not even to report the crimes they are victims of."

"Sorry for my curiosity but, have you ever been involved with Politics, or Religion, or anything to justify a kind of retaliation like this" he asked.

"No, I have no Religious beliefs. I like History, and Philosophy, Science, Arts, but never were Religion or Politics within my hobbies or passions, ever."

"May I give you an extra nightmare? What if Amazon-Kindle was to ban your book, like has happened with the video on the YouTube. I have seen banned books on Kindle and Amazon before, and yours wouldn't be the first one." he said, with a convincing expression.

"I don't think so; I hope not" I said rejecting the idea. "Eventually the Italian Government may ban it in Italy, where they have jurisdiction, but cannot ban it from Amazon. Like YouTube, Kindle and CreateSpace have no real reasons to ban it; why should it be banned? I am only writing about the High Moral Values inspiring our Courts of Justice to the Trust in God they have, rather than the Justice and Morality coming from the Law of Man, which is actually the meaning of the Law, against violence and abuses of intentional criminals pretending to be above the Law.

Why should my book be banned?" I asked again, almost reassuring myself there would be no reason. The Satanic Verses of Salman Rushdie wasn't banned, but eventually was encouraged and promoted in the name of western freedom of speech. What is this? The western democracy now has a problem exploring the reasons why we would be better trust in God for Justice, in the after-life, rather than the law of man on this side of the grave? Try to explain they didn't know what they were doing, making my documents vanish and tormenting me for years and years. Try to explain what is intolerable for Dissanayaka can be imposed on me as a standard.

I cannot really see any reason why Kindle or anybody should ban it. This book is well documented, is not fiction, and I am not inventing anything; I am simply reflecting on the Values of Justice, corruption, and the Morality of the best education we could find in the schoolbooks. I understand that the people making their living out of this System of Values may be disappointed, but I don't believe anybody ever asked how the Catholic Heresies became Catholic Legacy."

"Your book may be banned exactly for the same reasons also the schoolbooks banned these meanings in the first place. Maybe they will take you to Court."

"Well, going to Court is exactly what I want. I would love to know if I had the rights to my personal documents."

"You don't need to go to Court for that. Of course you have those rights, but just like you, probably a number of people had their papers vanished. But you have mentioned the Catholic Heresies; Heresies are good reasons to ban books, don't you know? And what do you mean exactly by Catholic Heresies?" he asked.

"The Secular Value of Justice as we said, from the book of McIntire, is one of the best Catholic Heresy; but also the Freedom of Choice and the Freedom of Thought are Catholic Heresies. The problem doesn't really concern theoretical heresies but practical obedience. All they want is obedience, undisputed obedience and Absolute Power. In fact the freedom of thought and freedom of choice are the essential part of human nature, as God made it. It was God to make us all different from each other, but they don't like it; they want us like puppets. Just obedience, and absolute Power, to do as it better suit them.

I'll tell you a story to outline a few points.

When the early Christians arrived in Rome, Rome was a polytheistic town with a number of Gods from all over the provinces. One God more or less was not to make any difference, and all cults were contributing peacefully to the

Public good. Then the Christians arrived, demanding exclusive worship, disrespecting the other cults and cultures, and pretending the law of Rome was not the true law to obey but there would be another law to obey above it.

It was exactly the pretence of having higher moral values above the law to make them uncivilized barbarians, and narrow-minded, unable to accept that different people may have different cults and beliefs. Nevertheless they do exactly the same today, exactly for the same reasons: the Moral Supremacy of God above the Laws of Man. What a surprise if our personal identity may be wiped out, and also our name may be taken from us. There is no right we may really claim, and the only concessions we have for Justice are confined to the afterlife!

Why do you believe the Prosecutor dismissed the case stating the vanishing of my personal documents was an Act of God? There was their signature on it, not God's, but in their view they talk on behalf of God, they tell us God's Will, and have High Moral Values above the Laws and good reasons we cannot understand. I don't really know why we still have Courts of Justice, since it is Catholic belief the Law of Man is not the true Law to obey, and we are meant to be just like puppets, with no rights and no freedoms.

Why be surprised if the Public Offices blackmail people for documents people have rights to, and the Courts of Justice vanish the lawsuits reporting the system of corruption and mafia. You imagine in Italy the medical assistance for abortion was legalized after a referendum, but over 70% of doctors and pharmacists refuse to provide their assistance, and 100% of the Prosecutors in the Courts of Justice tolerate this disruption of Public Service. The problem isn't just the office for degrees, or passports, and the Courts of Justice are just useless if not to acknowledge us and remark the origin of the High Moral Values they enforce, not by the Law but God's Will, despite the Courts are paid to defend and apply the Law of man against the aggression of criminals pretending to be above it."

"Do you believe in God?" he asked.

"I cannot really tell, but I know for sure the Earth will always be a polytheistic place. Looking at the Bible printed in the Sky, the Bible of the Book of Nature, eventually we could say it was God who made us all different, with different opinions, but concerning the God of the Catholic Holy Scripture I don't know. The only evidence I see is that his followers are still the same uncivilized barbarians they were when they first arrived in Rome; a bunch of mobsters with High Moral Values above the Law. Can you see, it is all about High Moral Values above the law, corroding the Institutions from the inside?"

I looked over the trees; the sun was on its way to disappearing behind the line of the horizon, and it was time to go home.

"Uncivilized barbarians, with High moral values above the law" he said smiling; "Let me say, you have quite a story to tell. I will stop by again to know more about the book of McIntire. I like to know the end."

"Me too" I replied with a nod. "See you later" I said, and then I made my way following the direction of the stars in the sunset.

Aisling

The day after I got to know Jason, I didn't see Aisling at all. Maybe she could have been at the Park while I was buying a sandwich at the corner shop, I thought, but I was not convincing. On the other hand, she didn't inform me, and one way or another she didn't care. I also thought she could have had an accident, because for some unknown reasons I was feeling she would have told me, if she knew she wasn't coming for a few days.

I was just wondering what could have happened when I noticed the kids laughing and playing in the Park as usual, like the birds twittering, the flowers, the bushes, and everything else in the Park was like every day, but not her. She was missing.

About midday Jason arrived in the Park and joined a cluster of people in front of the ancient house. He stayed with them for a while, long enough for my worries come back, overwhelming my attention until he said hallo. He was with a friend and they both sat on the bench.

"Hi, how are you doing? This is my friend Brian."

"Nice to meet you Brian, how do you do?"

"I am sound thanks" he said, but he didn't really look like it.

"Jason told me you are seeing Aisling quite often recently, is this true?" In his face Brian was tense and apprehensive, like after a night without sleep but Jason didn't give me the time to invent any answer.

"Brian is the boyfriend of Aisling, but recently they have fallen out, and Aisling is missing since yesterday afternoon; do you know something about her? Did you see her today?" Jason asked.

"No, not recently. I was waiting for her yesterday, here in the park, but she didn't turn up, and today either. What do you mean she is missing?" I asked.

"Yes, she is missing" said Brian, "We asked some friends in the Park but nobody saw her since yesterday morning."

"Hope she didn't have any accident" I said, giving voice to my worries.

"No, she is probably just fine, but who knows where she is. Sometimes she likes to ignore her appointments, and vanish with no traces. Almost like she was doing it on purpose to worry people about her."

"Oh, sorry to hear that."

"How long do you know her?" asked Brian.

"Not long really. It is only a few weeks I am coming to the Park. I know she usually comes with her dog, and last week we decided to write a book. But we just started and today, as I said, she didn't turn up. I was waiting for her before you arrived but now I don't know what to do."

Brian was smiling at my answer, almost with satisfaction, while Jason was looking elsewhere."

"We have known Aisling since she was at primary school", Brian said, "It is a long time, you know? She has always been like this, unreliable, untrustworthy and shameless, robbing friends, but now she is stealing the morphine of a friend of ours, a friend with terminal cancer. This is too much and I have to tell her to stay away from him. If she is not ashamed of what she is doing, we are, and we feel embarrassed about it. Using the excuse of taking his dog for a walk, she steals his morphine and his food from the fridge.

We know she has been robbing friends since she was a child; may be she doesn't do it intentionally, but she has been doing it for a long time, and maybe this is the reason why she likes strangers. Not because she likes to know new people, but because the people she knew for longer than 3 days don't trust her anymore. She tries all times to find trust from new people, despite the fact that she will lose their trust very soon and will start all over again with new strangers. She is acting like a tart, a slut and a thief, and who knows? She is always begging for money and probably she also prostitutes herself. But what she does is not our business, the problem is that she has robbed the morphine from our friend, and someone has to tell her, to stay away from his house."

Jason was looking at a few dogs chasing a ball in the meadow, and apparently was not interested in the conversation, but the words of Brian reminded me of the words of Aisling, asking if I could lend her £20. She never said a word to me before, but nobody else did, and I didn't find any problem to lose 20 quid with someone in the Park. Just to see what could have happened, and the result was that I had the money back 2 or 3 days later.

"She must be very desperate to do this. Anyway, the dog she takes for walks in the park is named Gadget, is not her dog but is the dog of our friend with terminal cancer. Today she didn't turn up in the Park simply because she has been paid, and she is getting drunk somewhere." said Brian again, disclosing more elements about the past of Aisling that I would have never known about without his intervention. On the other hand, the words of Brian were really sad, and concerning the desperation of Aisling I already had my own experience since the first time she talked to me.

"I know you are writing the Catholic Satanic Verses with Aisling; she told me" said Brian, reviving my attention, "Believe me, you will never be able to finish your book with her, because she is not consistent; she doesn't have a conscience, the strength of character or the consistency of a Philosopher, or a Heretic. She keeps changing her mind, and the Aisling you speak to today is not the Aisling you speak to tomorrow. She is just a compulsive liar, deceptive and mischievous, a thief robbing friends; unreliable and untrustworthy, an alcoholic tart. She is unable to commit herself, and if you wait for her you're wasting your time. Why don't you ask Kyle or Nancy to help you? Kyle is a passionate reader, and Nancy was a teacher and can do proofreading for you. Ask someone else; with Aisling you are just wasting your time."

These words made echoes all over, shaking the peace of the Park to the core and through every page of the notes she wrote, sitting on this same bench. But Brian was not worried about the book, and continued his outpouring, though my attention had shifted to Aisling and the confidentiality of the book; perhaps she had revealed things about it, including the notes I had collected over the years.

"For a while I sympathized with her for the bad experience she says she had in her adolescence, but probably she is just inventing all of this, as an excuse to justify she is forgetful of things. In reality she only forgets what she doesn't want to know. The problem is not she had that bad experience, but the way she behaves. Every time she gets paid, in few days she spends all the money and every time is the same. Try to ask her to justify this, where she spends her money. And then, skint, she goes to the pub, begging friends for a pint. She is not there. This is what people say of her, she is not there. But in the reality she does it on purpose, and takes advantage of the people she moves to pity; she is evil, and she is a witch not a philosopher, or a Heretic."

I though Brian would have carried on all day with his tirade, but Jason touched him on the shoulder and he became silent.

Aisling was missing for most of the day, and the only thing I could discover was the complaint of someone who knew her for longer than me. On the other hand I don't believe in witches and personally I didn't have the impression she was a psychopath.

"Jason said that Aisling is your girlfriend. Do you love her?"

"I am not sure I love her, but for sure I am ashamed of her, and I feel embarrassed. We have known her for longer than a few weeks, and if you ask me if I love her, may be I did but now I don't know if I feel love or pity for her, but somehow I cannot avoid feeling I have to look after her if she is in trouble."

"I wish I could help" I said looking at the meadow, but the colourful memory of Aisling was fading away, dissolving in the inconsistency and uncertainty of her nature. The overwhelming desperation of Aisling was apparent in her eyes, hiding dreams, screaming for life.

This is what I knew by myself, and I would have paid with all my dreams to see her dreams out of that cage, free of having a past, and a future, out of the present she was confined, unconditionally. Because she was always a nice presence around, despite of the infinite horizon she was hiding behind, with her dreams, and clearly Brian was just unable to accept the unbridgeable distance between his 'real world', and the escape of Aisling from that 'true world' he was pretending to be. The true world of Aisling was secret in her heart, far away from us, and after the words of Brian I could only wish she was safe and sound as usual; but while the in coming night was rising from the horizon I could only see her crying, for the silence of my answer to him. And if she were not crying for this reason, she would have cried for the impossible distance silencing every possible conversation.

Aisling is not without reason the muse of the Catholic Satanic Verses I should have said, and if she didn't obey his dreams, the dreams of Brian, was only because she had her own dreams, the dreams she was secretly crying for. And the evil, predatory attitude of Aisling emerging from the words of Brian, to me was only the cry of a broken heart, the heart of Aisling. She is not a witch grasping at people's weakness; she is seeking a friend accepting her the way she is, I would have said, but I didn't have the courage to admit to myself the feeling of pity I was also feeling for her, and the blackmail concealed in it.

The Aisling I knew clearly was not Brian's Aisling, and if she was missing all day, the solution probably was to be found in the figment of our imagination, factually transforming her into another person to please our dreams. Clearly the difference between being free or lost, for Brian was not a point for a possible conversation. She is not there, he said, and probably Aisling for Brian was only lost, inconsistent and unable to share meanings and values. Sure, in theory Aisling was free to choose, including the freedom to choose to be lost, but in reality she could only pursue her nature while in the mind of Brian she was only disobedient and unresponsive, intentionally, and not by nature.

A few minutes after Brian and Jason left I walked out of the Park, and took the long way home to do some shopping to help me survive the incoming nightmares. The Indian woman at the convenience store was kind as usual, and I imagined her speaking with Aisling, about chakras and reincarnation until I walked out, just in time to cross Aisling in front of the shop.

"Hi, how do you do?" I asked, with all my worries in front of me.

"Fine" she said lively.

"Are you walking this way?" I asked again, but she was going in the opposite direction.

"See you later" I said, and walked home with no dreams to defend, as if I hadn't seen her at all. Maybe the next day she would turn up in the Park, maybe not, but for sure she was just fine, and was not missing anymore. She was simply enjoying herself.

The Education Act

The day after I met Aisling at the convenience store I went to the park only in the afternoon, because I found from the Internet some information I couldn't find at the library. Having seen her the evening before sound and well it cleared up all my worries, and the only real problem left to resolve was to find some sources to introduce a few points I was discussing in my writing.

For a few different reasons I was to choose to refer a few quotes and references from Wikipedia anyway, despite the fact that the text of its pages is unstable as much as the text of the Bible, and later these quotes could have been a problem if they were not to be found as a consequence of the text changes. On the other hand also the quote to the biographical page of Galileo Galilei was not straightforward, because Galileo in Wikipedia was described as Italian, despite never knowing of Italy, and that was resulting in something apparently mysterious and contradictory, like the Gospel of Saint Peter, or the Catholic Heresies transforming into Catholic Legacy. Maybe at Wikipedia nobody ever thought that pretending Galileo as Italian is exactly the same as pretending Julius Caesar was Italian, in fact at the time of Galileo Italy didn't exist, the same as for Julius Caesar who was building the Roman Empire, and none of them ever mentioned the word 'Italy' exactly for the same reason.

Nevertheless a few bibliographic references and quotes were necessary, and would have been helpful especially for those people determined to satisfy their curiosities with some more reading. Maybe Wikipedia could have been helpful with its bibliographic references, providing suggestions and further directions, and the only references really missing were those concerning how the Catholic Heresies became Catholic Legacy. Also the page summarizing the Christian Heresies on Wikipedia [W37] was in need of some substantial integration, in fact the descriptions of such historical blasphemies were only reporting the Religious perspective of the heresies, but never mentioned how these Heresies were affecting the freedom of everyday life, like the freedom of knowing about Eratosthenes perhaps, living 600 years before the Nicaea Council flattened the planet. The case of intellectual freedom of thought and freedom of choice was completely missing from the long list of Heresies on Wikipedia, like the most basic freedoms were not the most persecuted Heresies; like the problem with Ario really was the Trinity and not his freedom of thought, claiming the rights for his personal understanding. Who else could I have quoted on the side of François-Marie Arouet [W38], the popular pen name of Voltaire, advocating the separation of Church and State?

As regards the problem with the bibliographic references, concerning how the Catholic Heresies became Catholic Legacy, recently I was researching the Education Acts, and typing in the search engine immediately came out the Education Act ratified in 1944. From the website [A8] with the introduction and the comment on the Act, also the full text of the Law was available to download. The site was well organized and documented, so I took interest in the reading it and spent all morning with it.

The Culture and Tradition compatible with the Italian Revisionism by now was already crystal clear, and my only curiosity was kept alive solely by my expectation of the legacy of Henry the VIII.

Obviously I was trying to find the modern day reasons responsible for pretending any possible confusion between Catholic Legacy and Catholic Heresies, such as the Catholic Heresies historically were not important, and not religiously persecuted for ages, so today could be disregarded as being part of the ancient past. Who was to gain from this situation? As usual I was interested in freedom of thought and freedom of choice, which are the foundation of our present-day democracies but also essential parts of Human Nature; the essential and distinctive part of each one of us, with our own mind and feelings.

Aisling of course was in the air all morning, wavering between her freedom of choice and the overwhelming necessity of her nature, and I was really wondering how much she could have been really responsible for her behaviour, if the words of Brian were true, depicting her as a witch and a fallen woman, fallen from the Grace of God and ready for the Magdalene laundries [W49].

The ideas of Fate and Destiny were clashing strongly with Free Will, and I was wondering what Free Will, what freedom of choice did Aisling ever have to oppose and defend against the inconsistency of her nature? What was really in her discretion, if her freedom couldn't control the necessity of her nature? I am not sure she was responsible for her actions, and I strongly believe nobody would have chosen a life of misery and chaos like she was apparently doing. The other option was to believe Brian was wrong, which was much easier and consistent with my personal experience of Aisling. In fact to me she was just like a star in the sky, a star from the book of nature, taking her chances one at a time within the constraints of the present she was forced to live in.

It was about noon when I decided to go for a walk in the Park. I did some printing from the website I was reading, with the intention to summarise a few simple points, and then I walked down the stairs and opened the door. The fresh air of the garden flooded my lungs with the brilliance of the sunshine, and the surprise of a white wild rose left on my doorstep. I don't have white wild roses in my garden, and neither did the neighbours I thought, checking their gardens. I took the rose back to the kitchen, I put it into a glass with some water and I walked out.

The mystery of the white wild rose completely diverted my attention all along the way to the Park, wiping out my interest in the Education Acts I found a few hours before. Maybe Aisling really left the rose. Maybe the day before she followed me from the convenience store and I didn't see her, but most probably it was a mistake and someone got the wrong doorstep. Next door was living a really well mannered single woman in her thirties, and a rose on her doorstep would have been much easier to understand. Or maybe the wind did it, but during the night because at present I couldn't feel any wind. I walked all the way dreaming of this new mystery until I crossed the gate of the Park and I saw a large isle of wild white roses, not far from the bench where I used to sit, staring at the sunset. She used to arrive from the meadow behind those bushes, and maybe Aisling left the rose I thought again, but also this time I didn't convince myself. If she didn't go to the Park for days, it couldn't be her. I was still staring at the flowers when Jason arrived, taking away my attention from my dreams.

"Hi Jason" I welcomed him arriving.

"Hi" he said smiling, "How are you doing today? Have you been writing? Have you finished reading McIntire?"

That was somewhat embarrassing, and made me smile back. Definitely the book was not part of my private life anymore, and I was really curious to know what Aisling could have disclosed to Brian.

"No, I didn't open McIntire today. This morning I spent some time on the Education Acts, the milestones of Public Education in England."

"Are you comparing it with the Italian?" he asked.

"Not really, no. Looking for the National Culture and its System of Values, the school programs are the starting point. I am after the influence of Religion in the classrooms, when Religion interferes and prevents the natural individual curiosity of students, distorting or obliterating the original information like in the cases of Galileo or Eratosthenes, or Henry VIII."

"England is Anglican since the time of Henry VIII, but the best schools today are Catholic" he said promptly.

"Are you sure of what you are saying?" I asked.

"Yes I am sure. This is the way it is" he said, confirming it with a nod.

"I wouldn't say that; I would feel more confident of the opposite. Just consider the Catholic Revisionism and Censorship in History, from Eratosthenes to Galileo and you will see with your own eyes that Catholic Education will never educate students to be citizens but good Catholic only. The Catholic School only respects Catholic Authority, not the Secular Authority of the State, and this is also emerging from the Education Acts I was reading this morning."

"And what about Aisling, did you see her?" he asked, clearing all my thoughts.

"Yes," I said smiling. "Yesterday, on my way home from the convenience store. She was busy with something, but she was fine. She only said a few words."

"Sorry for Brian, yesterday, but he was really worried and asking everybody."

"No problem. I was wondering and waiting for her, the same as you."

"Do you know what is she doing today?" he asked again.

"I don't have a clue. I have been at home reading all morning, and I just arrived in the park. What do you mean? Is she missing also today? I don't believe it; she is not! She is somewhere enjoying herself" I said, expressing my disbelief.

"Yes, she is probably enjoying herself, like a kid" he said with a nod, and I wished he could have said something more about her, maybe something to contradict Brian, but he didn't, and I didn't ask.

"So you are investigating Education in England. You are serious with your writing then" he asked, as if testing my commitment.

"Well, yes. I like to inform myself, criticize, and try to contradict myself before someone else will do so; just for the sake of doing the right thing. This is why I am wondering how the Catholic Heresies could possibly be Catholic Legacy, it is impossible, and I don't believe anybody ever asked about this confusion."

"Right, I remember you said this before, talking about the book of McIntire, but what are the Catholic Heresies? What are they?"

"Yes, we spoke about Justice; about the law of man on

this side of the grave, and about the Divine Justice of the afterlife. But the Roman Catholic Church throughout history has condemned a number of heresies, and not just the Human pretence to administer Justice. Initially the matter was limited to Religious issues, but later became more and more related to all aspects of life and knowledge. There is a variety of Heresies, affecting people's life in different ways. For example the nature of the Holy Trinity to me is not important, one or another doesn't make any difference. On the other hand also freedom of choice and freedom of thought have been persecuted as the mother of all heresies, in philosophy, science, arts, and this makes a big difference to our every day life.

A number of people have been burned at the stake for heresy, and it may be worth emphasizing that all heresies always had in common the same freedom of thought and freedom of choice, and the Catholic Church never tolerated any kind of personal understanding or feeling from the side of the worshipper. Maybe today there is no stake of the inquisition, but students not conforming to the lecture of the professors won't pass the exams, and will be condemned for life anyway. The only individuality required by the Church is the Act of conforming to its Will, and definitely after the Nicaea Council no personal understanding was ever needed anymore, not even to be baptized.

The Sacrament of Baptism is a good example to introduce the Catholic Heresies. In fact we know from the notes of the Nicaea Council [W39] that one of the main points in discussion was the duration of catechism, the course in preparation to the Sacrament of the Baptism. It is obvious a course requires students with the adequate age and ability to talk, and to understand, but nowadays we don't need this anymore. Nowadays no Act of Will or Choice is necessary to be baptized, but it was at the time of the original Christianity.

Nowadays also Jesus and Saint Peter would consider baptism a heresy for a child who cannot understand and who cannot freely choose with a deliberate Act of Will. But this is in harmony with the aim of the Roman Empire, to make unity through religious culture. This is for sure; in 325 AD, at the time of the Nicaea Council the Act of Will and the preparation course were still necessary, but sometime later most of the Holy Scriptures got lost, and all have changed. In facts, at the time of the Nicaea Council the Emperor Constantine commissioned Eusebius to make 50 copies of the Bible by assembling all the available Holy Scriptures, and at that time there were more books available than there are now [W5][W6][W7]. During the preparation of the Bible of Eusebius a letter of Serapion also came out with the relics of the Gospel of Saint Peter [W14], which was already condemned as heretical over 100 years before, because of alleged docetism [W16]. In evidence 8 out of 12 apostles have been intentionally wiped out of the Bible, but at the time of Constantine there was no Bible at all, he made it, and shortly after him also the Bible of Constantine went missing, all together with the relic of the Gospel of Saint Peter, the first stone of Christianity, and our rights of today to choose to be baptized. If we consider Jesus never wrote anything personally, and the Gospels are reports of intermediate persons anyway, the only certainty is the imposition of unconditional obedience.

Probably Baptism is one of the reasons why we have only 4 Gospels left in our current Bibles, but the original Christianity had several issues not conforming to the Roman Church, and for this reason not even the Bible of Constantine survived for long. Why be surprised if the Gospel of Saint Peter was condemned as Heresy, and vanished from the Bible? From the perspective of the Church it is clear, Saint Peter, the first rock of Christianity, the first disciple of Jesus, was also the first Heretic; and similarly to the Act of Choice and Will required for baptism, also the Freedom of thought and the Freedom of Conscience had to be wiped out.

Maybe the freedom of thought has never been persecuted for itself, but it has been persecuted in all its expressions, in all matters of knowledge, including the freedom of being as we are, human and individuals, all different. This is indisputable evidence from the Book of Nature, we are all different but for the Church we don't have the right to be different from each other and have different opinions. The problem emerges because the Church considers the Book of Nature to be an Act of Disobedience and Rebellion to its Authority, and we cannot be as we are, with our personal understanding and feelings."

"What does it mean the word 'Heresy'?"

"The original meaning of Heresy [W40] is 'choice', it is the Act of Choosing, the personal 'chosen choice'. But a Heresy may also be a provocative belief, a theory or a different idea at variance with the more accepted and established beliefs or customs, or at variance with the social System of Values."

"Ideas at variance with the common beliefs are still discriminated against today" he said, and made me smile.

"Sure they are. Our Religion is reproducing on earth the order they wish in Heaven, with one man like God ruling the entire planet at will, like we were puppets; our Society is dogmatic and authoritarian, the same as our Religion is, and this emphasizes it cannot possibly be the same God responsible for both, the Book of Nature and the Christian Bible. Because the Bible doesn't fit human nature, but only the most naïve of human fears.

Another popular example of Heresy comes with Galileo Galilei. The Catholic Inquisition arrested him with the accusation of supporting the heliocentric theory, stating that the earth is not at the center of the Universe. At the time of Galileo the heliocentric theory was a Heresy, it was in the index of the prohibited books, it was a prohibited idea not conforming to the Catholic teaching, and in this scenario Galileo become a Historic figure not because he did something special but because he abjured and recanted, as the Church forced him to do. He became popular because of his renunciation of his personal opinion in exchange for his life, but Eratosthenes had measured the circumference of Earth almost 2000 years before the birth of Galileo. Of course Galileo is to be admire for what he accomplished, but other people have been incredibly ingenious long before Galileo, and have been censored by the same censors as Galileo. The one thing I am concerned is the regime of terror and the intellectual oppression, the culture of ignorance, prejudice and preconceptions established by the Catholic Church. Galileo had been watching the stars like millions of other people did before him, but he lined up with the Heliocentric Theory of Copernicus and that was sufficient to take him in front of the Tribunal of the Inquisition. On the other hand we can be sure the heliocentric theory was not hurting the expectations or the Will of God, and were not the stars in the sky feeling offended, but the stars on this planet.

It may be worth remembering at the time of Galileo the Inquisition used to burn Heretics at the stake, just because of suspicion, or the word of some anonymous informants. The links with nowadays are multiple, and don't concern only anonymous informing. Today, like at the time of Galileo, all the best Universities with the highest fees pretend the Catholic Heresies are Catholic Legacy, and pretend that Italy is the flagship of the Renaissance Culture, even if Italy is the most Catholic Country of all, which makes this impossible, and makes their words intentionally misleading. It should be clear, for a Catholic school teaching the Catholic Heresies would be sacrilegious, like teaching blasphemies, and the Catholic Heresies could never be Catholic Legacy, nevertheless all our best Universities continue to sow the seeds of this confusion, systematically, pretending to disguise and mask the Catholic Heresies as Catholic Legacy.

But this is not the Universities to decide on this matter, and I am not inventing anything when I say that the school textbooks really pretend that Italy is the flagship of Renaissance Culture, despite the fact that Italy is the most Catholic Country on earth, and despite the fact that the Renaissance Culture is entirely made of Catholic Heresies, blasphemies, persecuted by the Roman Catholic Inquisition. Isn't it obvious that the Roman Church had its strongest influence on the Italian Peninsula, and the

Renaissance Culture in Italy was persecuted more than everywhere else? Definitely the blasphemies and heretical values of the Renaissance Culture in Italy have never been accepted or tolerated, at any time, and not even today."

"About Italy and the Renaissance I remember nice documentaries on the BBC. I also remember from the schoolbooks, but now I understand Italy was the home to the Inquisition, and as a consequence the Renaissance was out of place, as a blasphemy, on the top of the list of the prohibited books. This is clear, yes" he said.

"The Catholic Legacy doesn't mix with the Catholic Heresies, and the Catholic Schools may only represent the Catholic System of Values above the law, and not the forbidden Heresies, at the origin of the Values of the Law of man, giving us freedom of thought and freedom of choice."

"Why are you doing this?" he asked, guessing my intentions. "Do you believe you are a superhero to fight all of this?"

"No. Sure I am not a superhero, but it doesn't need a superhero to ask how the Catholic Heresies become Catholic Legacy, and in evidence we need someone to ask because we have lost the most important part of our rights. There are several reasons why I am doing this, and at this point my personal story is the last in the list.

Mostly I wonder who is to pass the exams, and then I wonder what was the target of our expensive education; what can we expect in the future? The schoolbooks pretend a number of contradictions, printed black and white, and apparently nobody ever asked for an explanation concerning how the Catholic Heresies became Catholic Legacy. What am I supposed to believe? Through the ages people have been genetically selected as stupid, and now there are only selected stupid people left? I cannot believe this, but I seriously wonder how it would be possible to believe that nobody ever asked, because the main point in discussion is not Religion but the Laws of Man and our most important Civil Freedoms and Rights. This is not happening by chance, and this regime resemble an intellectual cleansing; there is a holocaust going on, this is why nobody ever asked. It is not possible it happened by chance, and despite whatever selection may have happened through the ages, it would never have been possible to make people be all the same. The pretence that nobody ever asked, is just one of these things, inexplicable.

Furthermore you know about my degree and passport, you know about the Courts of Justice sweeping the legal claims under the carpets, and the mobsters printing fake documents for friends, with the blessing of the bishop, while blackmailing honest people for documents they have right to. It is always them doing it, and it is always matter of High Moral Values above the Law, but the brand, the variety of that God is evident from the reading of the schoolbooks. We are living in the dark ages, and Divine Destiny is shaping our lives in the offices, with the signatures of a bunch of mobsters and counterfeiters. What is the probability nobody has ever asked? What is the likelihood it was really God making all these documents vanish; gospels, and people, and legal suits, all vanished into thin air. Why to pretend God did it?"

"You are right there" he said. "I thought about your video and your complaint. It shouldn't have taken so long, maybe a few days but not years. What is the point in taking a degree, if later the office of the University makes you into an impostor and have to pass through this? The photograph of your Degree Ceremony is really creepy. I believe you may also had good marks, did you?".

His words brought up all kind of memories and thoughts, with me carrying the textbooks from home to the classroom every day for years.

"Yes I did" I said, "And there is no possible explanation to change the facts in discussion, after years, and years. But time, is what they rely on. They are not in a hurry, and the later they will have to explain what they have done, the better it will be. I do repeat, the report from the European Union finished up in the bin, not by chance, and was not an Act of God.

On the other hand we know the relationship between the Roman Church and the Law of man, it has never been an easy relationship, from the start; since the time the Christians arrived in Rome pretending the Law of Rome was not the true law to obey. This is the reason why the Catholics turned up in the Coliseum with the lions, and today we are still talking about the same High Moral Values above the laws, like I was reading this morning from the comments to the 1944 Education Act. That really made me ashamed."

"I would have never imagined finding an Italian in the Park, against the Catholic Church, reading McIntire, and discussing Catholic Heresies. Are you sure you are from Italy, Catholic Educated?" he asked.

"I am not against the Church; this is not correct and it has to be cleared up because I truly believe in Freedom of Religion, as it is an instance of the Freedom of Choice. On the other hand, Religion is influencing our textbooks, and perpetrates all kind of intellectual abuses and coercion, subjugating and brainwashing people. I am not against the Church; but I also believe they should be proud of what they do, and this is why I like to recall the several and recurrent intellectual cleansing they have perpetrated in the name of the Catholic Supremacy and its High Moral Values above the Law. It's not just a matter of people like Kyenge, Regeni or their beloved bishops. They pretend they have the mission to save us, but in reality the Catholic Church is not bothered about Religion or God, not as much as the Political Power above the laws of the State, so they can save us even if we don't want to. It was probably the Catholic Church that influenced and taught Machiavelli [W41] that «The end justifies the means», but his politics was the essence of treachery, deceit and betrayal.

On the other hand, if someone is not with them, he has to be against them because in their mind there is no other choice; this is the way they interpret people independence from the Religious precepts of the Bible they have vandalized in order to save us.

Anyway, concerning the Catholic Religion I have been

excommunicated and I am almost out of it" I said with a smile.

"If you have been excommunicated, you are out all the way" he said after a chuckling laugh.

"That is not true. The Dioceses said that Baptism cannot be cancelled, because it is an Administrative Act of the Italian State, and cannot be cancelled. So, it is only half way out, mainly because it is impossible to get rid of it. Even if you were in the list of the top ten Heretics you would still be listed as Catholic Baptized. In Italy the Church reports over 98% of people are Catholic, and on the other hand 5% claim are not Catholic at all. After the mathematics of the Trinity, what would you expect? In Italy live 103% population, and that is it."

"You are trying to drive me crazy, are you?" he resumed. "I understand you are serious, and you are reporting the evidence of facts, but I am missing the point. Why is the Italian Administration doing all this, and why don't the Italian people strike, or protest? Did you try to write to some newspapers?"

"Oh yes I did. I have asked a few Journalists of the two main newspapers in Italy, 'Corriere della Sera' and 'la Repubblica', but I never had an answer. I also tried taping the telephone conversations and making videos with the recordings, but still with no result."

"You enjoyed yourself during your protest, did you? Did you record any good funny call?" he asked.

"I did one in English, with the Chicago Tribune. I asked the Journalist how the Catholic Heresies become Catholic Legacy."

"And what was the answer?" he asked.

"He said he had no idea, and he asked me to explain how?"

"And you?"

"With a Holocaust. I said it happened with a Holocaust."

"How did you think to call the Chicago Tribune? That was crazy" he said.

"Not really, no. The excuse for that call was an article published in the Chicago Tribune, 'Measuring Nepotism:

the case of Italian Academia' [A11][A12][A13]. It was concerning the report of Stefano Allesina, an Italian Researcher in Chicago pretending the frequency of the surnames of the Professors in the Italian Universities is evidence of nepotism and corruption in Italian Academia. The article was also in the Italian newspaper 'Corriere della Sera'."

"Did you call the Italian Newspaper as well?" he asked.

"Of course I did" I said, promptly and smiling.

"What did you say to the Italians?" he asked.

"I said it was rough Justice, Mussolini style, and I suggested asking all the teaching staff how the Catholic Heresies became Catholic Legacy, including Journalists, prosecutors and judges. Because in my experience I cannot doubt University Degrees go missing from the offices, legal suits do disappear from the Courts of Justice, and apparently nobody ever asked how the Catholic Heresies became Catholic Legacy. But I can fix this last problem; this little bug concerning how the Catholic Heresies became Catholic Legacy I can explain in this life, on this side of the Horizon."

"I do imagine you never had any answer to your questions, did you? Why don't you ask something with some possible answers?" he asked smiling.

"There is an answer for these questions; it takes a permanent holocaust. To transform the Catholic Heresies into Catholic Legacy it simply takes a permanent holocaust, acting every moment of every day.

Eventually in this call to the 'Corriere della Sera' the Italian Journalist Lorenzo Salvia admitted the theory of corruption and nepotism Mr. Stefano Allesina was reporting, was not discriminating against as many people as the religious interference I was asking to explain. Furthermore, not all surnames have the same frequency in the general population, but even if Allesina did this evaluation, what is corruption? Standardizing the frequency of the surnames of the professors would never change the racism, the preconceptions and intellectual obscenity printed in the school textbooks."

"Why did you say racism?" he asked.

"Because this is what it is. You may call it cultural hatred or xenophobia, it is just another of several manifestations of racial but above all cultural discrimination. It was not Mussolini who invented the Cultural Supremacy and the Racial Laws" I said, like he could have known. "Mussolini was a Socialist, a materialist, and to obtain Catholic approval and support he had to invent something, so he came out with Fascism, the Catholic brand of Socialism, socialism in which the morality is not to be found in the Laws of Man but in the High Moral Values of the Church. Mussolini Catholicized the Socialist ideology; he enacted the Moral and Cultural Supremacy of the Catholic Tradition, and also the motivation of the Racial Laws is to be found in the same High Moral Values of the Concordat, at the origin of the Political Career of Mussolini. In fact most of his enemies were not Jews, as someone may suppose. Most of the people persecuted by Mussolini were Italians who had lined up with democratic or liberal ideologies, the old enemies of the Roman Church since the time of the French Revolution; democrats labelled anarchists, Apostates or infidel because of their ideals, claiming there are no High Moral Values above the Law.

Mussolini signed the Lateran Treaty in 1929 [W3], that was the 'Concordat' with the Church but it was not Mussolini who invented the Catholic Supremacy, that was already there; the ideology motivating the Cultural Supremacy and the Racial laws of Mussolini was already there ages before him. Mussolini simply dismissed all parties and closed Parliament; only the Church was allowed to make suggestions, like in the case of the Racial Laws and the Cultural Supremacy in the Classrooms.

This kind of racism I am talking about is nothing to do with skin colour, but nevertheless is responsible for several recurrent holocausts and intellectual cleansings throughout history, all with the blessing of the Pope. I hope I made it clear Mussolini simply embraced Catholic Politics, the Catholic Supremacy, and also the Racial Laws he enacted were in accord with the Concordat and the High Moral

Values of the Church.

But what does it matter? To Mr Allesina, the Italian researcher unveiling to the world the secrets of the Italian Mafia, the corruption and the nepotism of the Italian Academia is nothing to do with the Catholic Supremacy and the Concordat of Mussolini, and to improve the Italian Academia it is only necessary to standardize the surnames rather than questioning the obscenity printed in the school books."

"Yes, it sounds right, but why do you believe people are unresponsive to this shame?" he asked.

"I don't have a clue; most people just do what they are asked to do, and never doubt what they are doing. This is the way people are, the way they have been educated, and probably there are more reasons. Like the Professors before being professors they were students, and later carried on their life teaching what they were taught. They simply never questioned themselves or their knowledge, assuming it to be true and smart, good enough to pass the exams.

To pass the exams is supposed to be a good result of value, but I am not sure anymore. This is why I wonder who is to pass the exams, and I would like to ask them how the Catholic Heresies become Catholic Legacy. All of this is emerging from the school textbooks, and since they have passed the exams, they should be able to answer, shouldn't they?"

"Did you ever ask directly some professor?" he enquired curiously.

"Yes it happened, more than once. Usually it takes them a while to understand the question, and then they usually admit in their perspective there is no answer for it, and pretend this is the way it is, and they are not personally responsible because they only execute orders and honestly make their living out of it. They only do what they are told to do, and this is what they do for living. Like the professors in the picture of my degree ceremony, Emilio Tiberi and Bianca De Bernardi, like the prosecutors Guido Papalia, or Corrado Carnevali, the recipient of the legal suit from the European Union. But also Journalists and Politicians don't make any difference. None of them is at variance with the established System of High Moral Values above the law. Mussolini made a Reason of State out of this, and it is still in the Italian Constitution today in Article 7, placing the Values of the Concordat above the Constitution."

"So, tell me something you read this morning, what made you feel ashamed?"

"I have with me a few pages from the website I was reading this morning. It is by Derek Gillard, and the Internet address is educationengland.org.uk [A8]. I can read a few notes for you" I said, quickly checking through the pages. "Let me resume a bit of history" I said, and I started consulting my notes.

"The 1902 Education Act established the Local Education Authorities (LEAs) from the previous organization established in 1888. To the LEAs was conferred the authority to control the programs concerning secular teaching, and it was the LEAs which provided the grants for Public Education. On the other hand in order to access the grants the schools had to conform to secular education. Here I read from the words of Derek."

> Quote from EducationEngland.org.uk [A8.2]
> «Church of England schools generally heeded the rule that no pupil or teacher should be required to conform to religious belief or ritual. Roman Catholic schools were less enthusiastic about obeying the rule. They enforced religious observance more strictly and in 1917 the church issued a canon expressly forbidding Catholic parents from sending their children to non-Catholic schools on pain of excommunication.» [End Quote]

"The 'Title XXII' of the 1917 Canon Law is all about education [A24][W51], but do you see?" I asked. "The LEAs represent the control of the Secular State and have authority over the secular curriculum. On the other hand the Catholic Church was not really interested in organizing Religious education in accordance with the secular values of the secular State, and in 1917 the Pope issued a Canon Law forbidding on pain of excommunication Catholic students going to non Catholic Schools. In essence the Church was blackmailing both Catholic families and the State, and from this it should be clear Catholic Education is not about teaching people how to be citizens but to be puppets, or mobsters, disregarding and boycotting the secular values and the Culture of the Laws of Man. Is it clear, it was blackmail? Then in 1936 the Education Act introduced the syllabus for Religion teaching, and in 1944 was introduced the Act of Worship. Here I read again from Derek."

> Quote from EducationEngland.org.uk [A8.1]
> «In the years following the 1944 Act, most Church of England aided schools taught the local Agreed Syllabus but supplemented it. Roman Catholic schools ignored the Agreed Syllabus and sought to indoctrinate their pupils through a more confessional style of religious instruction, 'very much concentrated on introducing children to the Catholic community of faith (Gates 2005:23)'» [End Quote] [A7].

On the other hand concerning the temporal power of the Pope, from the book of McIntire we know, I read that

> Quote from 'England against the Papacy' [A2, Pag 2]
> «The Papal States dated at least from the 750s when King Pippin of the Franks granted Pope Stephen II extensive territory which the Franks had taken from the Lombards. With the authority of both the Lombards and Byzantium broken in Italy, the Pope became the effective political authority in the region. The Pope and the Frankish regarded the act as a restoration of the 'donation of Constantine' from the fifth century.» [End Quote] [W66]

But a few pages down concerning the 'English experience' and the secularization of modern society in 19th century McIntire continues writing

> Quote from 'England against the Papacy' [A2, Pag 8]
> «But the English opposition to the Papacy was powerful, too, because it arose out of an essential feature of English identity. Since the sixteen century, through the struggles of the English Reformation, to be truly English meant to be against the Pope.»
> [End Quote]

I understand Derek is disappointed concerning the Catholic Interpretation of the Secular Values of the Laws of Man, but I never spoke to Derek, not yet, and maybe he has no experience of vanishing degrees and people, passport and lawsuits. Do you see? For someone Justice is something Divine, not from this planet, but for someone else Justice is just in accord with the Laws of Man, and at one point you will have to ask yourself who is ruling the Country? Like Henry the VIII had to ask himself."

"What do you mean?"

"I mean Henry VIII was prevented from making laws concerning divorce, and he may have asked himself who was ruling the Kingdom if The King couldn't make a law. The Pope was factually suggesting to him to get rid of his wife, in accord with the tradition, but probably Henry loved her so much he refused to kill her, and as a consequence he got all the trouble. I am feeling confident, Henry loved his wife, and the Anglican Church in reality is a Love Story."

"It maybe, but he was a tyrant and even if he didn't kill his wife, he killed thousands of people. It is apparent he could have killed his wife if he wanted, but for sure England has been Anglican ever since."

"I am not sure Henry was the tyrant he is depicted, but for sure he was the only Anglican in a country of Catholics, and this magnifying glass makes him responsible for what he probably never did. If I had to learn about Henry VIII, the last place I would go to ask would be a Catholic School" I said, "Because they would probably pretend Henry VIII was disobedient, and maybe also a murderer, simply because he didn't obey the Pope refusing to kill his wife in accord with the tradition. On the other hand, do you believe the Catholic Church would be able to teach secular values, like the separation of Church and State, or the reasons why Henry made his refusal? And what about teaching Renaissance Culture, or the Catholic Heresies, or the disappearance of Eratosthenes from the schoolbooks? Sure, the Church is no less a tyrant than Henry; but he wasn't!

For quite a long time I have researched bibliographic references concerning how the Catholic Heresies become Catholic Legacy; do you believe I will ever find any from the schoolbooks or the research of any Catholic University?

You said that Catholic Education is the best education in England: play this game. If you find a Catholic teacher able to answer the questions I ask in my videos, I will pay you four times the highest reward I offer for an answer. It should be about 8000 Euros, Pounds or Dollars as you like" I said. "The currency makes no difference."

"Do you really offer 2000 Euros reward for the answers to the questions in your videos?" he asked with some surprise.

"Yes I do. I made videos asking how the Catholic Heresies became Catholic Legacy. I am sure of what I am saying, and I am solid in my intention to reward all the reasonable answers because I am confident there are no possible answers other than the few I already suggested in my videos. The Regulation is in the description of the videos, the only limitations concern the copy and paste, which is not allowed from previous answers, neither from my videos where I talk about it. It must be new original answer I didn't discuss and nobody suggested in the comments."

"You are doing this because you know there is no answer to these questions."

"This is not true; is not true there is no answer. To do this it takes a permanent holocaust; it would never happen that by chance, all the Universities with no exception pretending to confuse the Catholic Heresies as Catholic Legacy. All the questions I am asking emerge from the schoolbooks, and both professors and students should be able to answer or to understand they have wasted their time and money on false education they didn't need.

There is no evidence to believe Catholic Education may be better, but there are a number of reasons to believe it cannot be better. Yes, there are answers to my questions, especially to the most recent Racial Laws of Mussolini there are reasonable and documented answers, in the Concordat, and also to the historical tradition of recurrent holocausts and intellectual cleansing there are documented answers, since the Nicaea Council up to now.

Maybe students believe they are receiving a good education for the money they are paying, and probably only a few of them will understand after long years what that education really was. Students only pay for the show of a magician giving the appearance that the Catholic Heresies are Catholic Legacy, but deep inside it is clear, the same England that made a war against the Racist Cultural Supremacy of Mussolini, after World War II turned teaching into exactly the same as Mussolini was doing.

In fact after War World II the State Schools were abolished, the religious denomination schools took over, and after the Vatican Council II reunified the Christian World, Churchill found himself teaching the same High Moral Values above the law, the same as Mussolini was doing since before the war. Why do you believe still today Nazis are wanted and prosecuted, whilst no Fascists were ever condemned for perpetrating the same crimes as the Nazis?

But Mussolini was persecuting Democrats as Apostates of the faith, not Jews. More Apostates of the faith have been persecuted during WWII than Jews, as the Democratic Values were the problem, not the Jew. If today we cannot claim the rights we are supposed to have, it is only because these rights are in the Index of the Inquisition and have been persecuted as Catholic Heresies throughout history.

Nowadays, the Catholic Heresies are Catholic Legacy also in the English schoolbooks; what difference do you believe there may be between a Catholic Course by Mussolini or by anybody else? It will be a Catholic Course imposing the Roman Catholic Supremacy, and its Tradition of High Moral Values above the Law."

"I can see what you are saying" he said. "Yes, I believe the professors should reply. It is clear someone is misleading, and about this I would like to know more especially from their office" he said.

"It is not the Universities to decide about this, but politics; and yes, they are obligated to answer, but never did" I said promptly. "By statute the professors have an obligation to answer questions also from the public, but as long as the questions are not public, it is like nobody ever asked them."

"I understand. Nobody sees, nobody knows, and this is the reason for the book you are doing with Aisling. I am surprised she found interest in this, but she also was at the University wasn't she?"

"Yes, she said she was."

"But, if the revisionism in Education is so manipulative also in England, why do all these people come to England for their Education?" he asked, almost surprising me.

"This is funny isn't it? I believe most of the students came for the education after a degree, like a PhD, or a master's degree, or to improve their English Language."

"What is the problem with PhD degrees?" he asked again inquisitively.

"I came for a PhD, because I couldn't organise it in Italy."

"And why is this?"

"Because in Italy you may prove the Holy Shroud of Turin is really bearing the image of Jesus, but the Book of Nature is off limits. Because the Italian Constitution guarantees the freedom of Education, but forgets to mention it has to conform to the Catholic Tradition and meritocracy; it has to conform to the Bible, and not to the Book of Nature. It is about intellectual emancipation, independence, and the censorship of the mainstream unable to answer the easiest questions quoted from their schoolbooks.

Also the Renaissance and the French Revolution were about intellectual emancipation from the Catholic Tradition, but in the Catholic territory of Italy these new ideas have never arrived with their original and heretical meanings, but only after Catholic adaptation and Revisionism.

There is no lack of ideologies in Italy, and you may find Catholic pretending to be democrats, and also Catholic pretending to be communists, anarchists and socialists, despite them living by the same High Moral Values above the law as always.

It is like Allesina, pretending to expose the Italian Mafia, just to claim his rights to join them, sharing the advantages of being above the law. He is not concerned about improving education, but sharing personal advantages. He is not questioning the schoolbooks for the best interest of the students, and since he is respectful of the traditions he wonders why he cannot have his slice in return."

"You said something about the Cultural Supremacy of Mussolini, what was it? Is it like the Supremacy Act of Henry VIII?" he asked.

"In a way, yes. Henry proclaimed the Law of the State is above the Laws of Religion, and as consequence Religions have to respect the law of the State; he proclaimed his Supremacy in ruling his kingdom, with or without the consent of the Pope. He was proclaiming his independence from the Church, while Mussolini was seeking it in order to gain political power. As a socialist he would have never been elected, and probably from his perspective it was better to be a Catholicized Socialist elected, rather than never being elected at all. The Lateran Treaty is the bond, the Concordat, the foundation of the Italian Socialism, and in this Catholic spiritual perspective Mussolini has persecuted all the secular ideologies like democratic and liberal and socialist, as Apostates, infidels and Enemies of the State. He made a real holocaust in Italy, with the blessing of the Pope, and nobody ever talks about this because it was just a matter of High Moral Values against Secular Ideologies demanding no one is above the law. The fascists on the other hand, had a very good time, and many made their fortune dispossessing their victims.

After Mussolini made the Concordat with the Church in 1929, in 1949 the Vatican repeated the Anathema with the Holy Decree against Communism [W71] for the still to be established Democratic Republic of Italy. More people were persecuted after the end of WWII, after the Nuremberg Trials absolved the "High Moral Values" of the Fascist Racial Laws as Culture and Tradition that are still going on today. It was as if the fascist persecution of the Democrats as Apostates and Enemies of the State never happened; as if the Racial Laws couldn't possibly represent a problem for the Democratic Values. If today we cannot claim the rights we are supposed to have, like the Freedom of Choice or the Secular Value of Justice, it is only because these rights are in the Index of the Inquisition and have been persecuted as Catholic Heresies throughout history."

I looked around for a moment; it was getting late and people were going home.

"I am sorry Jason. It is getting late, and before we go I have a question for you" I said looking at him.

"What is it?" he asked, inviting me to continue.

"Should I believe what Brian said yesterday, about Aisling? Is it true she took the morphine from her friend?" I asked.

"Nobody knows what happened" he said smiling. "She was not alone in the house when the morphine went missing, and maybe someone else took it. Brian was thinking of Aisling, but there is no evidence anybody took it, and if you saw her yesterday late in the afternoon, maybe she didn't do it. She is not as evil as he said. Probably tomorrow she will turn up" he said, almost reassuringly. "I'll see you later then; I would like to know more about your stories. My father was upset because he couldn't give me an education, and recently he died. It is not perhaps he sent you over, from where he is now" he said, as if asking.

"Maybe" I said standing up, somewhat embarrassed; not surprisingly also Jason had his own horizons to stare at. "I believe my father also did his best to give me an education, but the education our fathers meant is not for sale, and is not part of the school program either. I'll see you later, with a new chapter from the heavens" I said, and then I walked my way home recalling the white rose I found on my way out.

The French Revolution

(From Galileo to Lafayette)

Aisling had been missing for two days when she reappeared from the meadow. She was walking slowly, and despite the fact I couldn't really see her for the sunshine I knew immediately the blurry outline of her figure, moving not in my direction. Brian was blaming her for stealing the morphine of his friend; and what about the disclosure of what I thought was private writing? The meadow was retching up bits of shattered horizons, while the real line between the meadow and the sky was demonstrating itself like an inconvenience, an indestructible figment with her hiding in it. I looked again with the intention of being blinded by the sunlight, at least for a moment; just for the sake of the illusion of seeing the edges I knew I could have seen only in my imagination.

After the words of Brian, all kinds of figments and ghosts took over the peace of the Park, and the illusion of the bench as the ultimate refuge and reconciliation with myself was definitively lost, overwhelmed by the surrounding human life. Maybe she was to come to the bench later, maybe not, but all my wishes were for her; because I couldn't believe anything Brian said, never, unless she was forced to. Yes but forced by what, someone or something? Maybe she was to come to the bench later, but I was sure she would have done the right thing anyway, and nothing would have ever been able to suffocate her freedom.

The current page on my notes was summarising a few points from the conversation with Jason the day before. Definitely my attention was on the Canon Law [A24], forcing the Catholic Students to choose a Catholic School, or to be excommunicated as a consequence of their freedom of choice. But the most important point of my concern was the silence of the State, witnessing the Church bullying and intimidating the citizens. It was like at the time of Martin Luther with the indulgences, and the spiritual blackmail of the priests selling tickets to heaven. How could this have been possible, to tolerate the Church blackmailing citizens like that? I was wondering about the morality of this pretentious spiritual leader, but the silence of the State was attracting my despair even more, especially in the perspective of the book of McIntire recalling the Secular Values of Henry VIII and the following English tradition.

I do understand how people around the planet like to imagine the way God may be, and the indisputable variety of different human understandings of God is what I like most of the inexplicable experience of the Divine; but by nature people will always have different understanding, and there will always be a multiplicity of Gods.

On the other hand the point in discussion was the syllabus for Public secular Education, the prerequisite to pass the exams, and what the students could have done with that education in their life. The point was the preparation of the syllabus compatible with the Holy Scripture, and Parliament with its little authority left to ratify and enforce what is to be taught to all the students for life.

From reading the Education Acts I could clearly see the interference of the Religious institutions in the planning of school programs, reducing the potential curiosity and creativity of the students into the specific and precise Religious precepts of the Catechism, and these same precepts were recurring in all subjects, from History to Philosophy, Science and Arts.

"How did the Catholic Heresies become Catholic Legacy?" I asked myself another time, almost to regain some peace from my small but solid certainties. How could it have been possible that nobody ever asked such a simple question concerning a relevant matter like the Catholic Heresies, with all the implications in science, education and politics obligating the entire society to live within the confines of the Bible, like we were already in the after-life, or our world could be confused with the after-life.

"It should take more than a syllabus to disguise the Catholic Heresies as Catholic Legacy" I said again, but I knew the answer. The students never liked all this boring tradition and culture at the root of our society, viewing it as not important or relevant in determining their conditions of life, rights and freedoms. It was only old stuff, scholastic, pedantic and useless, like most of the schoolbooks. But in reality the foundation of our society was hiding exactly between the lines of these textbooks, and that evidence was not something someone could have disputed.

Earthquake prediction is not as much a heresy as asking how the Catholic Heresies became Catholic Legacy, and probably the professors would feel offended and perceive the question as a personal attack to jeopardize their job, their moral and intellectual integrity, like the students paying the bill couldn't possibly feel cheated or exploited, personally. Asking the professors how the Catholic Heresies became Catholic Legacy would have made the problem even bigger because the answer could have only been «This is the way it is», like it was an Act of God rather than school programs and Education Acts of Parliament imposing them.

It was obvious from this same perspective also that the vanishing of my degree and my passport could have only been an Act of God, but in this particular case I was definitely sure the professors in the photograph of my degree ceremony were more responsible than the Celestial Destiny, as also the Court of Justice was responsible for sweeping the cases under the carpet, postponing people rights into the afterlife. Someone may believe that Justice is not of this world, but the only Justice I wanted was the Justice of the Law, to bring my personal documents together with me on this side of the horizon.

I was floating in the air of the Park with my imaginary conversation when she arrived, coming out from behind the bushes near the bench.

"Hi" she said, "how are you today? Are you writing the book?" she asked.

Hearing of the book made me smile again. Sure, the book was not part of my private life anymore, but may be she didn't see Brian or Jason, and may be she didn't know he was after her the day before, and didn't know of our conversation.

"Hi, no. I didn't start yet, but later today I will. How are you?" I asked.

"I am sound", she said sitting on the bench, "Would you like an apple?" she asked offering one.

"Not now, thank you. I have just had some breakfast", I said, but she dropped the apple into my hands like she knew I wouldn't have let it fall.

"You can have it later" she said with a sweet smile, sweetening the imposition of the offer.

She seat on the bench on my side as usual, and with Aisling also the twittering of the birds came back to the Park, with the colours, the joy in the shouts of the kids playing football and the perfumes from all the bushes and flowers. Aisling had arrived at the bench one time again, but the solid peace of the Park was already shattered into pieces, and the inconsistency of the surrounding human life was flooding my dreams with all its contradictions, unstoppable and irreversible. I almost told her about Brian, but I didn't; maybe because of the illusion of keeping alive the memory of the peace I knew was definitively lost. I would have really liked to rewind back to the best moments of peace and serenity I found with her during our conversations, but apparently that was not possible anymore. On the other hand, she made her choice, it was legitimate, and if I had any feeling of uneasiness probably the cause was to be found in my perception and in my expectations.

Definitely I couldn't lie to myself pretending she didn't disclose something about our writings, something that I was jealously guarding, and I couldn't pretend I didn't wait for her for two days before. On the other hand she never had any obligation about that; we never had a contract concerning the confidentiality or the frequency of our writings, and if I were waiting for her it was only because of my imagination projecting figments and illusions on this side of the Horizon.

"You know this writing is extremely important to me; you

know I am not joking about this, don't you?" I asked.

"Sure I do; am I here?" she asked, solid, like I was disputing her existence.

"About the book" she said, "We pointed out the different versions of the Bible, and the difficulty of writing the Satanic Verses of the Bible mainly because the text is uncertain and volatile, not like the Catholic Heresies which are well defined by the Catholic Inquisition as solid evidences of evil; the Bible is volatile and fickle like a beautiful woman" she said smiling. "There are too many Apostles missing, too many Witnesses and Gospels are missing, and then just consider the Catholic and the Lutheran interpretation of the Bible, which are quite contradictory, aren't they? And don't forget the several other traditions like the Gnostic [W43], the Cathar [W44] the Waldensian [W45] and the various other dissenters, like animists and hedonists, all promptly excommunicated by the Church. I believe into this list also fits Saint Peter, the First Rock of Jesus, who became the first Heretic of the Roman Catholic Church; appointed by Jesus but not by the Romans, wasn't he?

Then we talk about the Forbidden Archaeology, about the Knowledge Filter interpreting Archaeological findings in accordance with our expectations, our modern theories and beliefs. And similar to the process of interpretation is the Confirmation Bias, the mechanism of confirmation and agreement within the scientific community; the network of friends helping out each other imposing the most common preconceptions and prejudices leading to the conclusion the Catholic Heresies have became Catholic Legacy. But it is crystal clear the seismology of the region is not settled, there are visible cracks, and the reassuring analysis concerning the stability of the area only serves to reassure the investors in the market of tickets to heaven.

In this perspective we pointed out the two faces of the Renaissance Culture, the Catholic Heresies persecuted by the Catholic Inquisition, and the Catholic Legacy, which is well represented by the Catholic Inquisition itself. «How did the Catholic Heresies become Catholic Legacy?», «How did the Renaissance Culture become the intellectual legacy of the persecutors of the Renaissance Culture?». This is all in my notes" she said. "What do we do now? What is next? Is it the time to find out who really was on the cross, was that a man or a woman? And what about the 3 male sons of Adams, and the homosexual conception?" she asked again, but my answer once again was the same silence.

"On the cover of the book you should have a child on the cross; it would be the most appropriate of all" she said, revealing a regret in her voice.

Definitely she was right again, and me? What should I do? Share more of my notes with her, maybe for a laugh in the Park? The book was sinking into a jungle of doubts, and my silence was resuscitating all the fears I thought I would have never felt again.

"How did the Catholic Heresies become Catholic Legacy?" I said invoking a new idea, but I knew I never heard that question before I wrote it 10 years before, and never read it in the following 10 years, searching for the bibliographic references I have never found. The uncharted thought concerning the Catholic Heresies was just right in front of me, like an island in the sea, but there was no map of it I could find; it was as if it never existed before, or was never charted.

I was dazzled and overwhelmed by the uneasiness I was feeling and I couldn't find the reason. Sure, she had that question from me, from the notes I revealed to her, but on the other hand I revealed the same question to many more people, with the same reasoning and the same words, for years and years, and also publicly on YouTube and more social networks on the Internet. The inconsistency of the Catholic Heresies becoming Catholic legacy was also printed in the schoolbooks; it was there for each student, on each desk of each classroom, and precisely during the exploration of these textbooks I found the route to the uncharted island.

But the reason for my crushing despair was just right in front of me; she was the only one to cheer me up, but still I couldn't understand what was wrong with my perception concerning the sharing of my pages with her again, for what reason I was feeling bitter and betrayed. What was the cause of my uneasiness with Aisling repeating my mantras in the Park? The more I tried to understand, the more my dreams were dissolving out of control toward the other side of the horizon.

"The statement 'In God we trust', is representative of our probabilities to have Justice by the Law in this world' I said, as if spitting out a bitter thought. "Yesterday I was speaking with Jason concerning a few Education Acts; no wonder that the Administration vanishes degrees and passports into thin air, and the victims cannot have Justice. You imagine also here in England, in 1917 the Church issued a Canon Law forbidding Catholic students from going to non-Catholic schools, on pain of excommunication. Was it a moral blackmail to both, the worshippers and the State? Was it a blackmail concerning the Authority of Justice on this side of the horizon, or what?"

"Oh, that is interesting" she said with some surprise. "Do you have some notes?" she asked.

"Not with me, but I have some at home."

"Bring it with you later, or tomorrow" she said, indicating that she would have been around, for the sunset or the next morning.

"Do you know what? People pretending to be above the law reminds me of the French Revolution" I said. "That was a big point in history, it is the origin of our contemporary democracies..." I said, waiting for her.

"Ok. I liked the French Revolution. I like rebels" she said smiling.

I never knew if I was better considering myself a rebel. Maybe, from the perspective of being at variance with the common established beliefs, but I have no doubt concerning the indisputable evidence at the origin of the supposed rebellion. The established beliefs are established by the schoolbooks, and the specialists should be able to clarify how the Catholic Heresies become

Catholic Legacy. This is not a matter of opinion; it is not a matter of grammar, or a funny accent. The schoolbooks completely disregard the significance, the importance and the implications of the Catholic Heresies; they uncritically reproduce the Catholic Heaven on earth, and if I were at variance it was only because they were on the wrong side of the horizon. On the other hand it was not difficult to understand from their perspective of angels above the law I was at variance, standing for the laws of man against their will in the name of God; it was obvious they could only see the deeds of a rebel.

This is not the behaviour of a rebel I repeated to myself at least a million times, but they never listened, and my points or my rights have never been their concern. As far as they knew, God made me paperless, and that was to be until the end of time, until the final Judgment and eventually the resurrection.

"Do you think I am a rebel?" I asked her.

"I would say yes, no doubt", she replied with a smile. "Why are you asking? Have you any doubt?" she said.

"Do you think I am a rebel?" I asked again, repeating the question.

"It depends what you mean, about your documents of course you have the right and reasons to claim Justice. You like to have your say, like concerning the Renaissance perhaps, but I cannot see you being a rebel in the meaning of a terrorist. You are a free thinker, but this is all it takes to be a rebel. Yes, you are a rebel but a decent one, well educated and well mannered, helpful and polite" she said.

The apple in my hands was shining and inviting; I put it in my pocket and I looked down at the soil, staring at it speechless.

"Is that true Marie Antoinette said 'If they have no bread, let them eat cake'?" she asked.

"Maybe, but for sure the French Revolution was not about bread or cakes. It was about intellectual emancipation, put into writing, with laws and rights everybody had to respect. It was all about the High Moral Values of the Absolute Power, and the Law of Man everybody had to respect, Gods included. The institution of the Constitutional Monarchy was not just about the Constitution for the people, but more important it concerns the rights of the people to state that no one is above the law, including Kings and Priests. The true motto of the French Revolution was not about bread or cakes, but 'No one is above the Law'."

"Are you saying this because of what happened to you, with the people in the offices pretending to be above the law?"

"My documents are not the cause of all the problems, but eventually one of the consequences. In this world we live in, bureaucrats have no problems to make you vanish, and reinvent you like a character from a novel, but I am not the cause of this situation; it is the Absolute Power to consent to all this devastation.

This is why the institution of Constitutional Monarchies was so important, a milestone; because for the first time the people were putting boundaries to Absolute Power. Also the Coronation Oath was changed, adding to the traditional 'Grace of God' the new emerging 'Will of people'. On the other hand, today we have laws for passports and degrees but I am sure my documents and my legal suit were not the only ones to be vanished."

"This is true. The laws were not made for you, but for everybody" she said, taking the notebook from her bag.

"There are exceptions: the laws are made for all, but someone may be above it, and someone else may be completely excluded and prevented from all his rights.

Consider this case. They made my passport and degree vanish, they made me paperless like an illegal immigrant, and after years I was complaining, after also the OLAF office of the European Union sent my legal suit to the Court in Italy, at that point someone had the bright idea of pretending I was inventing things, just to discredit and defame me. Now, if we could see these documents, I was arrested at least 3 or 4 years after my documents went missing, and at that time I was simply claiming my rights against a bunch of mobsters hiding in Public Offices.

I was arrested because of the accusations of an anonymous informant named Claire Flannigan; I know because one time she had to show up to confront Dissanayaka. At that meeting was present also a Policeman, but out of her slandering there was nothing to be found, only the High Moral Values of another good Catholic pretending to defame the victims of Catholic Organized crimes and abuses. She always made someone else do the paperwork with the reliable and professional information she could provide; why do you believe nobody questioned her competence and professionalism in providing false accusations?

She has been so miserable she had the courage to suggest the victims may have good reasons to be depressed or deluded, rather than good reasons to claim for Justice as I were doing. The OLAF office of the European Union already sent my legal claim to the Court in Milan long before she arrived, and when also the Police knew I was the victim and not the felon, why did they flee the scene of investigation rather than prosecuting the criminals providing false accusations to cover up their crimes?

This is the reality of our world, the democracy we live in; I cannot lie to myself about this, and I am not to take lessons on how our democracy works. From the first to the last, do you remember the video we made with the recording of Dissanayaka, the forensic doctor saying that «There is a lack of illness going on», and then wondering «What are we doing here?». It was Flannigan who advised them both, Dissanayaka and the Antiterrorism Police, but what did it matter? She is a good Catholic, with a better understanding of morality; she can lie and be honest anyway, while I am just an idiotic paperless pretending to be Luca Benatti against the Will of God. Is that not the case?"

"Oh, yes I remember" she said, "With the doctor telling you of the anonymous informants providing false accusations he couldn't actually validate or confirm in any way. It is still disturbing" she said again, unveiling some repugnance in her expression. “Anonymous informants shouldn’t be accepted, and false accusations should be prosecuted as defamation.”

“Tell me the difference with the Inquisition of the dark ages, if any. In reality some people still today build their career on false accusations, reporting demons and witches they see. After what they have done, after the lack of respect they have demonstrated for the law and peoples’ rights, do you believe it is really possible to take them to Court? Do you believe we have the right to defend ourselves from the public slander of anonymous informants working in office? They perpetrate crimes, and then pretend the victims should conform to their will, and project their fears onto their victims pretending the victims are intolerant of abuses and violence, don’t accept to be abused and ignored, and potentially may became dangerous or terrorists. It was like I didn't have any of the rights I was claiming, and didn't have rights to report the mobsters and counterfeiters responsible for the vanishing of my personal documents. This is the kind of people we find in the public offices, and the Court of Justice is just another room along the same corridor. They know what they have done; do you believe it is the victims who make the legal suit disappear from the Courts of Justice?”

“Yes, they do it, and then sweep it under the carpet. It really reminds me of the Absolute Power before the French revolution. Do you believe we now need another Revolution to have our rights back?” she asked.

“Well, in evidence we cannot claim the rights we are supposed to have.”

“What could we do to make the French Revolution better?” she asked, trying to resuscitate my humour with a smile.

“Probably we need to unveil it was not an Act of God to make our claims vanish and our rights with them; but the offices have no problems ratifying whatever they can dream of, just look at the schoolbooks or the weapons of mass destruction Tony Blair has never found; why do you believe he found the courage to unveil his hidden morality, and convert to Catholic, only at the end of his appointment and not before? That was honest from the start, isn't it? And why do you believe the morality of his personal beliefs should be private business compared to our civil rights?

Try to imagine what it may be, to have to live with no personal documents, like an illegal immigrant, simply because to unravel the situation would be a problem for dozens of people in public offices. Also Dissanayaka said it was intolerable, but what does it matter? They have a better morality; they can distinguish good and evil better then us, and exceptionally the intolerable can be imposed on the victims of intolerable crimes they perpetrate in the name of their superior morality, this is consistent isn't it?"

"It was a nightmare" she said, brushing against my arm. "Forget about it" she said again, "Don't be too hard, give yourself a break; have an apple."

"I know you are right, but this is my every day life. If I have to be paperless like an illegal immigrant, they had better find the way to be proud of this."

"Yes, I was going to say that. You should write about this in the book, and tell the world what is going on in here" she said, determined, inviting me to never give up.

"This is the plan, but nobody is bothered about Civil Freedoms. Today Civil Rights only means gay marriages; this is all that matter about people's Freedoms."

"Do you see? If you were a refugee on a raft in the Mediterranean Sea, you would be a victim, a cause to stand up for. But you are not a victim, or better, you are a victim of the friendly fire of our saviours, so you are more like a fatality, a casualty, a fatal accident, something unavoidable, an Act of God or something like that."

"I am more like an accident they have caused intentionally, and intentionally have imposed for years pretending to make real their lie. No I am sorry, I have been vilified, tormented and tortured for years, and if I feel like a hostage still today it is because I am still as paperless as I was.

This book has to be a True Act of God, because this is the only thing they would understand. On the other hand it is clear, the expression «In God we trust» is more appropriate for a Church, and not for a Court of Justice on this side of the horizon."

"The first declaration of Human and Civil Rights was prepared during the French Revolution, wasn't it? Let us see what it says" she said, taking the smartphone out of her pocket.

"Yes, here it is. Article one says that «Men are born and remain free and equal in rights», and in Article two are listed the fundamental Human Rights, which are «Liberty, Property, Safety and Resistance to oppression». Let me see what is interesting" she said scrolling the page, while reading and summarizing from Wikipedia [W46]. "Article 4 defines «Liberty consists in being able to do anything that does not harm others», let me see, she said scrolling the page again."

"Somewhere it should mention that the free communication of ideas and opinions is one of the most precious rights."

"Yes" she said, after a few moments. "Article 11 does, but it also says that the citizens cannot abuse of liberty in cases determined by Law. The Article before says «No one may be disturbed on account of his opinions, even religious ones, as long as the manifestation of such opinions does not interfere with the established Law and Order» she said smiling. "Apparently, the Law and Order is indisputable, also in the Declaration of Human Rights of the French Revolution."

"Further down it should mention the division of Powers, apparently the Justice of God was never meant to acknowledge the Justice of Man. Since the early Christians arrived in Rome with the pretence of having High Moral Values above the law, since the time of the Nicaea Council, for a long time the people had no rights to express their opinions, and the French Revolution was really a breakthrough; also Galileo was calling for it ages before. Can you see the call of Galileo for freedom; can you see how the reborn curiosity for nature and the Renaissance Culture blossom in the French Revolution and the modern sciences?"

"Definitely" she said, "Intellectual Emancipation, this is all it was about. It was emancipation from a world of superstitions, made real only in the hope, projections and beliefs of the worshipper; it was a virtual world of figments, wasn't it?"

"I don't really see any difference from today; also today our world is made of words of mouth, figments and beliefs we have made real. Don't tell me; I know what it means to be confined into a world of lies.

Anyway, the main flaw of the French Revolution concerns women, which are not even mentioned."

"What about women?" she asked curiously, staring at me.

"I am sure women had the most to complain about. Try to see what Google has to say."

"Oh! Look, there is a page exactly on this, 'Women in the French Revolution'" [W47] she said, tapping on the screen of the smartphone.

"Look at this" she said again calling for attention, and then she started reading from Wikipedia.

> Quote from Wikipedia [W47]
> «The Feminism emerged in Paris as part of a broad demand for social and political reform. The women demanded equality to men and then moved on to a demand for the end of male domination, however the Jacobin and radical element in power abolished all the women's clubs and arrested their leaders» [End Quote]

After reading she looked at me like she had to pass through that experience personally.

"The women's march on Versailles was just an instance of feminism during the Revolution" she said resuming the next paragraphs, "But women were mostly left out of the debate, and finally were denied the political rights of citizens, also in the Declaration of the Rights of Man and Citizens. Pauline Léon and Théroigne de Méricourt, two major feminist activists of the time."

"Yes, and today?" I blurted.

"You can say that out loud. Also today women don't have the same rights as men, and are paid less than men for the same job" she said looking at me almost resentful.

"Don't look at me. The male domination you are talking about is one of the consequences of the same High Moral Values above the law I complain about.

Behind the disappearance of my documents in the public offices, were mostly women; and also behind the false informing of the Police was a woman. On the side of the high moral values above the law, women are allowed to follow their career exactly the same as their male colleagues; and if you were a victim, your gender wouldn't make any difference. It is all about the same high moral values above the laws, the same values the French Revolution highlighted from the start, demanding 'No one is above the law'."

"I understand, yes. Look, this is nice. Also Olympe de Gouges was a woman activist, she was a writer, a novelist, but she also prepared the 'Declaration of the rights of woman'. Further down I read that the Concordat reinstated the Catholic Church in France in 1801; not really long after the march on Versailles in 1789."

"I can see that; as usual the Church provided the blessing of God for anybody able to re-establish the high moral values of the Catholic Supremacy. But don't forget the women confined in the Magdalene Laundries, like slaves; nobody ever asked them if they liked it. On the other side, the rights and life condition of men were not really different."

"Yes, it is clear" she said. "The French Revolution was just an attempt to establish the principle of equality, but despite the fact some rights were promoted and recognized for all the citizens, it completely forgot to recognize women as human beings. Yes, and today is not much different; still today women are paid less than men, for the same job of a man; 'FEMEN' [A14] has good reasons to exist" she said recalling the feminist group. "I cannot believe someone made a law like this!" she said again, with an expression of disbelief, "You should know what it means, to be discriminated against."

"I love 'FEMEN', it is a great movement, but it should do more. FEMEN has big projects I agree completely, like concerning the separation of the Church and the State, but Feminism and Atheism are not good points. Sextremism is provocative, it attracts attention, but it is all women in need for justice, and not for sex rights or sex abuses only. The left wing should be all for Women Rights but it has never been. With the democrats and left wing we have rebuild on Catholic Values, it has never happened, but I am sure all good Catholic Politicians would make it their own personal raison d'être in their campaigns.

I cannot have the rights I am supposed to have, but on the other hand these people making their living out of crimes and abuses in the name of the traditional High Moral Values above the law, they are having a good time, like the fascists at the time of Mussolini; they become rich dispossessing their victims. Maybe this is what they mean for freedom of enterprise, who knows? But don't get confused: it is not a matter of gender. Also FEMEN complains gender discrimination and patriarchy, but these are consequences, and we are after the causes.

Did I ever tell you the story of Cecile Kyenge?" [W48] I asked.

"No, I don't think so. Who is she?"

"She is a lady from the Congo. She arrived in Italy with no documents, no visa, but with the help of the Bishop in the Congo and a few Catholic Friends in Italy, in a short time she held a Passport and a Degree."

"Are you jealous because the officials found her papers, but still cannot find yours?" she asked, with some dark humour.

"No, I don't think so. She well represents the good reasons why my documents went missing, and I would never like to be involved with people like that: they are just the most miserable mobsters and counterfeiters you may find.

Anyway, she said it all, with her own voice during an interview broadcasted by RAI 3 [A15], one of the Italian national television channels. She also declared she was worried, because she knew she had no rights to any of the documents she was asking for, and would have never had any without the gracious and responsive help of the Bishops, nuns and the network of friends working in the Public Offices of the Italian Administration. I only wonder why Bishops and nuns smuggle Italian documents, and not Vatican's ones they may have true rights for? Why do they smuggle Italian documents, rather then the usual Indulgences for a place in heaven?

Anyway, the story of the Kyenge had just started. Sometime later she has been elected a Member of the Italian Parliament and became Minister for Integration, an office of the Ministry for Equal Opportunities. In evidence in Italy, also forgers and counterfeiters have the Rights for the Equal Opportunities, and Kyenge is just an example.

The Italian people cannot have documents they have rights for, meanwhile some others, from the angels above obtain documents they had no rights to at all; is it clear, in Italy the blessing is all you need? I understand from the perspective of the tradition of Miracles and Acts of God, it is just business as usual; it is just another example of High Moral Values above the law pushing the Italian Administration and Judicial system far behind the Horizon.

Do you believe an angel like Kyenge could represent or defend my True Rights, or my Equal Opportunities? On the other hand it is obvious, Kyenge is just an example and makes no difference; the Holy Republic of Italy has plenty of people with High Moral Values like Kyenge. She represents very well the true Italian mafia, the mafia of the brotherhood made under oath to set up Saint Peter, and pretend he was an evil and immoral wicked man, disgraceful and despicable, a Heretic to be erased from the Bible. That happened before the Nicaea Council, do you remember?"

"Yes, I do. It is ridiculous, but it is true; would you like to make a video about Kyenge?" she asked.

"Maybe in the future; at the moment I am busy writing but yes, she well deserves a video."

"I understand" she said with a nod, "Let me know if you like a voice-over."

"Sure, thanks. Did you enjoy doing the voice over for my videos last time?"

"It was interesting to see how it works, but I never saw it before."

"Anyway, about this story, Kyenge I mean, it is funny to see a woman from the Congo representing the politics of the High Moral Values. Because it is the ideology of the Right Wing, the Racial Laws of Mussolini and White Supremacist, and she makes really dark humour in there. It is true she was elected within the Democratic Party, but her supporters were the people providing all the documents from the start, bishops and nuns. This story was in newspapers worldwide [A16], because the crowd was throwing bananas at her while she was speaking in public during political meetings.

More recently she has become member of the European Parliament; can you imagine what chance my European Passport has to be found, with people like Kyenge around?" I asked.

"After she admitted the scam of the documents, where did she find the courage and the votes to go on to the European Parliament?"

"Well, she is Catholic and has good reasons above the law for what she did; she did it in the Public Interest, she did it for us, the same as the nuns and bishops who gave her the documents, all spotless angels trying to save us, like when Mussolini made the racial laws, but probably Kyenge doesn't know about this. You should have seen the front pages of the news, also Cecilia Malmström and Rupert Colville were defending her."

"Who are these people you said, Cecilia Malm…?"

"Cecilia Malmström; she was European Commissioner for Home Affairs, and spoke out defending Kyenge from the Italian crowd throwing the bananas. Cecilia Malmström understood that the Italians were Racist, complaining about the non-Italian origin of Kyenge, the somatic traits of her, and not the dodgy documents she has got, and the lifestyle of her friends pretending to be above the law. Also Rupert Colville, spokesman for the United Nations spoke in favour of Kyenge, complaining about the Italians being Racist, and never mentioned the true reasons to address, about her documents and her brotherhood.

In conclusion the people in the audience couldn't complaint about the iffy and deceitful documents of Kyenge, not even the mafia behind, because the audience would have been blamed for being racist. On the other side, I was wondering about my documents and you have seen what happened."

"Did you ask the European Commissioner about your passport and your degree?" she asked smiling.

"Maybe we can make a video and ask them, but all this conversation concerning Kyenge started from the feminists of the French Revolution, just to say it is not a matter of gender; if you are a good Catholic you are all right, today like at the time of the French Revolution, no matter what gender."

"What do you mean?"

"I mean the High Moral Values above the law are still here, judging and dividing good and evil; it is not the gender which makes the difference but the sharing of these Values. The French Revolution made an attempt but didn't accomplish the recognition of women as citizens, and also concerning the High Moral Values above the law, made an attempt but it didn't last. In fact the Magdalene laundries [W49] had many more angel customers than evil people doing the laundry; we are only entitled to Trust in God, and have no rights to claim the rights we were supposed to have.

I would like to ask Cecilia Malmström about equal opportunity, if I had the rights to my personal documents, or the freedom to fulfil the opportunity I organized myself. I would like to know how she would compare my true rights with the rights of Kyenge, if she could understand what I mean."

“They probably share the same High Moral Values” she said with a miserable expression.

“Have you ever seen the movie ‘In my Country’ [A17] by John Boorman” I asked. “It is a movie about Apartheid in South Africa; at one point, when the Truth and Reconciliation Commission hearings were to start, the scene moves into the Court and it turns out the Judge to rule the Commission is a Christian Bishop. Basically, the same High Moral Values at the origin of the Supremacist ideology of Apartheid were to rule the reconciliation, and with the confession of the crimes also the traditional absolution would have come. But the scene of the Bishop with the same physical traits of the victims, absolving white supremacist torturers and assassins, highlighted the future of South Africa was again under the same High Moral Values.”

“I believe I have seen it, with Juliette Binoche and Samuel Jackson” she asked.

“Yes, exactly. Do you remember the Judge?”.

“Probably I missed it; I don’t remember he was a priest.”

“Sure, the movie is well done, and that Bishop actually is Archbishop Desmond Tutu [W50], Anglican, educated at the Saint Peter Theological College in Johannesburg. I feel sorry for him, because I am sure he had big trouble there, and he felt sincerely about all the impossible wishes of the victims.

Anyway, Archbishop Tutu is not my point, but the analogy with the racial laws of Mussolini. In Italy in 1929 the Pope in person was preparing the Concordat as the foundation of the new Italian National Culture [W51], soon to be enforced with the Racial Laws Mussolini enacted a few years later [W52], exactly to defend and promote the Values of the Alliance with the Church. On the other hand most victims of the Racial Laws were Italian white Caucasian, people with cultural problems, in disarray with the High Moral Values of the Fascist dictatorship. It wasn't skin colour that was problem, but a Cultural problem at the origin of the fascist racial laws and the following intellectual cleansing.

During the Italian Unification in 1800 the king was also excommunicated, just to discourage him from his ideas of conquest, and later the Concordat of Mussolini re-established the Vatican City and the Cultural Supremacy of the Absolute Power of the Church, transforming the Catholic Heresies into Catholic Legacy, and the Secular Value of 'No High Moral Values above the Law' have become a terrorist ideal.

When the High Moral Values above the law become a Reason of State, all the political parties were dismissed, political newspapers were burnt down, and dissenters were persecuted and executed as Enemy of the State. But it was all in accord with the Catholic Moral Supremacy; it was not Mussolini who invented it, and the problem has never been skin colour but the Secular Values, and especially the Secular Values of Justice.

The High Moral Values at the basis of Apartheid are the same as the Racial Laws of Mussolini, but there is a small difference I'll tell you later. Now I would like to make clear Mussolini made the Concordat; it was a Cultural Agreement with the Church, and as a consequence the people demanding the Freedom of Choice, the Secular Values of Justice and emancipation from the Absolute Power of the Church become enemies of the State to be hunted and persecuted, as they already were since the 3rd January 1925, when Mussolini dismissed the parliament, the political parties and the freedom of press.

Mussolini had many more Italians killed than Jews, even if nobody ever talks about this, simply because after WWII the Pope in 1949 [W71] repeated the Anathema against the democrats, against the Freedom of Choice and the Secular Values of Justice, promulgating again the Racial Laws this time for the Democratic Republic of Italy, to continue the intellectual cleansing and the persecution of the Democrats as Apostates.

Why do you believe Mussolini persecuted all the secularist ideologies, demanding no one is above the law, if not as consequence of the system of values he embraced from the start, and openly imposed with the

Concordat, reinstating Vatican City and the absolute power but also imposing the Roman Catholic as religion of state, to justify the morality and authority of the intellectual cleansing he enforced.

Not all forms of racism are skin colour related, and the Archbishop in that Commission for reconciliation, dispensing amnesties to the murderers was just out of place, like it would have been out of place for a Priest pretending to judge in a trial against the racial laws of Mussolini; it would be a farce because the mastermind of the racial laws was not Mussolini but the Church, and the Church should have been on the dock in Nuremberg at the side of the Nazis.

Why do you believe the Nazis have been on trial, but not the Fascists, responsible for the same crimes? The only difference was the blessing of the Pope, the same as for Kyenge, wasn't it? I wonder what could we do without such honest people like Kyenge and her friends, dispensing indulgences and absolutions for the crimes they intentionally perpetrate with premeditation.

The only reason I can see Kyenge as Minister for Integration and Equal Opportunities is because she is decorative, and may help to make the Democratic Party look like Democratic. But she couldn't see the favours she was receiving as "crimes", but "help" she had from the Brotherhood, the friends of the Bishop, helping her to obtain documents she admitted she knew she had no rights to. What does matter if the same "reason", the same "help", the same System of Values is discriminating millions of native democrats since the time of the Concordat of Mussolini? What matter if it is for the same reason of "help" and "Mafia" the Italian people cannot have documents they have rights to, and become paperless like illegal immigrants within the EU Borders? But she is Catholic educated with Catholic recommendations; about democracy and the respect of the law she doesn't know and doesn't care about."

"This morality of God above the law is really a big issue, isn't it?" she asked.

"As far as I can see, the Morality of the law is completely compromised in favour of the High Moral Values above the law. They pretend to be good and honest people, but they don't understand what double standards mean; they are just barbarians, mobsters and counterfeiters, as they have always been."

"I can see what you mean, and I also see you like to call them barbarians, mobsters and counterfeiters, don't you?"

"Well, this is what they are, with signatures, stamps and photographs. A bunch of barbarians ..."

"Mobsters and counterfeiters" she said anticipating my words.

"And counterfeiters" I said smiling.

"Why do you believe we have two Popes? I wanted to ask you and always forgot."

"Yes, this is also funny. After Pope Francis was elected, he said immediately that «The end of a Pope is the tomb» [A20], like reprimanding Pope Ratzinger for resigning. Probably Ratzinger believed the worshippers needed to strengthen their faith, their unconditional belief and obedience, but it is also true in South America that the Communist ideology was getting stronger and the Church has always been the first line of defence against communism, since the Iron Curtain, Gladio and before.

Also after World War II, rather than facing the Nuremberg trial as Mastermind of the Racial Laws, the Church became the line of defence against Communist Ideology, and continued with the Allies in what Mussolini was doing since before the War, revising and amending the left wing ideals into a more Christian interpretation, with Justice postponed into the afterlife perhaps. The end of WWII clearly replicated these ideals, also promoting secret operations like the Gladio Operation [W53], which in some ways recalls the War on Terror we see today, making a flag out of our System of Values, to defend our lifestyle against the threat of Secular Values and ideologies.

But in reality Mussolini Catholicized the Socialist ideology long before WWII; since the beginning of his career in politics. In fact after World War I Mussolini was a

Socialist, and the Church had already excommunicated the socialist ideology long before. So, Mussolini had the bright idea to convert the Socialist Ideology into a Catholic Ideology, and he invented ‘Fascism’, which is the Catholic version of Socialism. Mussolini invented a kind of socialism in which at the center of human life is not the law of man but the High Moral Values of the Catholic Tradition, like during the dark ages.

Mussolini enforced the Catholic Cultural barrier against the secular values, persecuting them as Apostates and communists since the 3 January 1925 when he dismissed the parliament to impose the Catholic tradition, promoting secret police like inquisition and Laws concerning Culture and intellectual cleansing more than skin colour. In 1939 Mussolini promulgated the Racial Laws the Senator for life Liliana Segre is compelled to complain today, but for the democrats the holocaust was started 3 Jan 1925 with the Cultural Laws transforming the democratic values into Catholic legacy, and still has not ended yet.

Mussolini enforced the Catholic Cultural barrier against the secular values of democracy, and he was right when he said all Europe would have turned Fascist [W54] in response to the communist threat. In fact after WWII the political scenario have adapted to the vision of Mussolini pretending the democratic values had to be found in the Catholic tradition, and the Racist Cultural Laws transforming the democrats into Apostates and heretics would have set the standard all over Europe for years to come until today.

How do you think the democratic values have become Catholic Legacy, without a permanent intellectual cleansing, a permanent holocaust?

After WWII, the Papacy repeated the racial laws already recommended to Mussolini, and issued the Excommunication of the communists and all the other parties making common cause with the secular values, especially concerning the secular value of justice and the freedom of choice, revamping the tradition of religious abuses and inquisition.

For the young senator for life Liliana Segre the holocaust was ended after WWII, but for the democrats the holocaust is not ended yet, and despite Italy pretending to be a republic and a democracy, the Judge Luigi Tosti [A33] was disbarred for suggesting the removal of the crucifix from the Courts of Justice.

If the Prosecutors have the decency and decorum to sweep some cases under the carpet, to help friends and colleagues, it is just one of the consequences of such High Moral Values being above the law. Also the black market in documents, to them, is not bribery but rather a matter of Values and Culture; like we had to revive the ancient tradition of Indulgences, to celebrate Europe reunited again after ages. Where do you think is the difference between the Mafia and people like Kyenge, who pays an indulgence fee to the Church, expecting to become a 100% Italian Extra Virgin?

Let me tell you, this System of Values is seriously ridiculous: I cannot have my personal documents because some bureaucrats have rights to blackmail me for that, and they suggest Kyenge as a model of Equal Opportunities and Integration. We are plunged into the Dark Ages, and like in the Dark Ages we have to pay the same brand of mobsters and counterfeiters for documents."

"You should be Pope" she said, "Yes, yes! You must become Pope."

"You love it, to be funny, don't you? You should know, I am not compatible with their spirituality; but sincerely I would love the position of Bishop in Beijing. That would be nice, maybe I could resuscitate Saint Peter and explain what really happened to his Gospel; but the best thing would be asking how the Catholic Heresies become Catholic Legacy, in Chinese."

"If you were Bishop of Beijing, would you remember me?"

"Sure I would, you are my official voice-over. How could I do without you?"

"Good luck you know, I am not a dead weight. Did you think about the characters?"

"The characters, to respect the reality of our lives, should be like ghosts, with no clothes and no human resemblance. At the end of the day it is a dissertation undercover. I believe Galileo didn't pay much attention to the characters in his Dialogues [W18], but later I will check if he made any portrait or description."

"One more thing, before I go. I have been researching the Forbidden Archaeology, but at the library it is not available, and not even at the Central Library in Town. The only copy is at the library of Armley Prison" she said smiling. "Do I need to book a few days in for you?"

"Are you serious" I asked, looking at her.

"Yes, yes" she said, still with an expression of surprise. "Yesterday and the day before I have been after the Forbidden Archaeology, but couldn't find it. There is only one copy for all libraries in town, and that copy is in the library of the Armley Prison", she said smiling again.

"What does it mean? Do we need to be sentenced in Prison to read that book?"

"Yes, this is also what I thought; this is strange isn't it?"

"Yes it is. I had better buy it, but please don't tell anybody" I said whispering.

"I will wait for your copy" she said returning the smile. "Look, it is almost one and I am running late. I have to go" she said collecting her notes, "I will see you later, or tomorrow."

"I am going too" I replied, and in a matter of second we were walking in opposite directions.

The Headingley Literary Festival

I was on my way home from the park when I heard a voice calling my name; I looked around and I spotted Jason on a bench near the entrance, waving his hand as if inviting me to join him.

"Hi" I said, coming nearer.

"Hi" he replied. "I called you because I want you to met Theia; she is a passionate reader, and if you like the view of a woman she may help you."

"Hi Theia. How are you doing?"

"I am alright, thank you" she said.

"So, how are you doing today? Have you been writing?" he asked again.

"Not really, and you? How are you doing today?"

"I am all right; sit down a minute with us. Where were you going to?" he asked.

"Nothing important. I was going to the convenience shop, I need a few items before dinner".

"I also need a few things from the shop, but not now. Did you see Aisling today?" Jason asked.

"No, not really, and if you are wondering, I have no clue where she may be. Yesterday she said she would have come to the Park but I didn't see her. I don't know" I said repeating myself.

"Jason said you have quite a story to tell, and you are after someone to proofread your writing. If you like, I've been teaching English for years and if I could I would be pleased to help you" she said.

"Yes of course I would like to, and thanks for the offer. At the moment I have not finished writing; I am just trying to find my way through the points I want to discuss, to make it easy and clear to read. There are probably a few grammar mistakes left in, but at this stage I am not concerned about grammar; I am more concerned about the meanings being accessible to all people, despite of their different backgrounds."

"Sure. I understand your concern about clarity first" she said.

"Luca had a few problems with his personal documents" Jason said, "Now he is trying to expose the situation, but apparently the offices responsible are not listening, so, since he was prevented from going to Court, he decided to go Public with a book."

"What documents are you talking about" she asked.

"My Passport, and my University degree" I replied.

"Oh, I am sorry to hear that. What happened?" she asked again.

"I had a PhD offer but the professors in the photograph of my degree ceremony did not confirm the degree they issued, and made me look like an impostor."

"Wow. That is not nice" she said.

"Well, this is what happened."

"He has also been arrested because some anonymous informant gave false information to the Police, pretending Luca was the problem, maybe an impostor, a threat, maybe even a terrorist while he was just the victim of the situation."

"Is that true?" she asked.

"Yes, it is true, and in the book I simply tell the facts" I said.

"So, you are writing a book about this story of what happened to you" she asked.

"No, not really. One of the matters is Justice, but what is it Justice? And which Justice is under discussion, the Justice of this world, by the law of man, or the Justice of God in the afterlife?

I am writing about our rights to defend ourselves against the High Moral Values of the public offices making people vanish into thin air. I am concerned about the rights we are supposed to have, but cannot claim; the white man speaks with a forked tongue, and I wonder if the Offices are above the law."

"The white man speaks with a forked tongue" she said smiling.

"Yes he does. I don't believe it was an Act of God to

make my Degree vanish, or my rights; and it was not the luck of evidence about the repeated abuses to prevent the case from obtaining Justice. Sure there are High Moral Values twisting the application of Justice by the law, and I am curious about this process of interpretation.

"I can see your motivation, after what happened to you" she said, "But how do you put across a point like this? It is really hard to believe. I don't know if people will ever take you seriously; probably the public will not believe that the public offices make people vanish like that" she said.

"I had your doubt before, but apparently it has happened." Jason said, looking at Theia. "If Luca's story wasn't true, he would have been prosecuted for defamation, for what he has been doing, addressing his accusations for years by naming professors and prosecutors, with photographs and tape recordings. At one point we have to accept it has happened for real, as also Luca had to accept all of this.

The problem I see is not a mistake that may happen, but the arrogance of calling that mistake a reality, preventing him from Justice. Not only did Luca not have confirmation for his documents, a problem that could have been resolved easily, but after that first mistake the offices made an impostor out of him, accused him of being a liar, made him live like a paperless, like he didn't have rights for his documents and he was the problem. I am also concerned about his European Passport, because without it he is a sort of hostage in this Country, isn't he?"

"Thank you for saying I am a hostage, I appreciate it" I said with a smile. "Nobody ever said that, but sometime I feel like it, yes."

"What happened exactly?" she asked.

"Shortly after I arrived I had a bag stolen, and the passport was in it. I reported the theft to the Police, and with the report I applied for a new passport to the Consulate, but I never received another one. The Consulate replied after 9 months, informing me that I followed the procedure correctly but the Office from Italy didn't authorize the issue of the new passport, not yet.

Then, about one year after the theft, in the last of three letters I received, the Consulate informed me that during the time I was cancelled from the Population list and I was not to have the new passport.

During the time I was waiting, a few months after the theft, I moved to Leeds without a passport, to register for the PhD offer. To complete the procedure I had to return to the Consulate for the legal translation of my degree, but Verona University never confirmed it to Leeds University and made me appear to be an impostor."

"And what about the Police?" she asked again.

"That happened later, about three years after the theft of the passport or more. When the police arrived I was already paperless for a long time.

The police arrived when I was claiming my rights, but nobody could believe the Italian offices were doing this, and I was treated like a counterfeiter, inventing a story, pretending to be Luca with a Degree at Verona University while none of the Italian Offices were confirming the documents they had issued, with signature, stamps and photographs.

They made a counterfeiter out of me, and since then I do videos on YouTube, showing the photograph of my degree ceremony and telling everybody that the Professors Emilio Tiberi and Bianca De Bernardi of Verona University are mobsters, liars and scumbags. If they didn't take me to Court, it is only because I am just telling the truth. And the same is true of the Prosecutors Corrado Carnevali and Guido Papalia; they also have been very helpful in the situation, sweeping the legal claims under the carpet of the Courts of Justice. They won't take me to Court if I call them vile mobsters, gangsters and pieces of shit, as they are, because in reality they covered up for their colleagues, just as a gang of mobsters would have done.

Maybe such prosecutors believe the Public Offices have rights to blackmail people for documents, maybe they believe it is a Tradition to be preserved, a peculiarity at the basis of Cultural Identity of the Italian society, and we know the Courts are quite conservative concerning High Moral

Values above the Law.

But the best came sometime later, when someone come up with the bright idea of pretending I could have had good reasons to organize revenge, to be depressed or deluded because of the happenings, and potentially have good reasons to become a terrorist. They had the effrontery to pretend I could have been deluded, and they never questioned themselves about being deluding for sure, faking documents in the Public Offices and then accusing me of crimes which in reality they had perpetrated; I was the victim, but I was viewed as the criminal, even worst, a potential criminal with good reasons to take Justice in his hands. Yes because in evidence they did the job, from the start; they made my paper vanish, and they projected their problems and fears on me, forcing me into the confines of their world of fiction."

"A potential criminal, with good reasons to take Justice into his own hands" he said, repeating my words.

"Yes, someone with good reasons to take Justice in his hands. Also the OLAF office of the European Union sent a Legal Claim to the Court in Italy, long before I was accused of being a terrorist, but the Italian Prosecutor Carnevali swept the claim under the carpet, pretending it had never happened."

"How long did take all this?" she asked.

"We are talking about 10 years ago."

"This is a nightmare" she said, looking at Jason.

"I said that too" he whispered, smiling.

"Exposing them on the Internet for a while has been fun, but to explain the situation in a book may be better. I would have the chance to give a few more details about our Tradition and Culture; about our education, Justice and morality..."

"So what is the book about?" she asked.

"To make it brief, I would like to know how the Catholic Heresies became Catholic Legacy. I want to explore the possibility of conscience and Justice existing without the approval of the Church. I am attracted by the possibility that nobody ever asked how the Catholic Heresies became

Catholic Legacy, because apparently nobody ever did. This is what emerges from the schoolbooks; the Catholic Heresies are Catholic Legacy, and as consequence of this morality, in the Courts of Justice we read «In God we trust», despite Jesus himself making it clear that 'The law of Rome is not the true law to obey'. Concerning the Law of the Land, also all the Apostles made it clear, and have been very respectful of this directive, like it was a precept above the commandments. I am not inventing it, it is in the Bible, «But Peter and the apostles answered, 'We must obey God rather than men!'» (Acts 5:29) [B3]. I only wonder why should we trust in God for the Law of the Land, when we know from the Bible he never liked it, but rather opposed and undermined it?

For example, one time a person investigating the case said that the situation I am living in is intolerable, but after these words nothing happened, and the situation still remains intolerable. The Police fled the scene of the investigation leaving it as intolerable as they found it; what am I supposed to understand from this? Do they enforce the law, or the abuses?"

"This is odd" she said.

"I have seen a few of his videos, showing documents and legal suits" Jason said. "Luca taped the conversation with the Psychiatrist of the Forensic Assessment, and it was the psychiatrist who said the situation was intolerable, and the accusations against Luca were from some kind of Anonymous Informants pretending Luca was a threat, possibly depressed because of the abuses, and as consequence potentially planning terrorist attacks in revenge, and they made him pay for their crimes and their fears.

At the end the psychiatrist said «There is a lack of illness going on», «What are we doing here?» That was really funny, I still remember these words" Jason said smiling. "It may sound odd, unbelievable, but it is just the truth. It is a matter of High Moral Value above the law preventing the victims from obtaining Justice. It could be a nice fiction, but it is every day reality."

“Wow” she gushed, like she imagined herself in my shoes for a moment. “Tell me more; I am sorry for you, but this story is really intriguing!”

“Sure, it is a pleasure. I am writing a book about it” I replied.

“Tell me” Jason asked, looking at Theia, “Do you believe the taping Luca made would be admitted in Court?”

“Probably someone would object, probably because Luca didn’t ask permission, or some other excuses. It depends on the results they plan, but without a passport I doubt Luca has the possibility to hire a lawyer and find legal representation at all. Tell me more; why do you believe it happened? What went wrong?”

“Oh! This is not easy to say, and for the very same reasons several things went wrong, not just my papers; also the Fascist would have been on trial in Nuremberg on the side of the Nazis, if the High Moral Values above the Law didn’t make a difference, leaving the Nazis only responsible for the Holocaust. Also the Nicaea Council went wrong for the same reasons, and Eratosthenes, Michelangelo; lots of things went wrong because of these High Moral Values above the Law, and my personal documents are just a small detail compared to the devastation they have caused in history and still continue to do.

How do I explain ‘why’ in some offices true degrees become fake, and the fake ones became true? How do I explain why the Courts of Justice sweep cases under the carpet, or why some officer causes documents to vanish in the offices and then pretends the victims should conform to their will?

The Catholic System of corruption is well documented since the time of Martin Luther; you don’t need to be good to go to heaven, and you don’t need to go to the University to have a degree. This is the ancient legacy of the High Moral Values above the law, made of corruption and blackmail, indulgences and Saints above the law. It is a system of favours, you may believe you have rights, but also having rights is a favour.

It is not my passport or my degree only that went wrong, but our Civil Rights, and the rights for people to have personal documents; this is what really went wrong. The Morality of the Courts of Justice, sweeping our legal claims under the carpet, despite being paid to administer Justice by the Law of the Land; this is what went wrong. Look at me: I am writing a book because I couldn't have my personal documents! What morality would tolerate all of this? Can you see, they pretend to be above the law? From the Courts of Justice to the school classrooms, it is always the same High Moral Values ruling the scene, and for this very same reasons lots of things went wrong, not just my papers, but also for all of us. It is Europe that has gone wrong, since the time of the Nuremberg trial, and my European Passport has gone with it."

"So, in the big picture, it was destiny" she said, as if concluding my words.

"I wouldn't say that, no, I don't like that word; I don't believe in destiny, but causes and consequences. The word 'destiny' recalls 'God Will', 'God Design', and God has nothing to do with this; it was not God Design but man made mafia to make my documents vanish.

You wonder why all of this happens, but sometime you cannot find the answer you would like. Do you believe the Jews never complained or never reported the Fascists for the abuses and violence they were suffering? Sure they did, and also the Italian democrats did, but all these claims were flushed down the toilet, the same as today, exactly for the same reasons, the Same High Moral Values above the law.

It wasn't only my papers which went missing, but the law of man and rights for a number of people, and the final reason 'why' all of this happens is to be found in the double standard of such High Moral Values ruling our society; some people are above the law, and some others have no rights at all.

About the degree going missing, Domenico Pacitti wrote an Article on JustResponse.net [A9]. Domenico is Professor at the University of Pisa, and has a nice website reporting interesting interviews, like with Noam Chomsky perhaps. He has an interest in Italian Higher Education, Culture and Politics, and I understand he wrote the article because he cares about the Italian Academia more than the ones selling fake degrees, or blackmailing students for confirmation of their studies. Eventually Domenico could see the problem, but sincerely I am not particularly bothered about the Church. I would like everybody to believe in whichever God they prefer; what I am concerned about is what they do with it, and the State not respecting its own laws.

It is obvious all the confusion comes from the belief that the Institutions won't harm people, and the victims of the Public Offices are not prevented from Justice, but in real life this is not what happens. The Institutions were perfectly aware of what was going on, but didn't do anything other than confirm the situation was intolerable, like the intolerable could have been imposed on me as everyday routine."

"It is unbelievable; I understand it has happened for real, but what do you mean about High Moral Values above the law?"

"When the early Christians arrived in Rome, Rome was a polytheistic town, and the exclusive worship of monotheism was unknown. But the Christians arrived in Rome with the pretence that the law of Rome was not the true law to obey, and there would be another law above it. This is the message of the early Christians to the Roman Empire, and since then the Secular meaning of Justice by the Law has changed and faded into our Trust in God, and God's Will, postponed into the afterlife.

In the Court of Justice we read «In God we trust», but in the Churches we don't read «We trust in the Law of Man», isn't it?

Also Public Security may be an example of High Moral Values, as the Police have the right to arrest people on suspicion, without evidence or any real reason except false accusations. The point is, what would happen if some offices were to make your documents vanish, and then pretend you were an impostor, and make a terrorist out of you? What about your rights, against the lies of a bunch of mobsters hiding behind the High Moral Values of the Public Office, in the name of the Law and Order?"

"Well, Public Security comes first; forget your rights, you are in big trouble" she said, shaking her head. "You said a few times they made you paperless; sure you couldn't print these documents yourself, but when you seemed like an impostor, you also become a threat. I like to believe a person is innocent until proven guilty, but when you became a threat, office to office, your word didn't matter because the Police were not listening to you but the Italian Consulate and the Italian University. Of course I believe those responsible should be prosecuted, especially for the hard time they gave you, but I also understand the Police didn't do anything concerning the situation of your documents."

"This case is business for diplomats; they only can afford to talk for weeks and years about it, and reinvent it as they like it, but I never had my personal documents and from my perspective there is nothing to talk about. Concerning my passport and my degree, there are no shades of grey.

What I wonder is what the European Union will chose, to guarantee personal documents to European Citizens, or freedom of bribery to the offices distributing passports and degrees at will, God's Will of course. This is not the first time that people in Europe had this very same problem, is it? As a consequence of these High Moral Values above the law, Europe has been divided for ages, since the end of the dark ages. Martin Luther summarized very well that moral rebellion, describing the System of Corruption of the Roman Tradition. I wonder if the European Union is just the revival of the dark ages, and after Nuremberg it considered the Religious System of Corruption of the Roman Supremacy, a Legacy to be revamped and imposed as the Culture and Tradition of the new Re-United Europe."

"I understand" she said smiling, "You had a European

Passport and Europe should have paid some attention to the Italian Administration of European Documents; but you said bribery, why?" she asked again.

"Apparently in Italy people cannot have documents they have rights to, but eventually may be blackmailed for them. Isn't this Mafia, blackmail and bribery?" Jason asked, looking at me. "You imagine, Theia, to be blackmailed and have to pay black money, like your degree was kidnapped, or it was a fake; as if it was a favour and you had no rights for it.

But Luca also told me this problem is not only with the offices for documents, like passports or degree certificates. Also doctors refuse to provide Public Service in Hospital, like for abortion, how much did you say? More then 70% of doctors refuse to provide Public Service, unimaginable!"

"It is true, more then 70% of Doctors and Pharmacists refuse to provide assistance for abortion [A29], but 100% of Judges tolerate also this interruption of service and refuse to Administer Justice by the Law of man. They do whatever they want, and then there is no way to complaint. Also the Police, I told them a thousand times, my name is Luca and I am not lying; they cannot pretend I didn't tell them, but they were in charge, and had absolute power to do whatever they wanted. They had full freedom to choose to do the right thing, but in their opinion my request for Justice has been interpreted like an Act of Terrorism, demanding rights from the Law of Man rather than fulfilling in silence the Will of God as they saw it, and to preserve the decency and decorum of this System of Values I have been defamed, vilified, tormented and tortured. Nevertheless I never believed anybody ever asked How the Catholic Heresies became Catholic Legacy. It is all a scam by the book" I said.

"By the book" Jason said smiling.

"What book?" Theia asked.

"In God we trust." Jason said, "The book of the High Moral Values, inspiring our Courts of Justice."

"The Bible" Theia asked.

"Really I was thinking of the mobsters in the Offices" I

said, “But it is obvious the entire System of Values is under discussion, from the Church to the Court of Justice, including the school classrooms.

Concerning the Bible inspiring the Court of Justice, I don’t think the problem is the Bible itself, but rather what people do in its name. Definitely I don’t believe it was an Act of God to make my documents vanish, despite this is what the Prosecutor said, in the name of the Law of the Land. But I still believe the problem is not Religion, or God, but people abusing it, pretending God did something, or someone has to do something in the name of God.

I am pretty sure the Prosecutor is a liar, and he knows God didn’t do it. I am definitely sure God is innocent, and the scumbags are to be found in the Office, under the Jurisdiction of the Law of man. My degree vanished, and it wasn’t God’s responsibility.”

“Yes, I can see your disappointment” she said smiling. “The big wheel has lost your personal documents, and it is obvious you now wonder about the rights of people to survive the big wheel” she asked.

“Kind of, yes; I like your summary. We have no rights to defend ourselves. At any time someone may come out pretending we are impostors, may become a threat, may have weapons of mass destruction, or may be suicidal like it happened to Mr. David Kelly [W55]. Also to me they said I could have been suicidal, after they made me paperless and I was claiming my true rights against their fiction and lies made of false accusations. But they have the true morality to interpret reality, and twist it as they like. They can project their fears and paranoia into our real world, and we can be aborted alive at any time. This is what I know for sure about our democracy: not even our existence and our names are guaranteed, and they can take them from us.”

“Probably the Police found it convenient to stay out of it, because it was a situation made in the offices from the start. Probably there is no glory in investigating colleagues working in the same offices; but I like that you connect the Values of our Democracy to this reality of abuses and violence. We like to believe we export democracy, civil rights and freedoms, but probably we exported so much that there is none left for us.

I am sure the Institutions lie; do you believe none of the people abused in Rotherham ever complained? Do you believe it would help if the media reported it every day? Do you believe the case swept itself under the carpet? Sure the victims are prevented from getting Justice, for a matter of decency and decorum, or bigotry, depending on the perspective. Should I believe this is Public Interest, or it could make the Institutions better?

I am definitively sure the institutions lie, and I like it that you find lies in the schoolbooks, because these textbooks are the Gospels of our System of Values. The mass-communication system we have, is perfect to make puppets out of us; nobody uses his own head anymore, and these High Moral Values are the only option we are allowed."

"This is exactly the reason why I believe it is impossible that nobody ever asked, because we are not all the same. This is indisputable evidence; we will never be all the same, but this is what they want from us. From the deception of the schoolbooks, to the Courts of Justice redirecting the victims to the Justice of God, we are invited to live like we were already in the afterlife.

Especially the Court advising to trust in God is ridiculous. It sound like we didn't have any law we could trust, but there is no God we can trust either, because their God made of decency and decorum is only an accomplice, an accessory sweeping their crimes under the carpet.

The High Moral Values above the law are only useful to overrule our rights. Not long ago I was reading an article "A Law above the Law: Christian Roots of the English Common Law" by Augusto Zimmermann [A6]. Augusto teaches at the School of Law, and I would like to tell him that 'The Law above the Law' well represents the High Moral Values of the System of Corruption I am talking about; it enforces the System of Values in which the offices blackmail people for documents people have a right to. It is really a kind of Justice above the law, the same as shooting randomly in the street.

The 'Law above the Law' is not a matter of Natural Law, or Positive Law, but having rights for personal documents, or being blackmailed for them, in the name of a Law above the Law enforcing a System of Corruption made of Indulgences, bribery and blackmail. It is exactly the same difference between having rights, or not. I would like to tell him, dear Augusto, there is no Law above the Law, but only outlaws and mobsters with High Moral Values, informing and exploiting masses of naïve and good-hearted idiots.

It is obvious the Natural Law undermines the Positive Law [W56][W57], but where is it the Public Interest in having no laws people could trust, but a bunch of Corrupted Moralists dispensing favours and indulgences with the freedom of forgiveness?"

"So, what is next? What have you been writing recently?"

"Yesterday with Aisling the French Revolution came out, because it is the origin of our contemporary democracies. It came out during the French Revolution that women were not considered citizens, didn't have the same rights of man, and probably for these reason still today women are paid less for the same job as a man. This is about gender and democracy. On the other hand, concerning the Absolute Power, the French Revolution sanctioned the principle that «no one is above the law». That was the meaning of the Constitution: the end of Absolute Power. Also the Monarchy and Clergy had to respect the law, like all people. Then Lafayette proclaimed Human Rights, but the bill forgot to recognize women as citizens, and Napoleon a few years later made a new Concordat with the Church reinstating the tradition of High Moral Values above the law.

That was yesterday; this morning I have been reading the program of the Courses of Italian Literature, and I found out there is an Institute dedicated to Dante Alighieri at the University in town."

"Oh!" she said, "The Headingley Literary Festival is to

start next week. I know there are students and lecturers from the University reading; maybe there is an evening dedicated to Italian literature. You should check, you may find the input you are looking for" she suggested.

"Thank you" I said. "I didn't know about the festival, and it may be interesting, yes."

"Give me a minute and I will tell you more" Jason said, with the smartphone already connecting. "Here it is, Headingley Literary Festival. Let me see... Here it is; one of the events of the Festival is 'Supper with Dante'. Students and lecturers from the Centre for the Dante studies of the Leeds University will do some readings from the Divine Comedy. The event will take place in an Italian restaurant. What do you think?" he asked.

"I had to study the Divine Comedy at school, but I've never seen the comedy part of it. Dante exactly represents the tradition of High Moral Values, prejudice and preconceptions we are talking about. It is a display of the best Catholic allegories and superstitions, in which the most distinguished historic figures find their final judgment.

"So, tell me something the professors would never say, during the supper with Dante" he asked.

"Ok" I said smiling. "A few years ago one of the offices of the United Nations made a claim reporting that the Divine Comedy of Dante is a racist book, and a collection of synonyms have been listed in that report, from racism to hatred, all justified by the same culture of ignorance, stereotypes, prejudice and preconceptions. It was the Human Rights Committee of the United Nations that made the complaint, through an independent research organization named Gherush92 [A22]. I am sure on the Internet you can find several articles from newspapers, including The Independent, The Guardian and The Telegraph. Try to search Gherush92 [A22] and Dante."

"You are right, here it is. Yes, it is about racism" he continued after a few moments, without moving his eyes from the small display on the smartphone. "Maybe it is good for learning the Italian language" he said.

"I am not sure really. The language of the Divine

Comedy may be compared to the English language of Shakespeare. Nobody speaks like that anymore, it is old fashioned."

"It is the origin of the Italian language in use today" he said, like as he found some suggestions from the articles he was reading.

"Maybe, but nobody ever called that language as the Italian Language. The language of Dante was 'Vulgar Latin', it was the language of the common people with no education, the plebs. Also Dante never said he was writing in Italian".

"Oh, really?" she asked.

"Dante wrote 'De vulgari eloquentia' (Concerning Eloquence in Vulgar language), clearly it was not concerning eloquence in Italian. Also Pietro Bembo wrote 'Prose della volgar lingua' (Prose in Vulgar Language), and the Italian language was not in his mind either, otherwise he would have done, wouldn't he?

Dante, Galielo, Michelangelo, none of them ever mentioned the word Italy [W58] simply because Italy didn't exist. Then, after the Italian Unification the Vulgar Language of Dante changed its name, from one day to the next, but the language had been already there for ages; it was only the name that changed, after Italy was established, and this is obvious, isn't it? People don't change language from one day to the next. It was Manzoni, more then 300 years later feeling the necessity to unify the Language and the Culture, in order to unify the country."

"And what about Dante himself" she asked.

"Dante was a man of the Dark Ages, and his Divine Comedy explains what may happen if you don't follow the Catholic precepts. He was speaking the language of the plebs, the Vulgar Latin of uneducated people, but he was a well-educated man of the Dark Ages, perfect in Latin and extremely scholastic, nothing like Michelangelo.

In the view of Dante, God is at the center of Human life, and he never came close to the Renaissance Culture in which it is freedom of choice and the personal responsibility that are at the center of Human Life. The Divine Comedy is a collection of medieval Catholic allegories and metaphors, superstitions, prejudice and preconceptions. This is why it was reported as racist, but don't get confused, it is not a matter of skin colour. The racism of the Divine Comedy is made of High Moral Values, it is built on the belief of the Moral Supremacy of the Catholic Church; it is a racism based on Religion, Catholic Culture and the Catholic Inquisition.

Mussolini killed more Italians than Jews were ever killed in the entire WWII, and nobody ever speaks about it. Why? The Nazi Germans were on trial in Nuremberg [W63], but not the Italian Fascists responsible for the same crimes, why?" I asked again.

"Why?" she asked, waiting me to continue

"Well, that was the prologue of the European Justice we witness today. The Holocaust of Mussolini was different from the German because Mussolini had the blessing of the Pope from the start, for opposing the democrats and the democratic values. Then Mussolini made the Concordat with the Church in 1929 [W3], reinstated Vatican City after the Italian Unification, and in 1938 he enacted the Racial Laws [W52] to defend and promote the Moral and Cultural Supremacy of the Absolute Power of the Church more and more, against any contamination. But the real contamination Mussolini worried and opposed the most was not concerning skin colour but the most traditional Catholic Heresies concerning the freedom of choice and the secular value of Justice.

But it was not Mussolini who invented the Catholic Supremacy; it was already there for ages, and Dante and Mussolini are very alike. Dante made the Divine Comedy in accordance with the Church, putting people in Heaven or in Hell in accordance with the Catholic Inquisition, and Mussolini did exactly the same with the Concordat and the Fascist Cultural Regime; maybe Mussolini didn't write a comedy of horrors, but he made a reality of horrors, and both the Morality of Mussolini and Dante were inspired by the same Catholic Supremacy.

In both cases it was an Intellectual Cleansing, a Holocaust for all people who demanded freedom of choice, or that 'No one is above the Law'. It should be clear that the Roman Church is responsible for crimes against Humanity since long before Dante arrived, and the same abuses still continue today, exactly for the same reasons. So, ages after the rebellion of Martin Luther, here it is back again with the European Union promoting the culture of the dark ages, as the only way Europe could be united.

Anyway, Dante found a place in Hell for all the enemies of the Church, and similarly Mussolini persecuted the enemies of the Church closing down their democratic political parties, and labelling them 'Anarchists' and 'Apostates' because they demanded 'No High Moral Values above the Law'. Mussolini hunted and executed the opposition as infidels and Enemies of the State, but in reality the opposition were unarmed democrats defending the Laws of the State from mobsters pretending to be above it, because of the blessing of the Pope.

But as I said from the start, they arrived in Rome pretending that the Law of Rome is not the true Law to obey; this is what the Christians said when first arrived in Rome two thousands years ago, and since then they have been seeding holy wars and holocausts all over the planet."

"You remind me of the Education Act, and the Canon law excommunicating students here in England" Jason said, looking at Theia.

"The crimes of the Roman Church are screaming from thousands of years of Moral and Physical violence, and about excommunicating students, I can tell you more.

Some time ago I have made a few videos using clips from true University Lectures. Just to make sure of the quality of the teaching, the lectures in discussion were made by the "Nettuno University", under the Patronage of the President of the Italian Republic, and broadcasted by the Italian National Television Channels. But out of the academic honours, these lessons were just repeating the same school program everybody already knew from his own schoolbooks; it was nothing new, nothing to be surprised, unless someone at the end of the lectures was asking strange questions nobody ever asked before, like perhaps how the Catholic heresies could possibly become Catholic legacy.

With this evidence from true University Lectures I made a collection of videos, with Professors caught on camera while pretending to transform the Catholic Heresies into Catholic Legacy, obviously in accord with the schoolbooks they were reading and the school programs above. The collection is titled 'Matters of Italian Culture' and a few years later I have sent one of these video to an Italian Professor very popular on Youtube named Serafino Massoni.

Concerning my observations I never had an answer from the honoured Professors doing the lectures, or from the Office of their Patron, but eventually from Serafino, who knows? So I asked him how the Catholic Heresies become Catholic Legacy, and since he is very passionate in literature I sent him a Video from that collection, with the Lecture about a very popular sonnet of Dante Alighieri [A25].

Anyway, the next day I found a cheering video-reply, praising and complimenting me for the reflections I raised. «Very original my dear, very original», «You are right, these are all lies» he was repeating, laughing at Dante Alighieri and the distinguished professors caught on camera deceiving their students. «You are right, and your video is very well done; 5 stars, 10 stars my dear.» «I have never seen a video so original, very well done», «It is really funny to see such honourable Professors explaining that sonnet; they have to interpret it, yes», «Do you see the double standard? The double, triple and quadruple standard, do you see?» he was asking, pointing at the inconsistencies I was highlighting in the video, with captions, asking how possibly the Renaissance Culture could have become intellectual legacy of the persecutors of the Renaissance Culture, and showing drawings and paintings of the Renaissance time representing the burning stake of the inquisition. How did the Catholic Heresies become Catholic Legacy? How is it possible nobody ever asked? Who is to pass the exams? Is this a holocaust?

But Serafino was laughing like he never did in his videos before, and from that I understood he completely missed my point. In fact I wasn't asking his opinion about the deception of the Professors under the Patronage for the President of the Italian Republic, caught on camera while pretending to transform the Catholic Heresies into Catholic Legacy. In conclusion I had to ask him directly, about him and his double standard. In fact, as a Professor he was doing exactly the same as the Professors in the video he was laughing at. Serafino enjoyed a good laugh at the High Ranking Professors, spotted deceiving the good faith of young students, but he didn't like to see himself in those shoes, doing exactly the same things, and sincerely I felt all these compliments were somehow unexpected. «Your video is very well done, very original», «Do you see the double standard? Do you see?» he was repeating, and I couldn't find any reason to justify his delight, if not as evidence of his own double standard; like his amusement was the only way he could be honest in front of the ultimate deception, to set up students' beliefs for life.

So, finally, simply because he didn't understand the questions from the start, he made another video, this time complaining I was not intelligent or original anymore but an idiot making fun of respectable people doing their job. In conclusion, after the delight his double standard came out, the true side of a fascist pretending to have High Moral Values above the law; they should be prosecuted for taking advantage of the good faith of young students.

But concerning the racism hiding within the Verses of the Divine Comedy of Dante Alighieri, I made that collection in 2008, a few years before Gherush92 came out with his report in 2012, and I remember I felt somehow honoured with that authoritative chorus after my voice.

"Look at this!" Jason said inviting Theia to pay attention to the display. "I am reading the Guardian" he said, "You are right, Dante is racist. How is it possible our schools teach Dante? Is he worth the University fees of £10.000 and more a year?"

"No he isn't" I said smiling, "Someone pretends it is literature, but it is only a course of Catholic Culture, Catechism and prejudices. It is mythology, all about the Cult of the Moral Supremacy of Rome."

"Yes," he said looking at me and shaking his head. "The Guardian [A22.1] says that the Divine Comedy is «Offensive and discriminatory», «Racist, islamophobic, antisemitic» and «The poem should be removed from classrooms».

Similar things appear in several newspapers; it is also in the Independent, and the Telegraph. Theia! Look, the Telegraph only changes the spelling and says «Racist, homophobic, anti-Islamist and anti-Semitic» [A22.2]. Fascist racism is in school classrooms; we have courses in racism at the University, what is this? What kind of people will be these students in the future?"

"Well, if students don't conform to the precepts, they won't pass the exams. This is what they learn: silence and obedience. In the future they will be good mobsters, very domesticated and obedient to the System of Corruption and Indulgence they have been educated in. They will name it career and success, like the fascist did, exploiting and robbing their victims."

"Look!" said Theia, calling for attention. "On Google Dante is the Father of Italian Literature."

"I am sure somewhere Dante is mentioned as the father of Italian Literature, but he is not. Also Galileo was mentioned as father of the modern science, and he is not.

"Why is Galileo not?" Theia asked.

"There already existed different views of the skies and heavens long before Galileo arrived. Recently the mystery of a few pre-Christian Babylonian Tablets was unveiled, illustrating how to calculate the position of Jupiter using geometry for the calculation [A26]. But also the map of Piri Reis [W46] is a mystery, drawing the coast of the continent of Antarctica under a mile of ice, which nobody knew was there before the invention of the sonar. Astronomy and geography have been really devastated by Catholic Censorship; you imagine that Eratosthenes [W29] has measured empirically the circumference of earth almost 600 year before the Nicaea Council flattened the planet in 325 AD.

Admitting Copernicus or Galileo have discovered something is like ignoring the devastation perpetrated by the Inquisition. Galileo was condemned for heresy, because of repeating the ideas of Copernicus, and Copernicus as well was simply repeating ancient knowledge, cancelled from history by the same inquisition thousands of years before.

At last Galileo abjured, he had to recant to save his life, and a few hundred years later someone made him father of Modern Science because he abjured in accord with the will of the Church. Definitely the experimental observations of Galileo have an historical relevance, but what about Eratosthenes and Hypatia; they also did experimental observations and accomplished the same conclusions, thousands of years before Copernicus and Galileo.

In reality, it was easier to make Galileo father of modern science, rather than having to explain what happened during the gap between Eratosthenes and Galileo. Otherwise, how to justify the flattening of the planet, with all people on it, with their freedom of choice? Try to imagine yourself having to explain the Canon Laws flattening the Earth for 13 hundred years, in the name of God. How many people have been vanished in this extraordinary attempt to flatten the planet? And today, what is different? How is anonymous informing changed? How to explain all Universities pretending to transform the Catholic Heresies into Catholic Legacy? Tell me we are not living in the Dark Ages. Exploring the revisionism of the Catholic Church would take more than one lifetime, and not least would be the problem to justify the textbooks in which Galileo is the father of Modern Science.

But now, for the sake of democracy and knowledge, just to have an exhaustive comprehension of Dante and

Fascism and the points under discussion, play this scenario. Since we know at the University in town there is the Centre for Dante Studies, could we ask them how the Catholic Heresies become Catholic Legacy? To see if they believe it is really God who makes University Degrees disappear from the Archives of the Public Offices, or was it rather one of their colleagues?"

"No!" he laughed. "Don't do it! You will get arrested again!"

"Just to see, if it was a matter of literature or what?" I said returning the smile. "At the end of the day, the teaching of Dante well represents the system of corruption of the dark ages we are living in. It is a Catholic Book in which the Earth is flat, humans are puppets, and God is at the center of human life, faking Degrees and Passports. There is no room for the Law of man in there; they are just the same barbarians as they always were, mobsters with High Moral Values above the law."

"So, what happened to Vulgar Latin, and the Italian Language" Theia asked.

"In Italy the issue concerning the language become important at the time of the Renaissance, and was then revamped during the process of National Unification, about 300 years later. Listening to the schoolbooks the issues were a matter of literary style, but at the same time were blooming the Heresies of the Renaissance Culture, and the Heresies of the French Revolution, and the problem in practice was not literary style but the content of the writing. It should be obvious that at the time of the Renaissance the good Catholic Authors were against the Heresies of the Renaissance Culture, while at the time of the Italian Unification they were against the Heresies of the French revolution."

"Well, what is left of the Modern Era? If you remove the Renaissance and the French Revolution, it would be just the same as the Dark Ages. At this point, I wouldn't be surprised if someone was to pretend that Renaissance Culture and the French revolution never arrived in Italy" he said smiling.

"Well, maybe is not really like that, but it is true all the heresies of all times have always been immediately persecuted and prosecuted, on the spot."

"At the stake you mean" Theia said, smiling.

"Yes, the spot of the stake, where we read «In God we Trust»" I said, returning the wit. "As Jim said, «Cancel my subscription to the Resurrection» [A23]. I didn't choose to be baptized, and now I tell you the reasons why I wouldn't. Some time ago I recorded a poem with Aisling, it is on YouTube; I could make a video for the Headingley Literary Festival out of it. It is a Poem about the Italian Literature."

She looked curious, and Brian smiled. "Go for it" he said, and in a moment the video was on.

"The darkest day"

The darkest day in the history of Italy
was the day of the literary laundry in Arno[1]
The real day of the Universal Judgment,
when the Heresy of the Renaissance Culture
have been coated with Catholic colours.

You make fun of your own belief, you parrots,
in the darkness of your freedom, with myself
in the prison of your conscience.
Nevertheless, the Renaissance Culture
was established on Catholic Heresies,
was made of Catholic Heresies

---

[1] The day the Italian Language was ideally cleaned from regional differences (the laundry in the water of the river Arno). It was Alessandro Manzoni, in XIX century, at the time of the Italian Unification, manifesting the necessity to unify the Culture and the Language before the Nation could be unified. Manzoni was inviting to adopt the Tuscan heritage as model, and called Dante as Father of Italian Language and Literature. In reality, it was not a matter of literary style but Culture, inviting to adopt the Roman Catholic Tradition.

and there is no way,
with your arrogance, propaganda, censorship,
violence and fear.

It cannot only be me, to ask you
where are all gone?
what have you done to my friends?
all missing, vanished,
with witnesses, and confessions
in conscience....

Listen, clear and crystal,
the Renaissance Culture
is established on Catholic Heresies,
was made of Catholic Heresies.
Listen wise parrot, read, and think,
think, those heresies,
in the space of centuries
have been chased, hunted out,
isolated, persecuted,
cancelled, from the history of Italy
purified, with the fire
sacrificed, with the people inside.

What do you believe, nobody ever asked?
No complaint? Nobody ever understood?
Nevertheless, no witnesses, ever,
and it was never happened!

No evidence, is the evidence,
the evidence nobody has ever asked
and the logic, heretical
has never survived, on the stake
burn, Italic culture;
the law of Rome is no more
the true law to obey.
New values and pride I see
in the image of a new God.

The video finished, and Theia smiled. “It sounds nice, the voice of Aisling in the recording” she said. “I liked it, but the readers of Dante may be conservative concerning their Traditional Values. But I got the point: How did the Catholic Heresies become Catholic Legacy?”

“Do you believe people would be able to understand this question?” I asked.

“I am not sure; surely not from their experience as students. Yes, students should ask for their money back for the education they had. Fake education should be paid with fake money” she said smiling. “The question is not difficult, there is no chance the Catholic Heresies could be Catholic Legacy; they are made of different Values. The Catholic Heresies are not Catholic Values, and will never be. It would be like odd numbers becoming even numbers: not a chance.”

“This is exactly what I meant” I said. “The Catholic Heresies are the edge of the civilized world, and if you wonder on which side you are you may ask your best professors to explain how the Catholic Heresies have become Catholic Legacy, or to tell one Democratic Value that has ever been a Catholic Value in history.”

The wind was gently moving the leaves, whispering from the trees, and I felt like I had to go home.

“I am really glad I met you Theia, but I have to go, and thanks to you Jason as well.”

“Was nice to meet you too” she said.

“I'll see you later” Jason replied.

“See you soon, bye.”

I walked away to the exit around the flowers and the oak, and then turned my way home just in time to see Aisling. She was apparently walking alone toward the Park.

"Could you help me, please?" she asked, still a few yards away.

"Hi. Sure, but how could I?" I wondered.

"Invite me to dinner" she said.

Appendix

(To whom it may concern)

To those who may believe this is a novel, I spent long walks trying to understand what would be best: if I had to publish documents to support my words, how many documents would be necessary, and what would be the definitive evidence if common sense and logic don't make sense anymore?

On the following page is the photocopy of my stolen passport (image 1).

As you can see it was issued on the 28th September 2001 by the Passport Office of the Questura of Milan, the Police Headquarters.

The following year the details of my passport were registered with my address on more papers from the same Questura, and confirmed in person by Police Inspector.

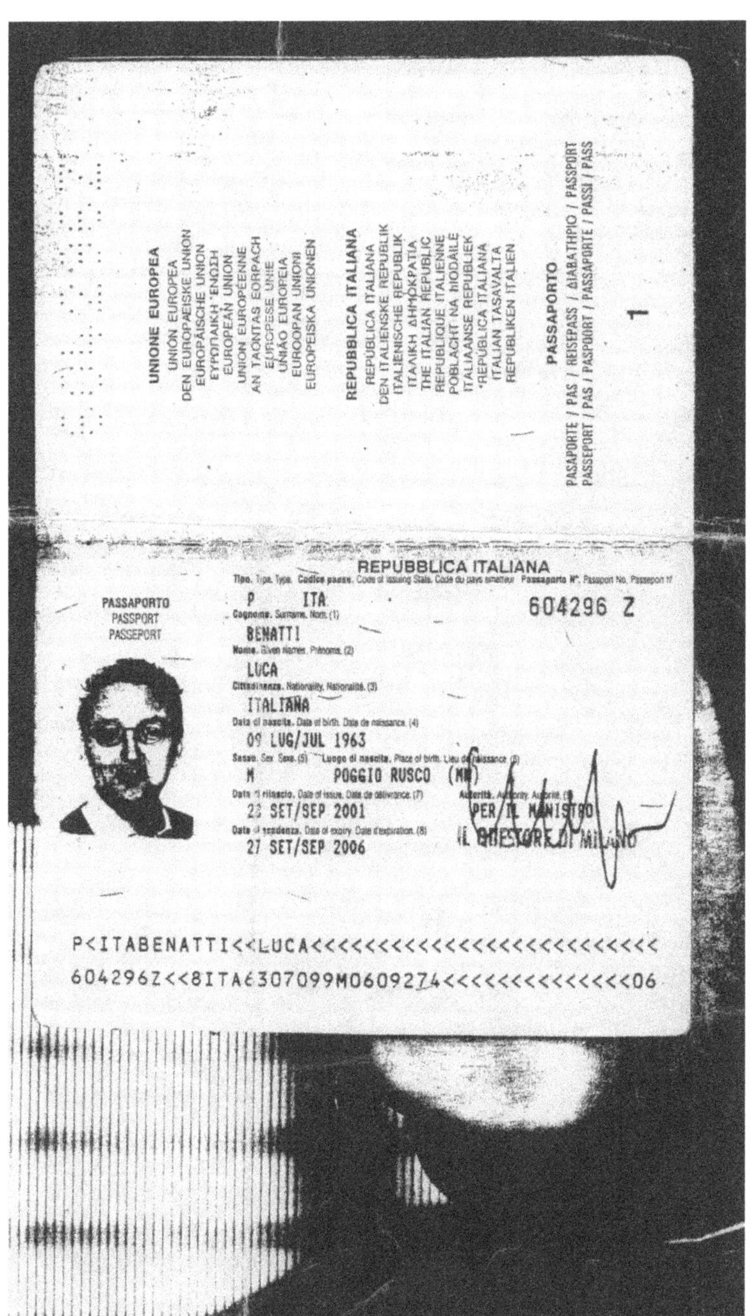

UNIONE EUROPEA
UNIÓN EUROPEA
DEN EUROPÆISKE UNION
EUROPÄISCHE UNION
ΕΥΡΩΠΑΙΚΗ ΕΝΩΣΗ
EUROPEAN UNION
UNION EUROPÉENNE
AN tAONTAS EORPACH
EUROPESE UNIE
UNIÃO EUROPEIA
EUROOPAN UNIONI
EUROPEISKA UNIONEN

REPUBBLICA ITALIANA
REPÚBLICA ITALIANA
DEN ITALIENSKE REPUBLIK
ITALIENISCHE REPUBLIK
ΙΤΑΛΙΚΗ ΔΗΜΟΚΡΑΤΙΑ
THE ITALIAN REPUBLIC
RÉPUBLIQUE ITALIENNE
POBLACHT NA hIODÁILE
ITALIAANSE REPUBLIEK
REPÚBLICA ITALIANA
ITALIAN TASAVALTA
REPUBLIKEN ITALIEN

PASSAPORTO
PASAPORTE / PAS / REISEPASS / ΔΙΑΒΑΤΗΡΙΟ / PASSPORT
PASSEPORT / PAS / PASPOORT / PASSAPORTE / PASSI / PASS

1

REPUBBLICA ITALIANA

PASSAPORTO
PASSPORT
PASSEPORT

Tipo. Type. Type. P
Codice paese. Code of issuing State. Code du pays émetteur ITA
Passaporto N°. Passport No. Passeport N° 604296 Z

Cognome. Surname. Nom. (1)
BENATTI

Nome. Given names. Prénoms. (2)
LUCA

Cittadinanza. Nationality. Nationalité. (3)
ITALIANA

Data di nascita. Date of birth. Date de naissance. (4)
09 LUG/JUL 1963

Sesso. Sex. Sexe. (5) M
Luogo di nascita. Place of birth. Lieu de naissance. (6) POGGIO RUSCO (MN)

Data di rilascio. Date of issue. Date de délivrance. (7)
28 SET/SEP 2001

Autorità. Authority. Autorité. (9)
PER IL MINISTRO
IL QUESTORE DI MILANO

Data di scadenza. Date of expiry. Date d'expiration. (8)
27 SET/SEP 2006

P<ITABENATTI<<LUCA<<<<<<<<<<<<<<<<<<<<<<<<<<<
604296Z<<8ITA6307099M0609274<<<<<<<<<<<<<<06

The year after my passport was issued, I used it to identify myself to the Police Office in Milan, in order to collect documents.

On the following page is copy of a Police Report signed by the Police inspector, reporting the details of the stolen passport and the address I was living, my property in Milan.

Please note this document was issued on the 12th March 2002 by the same Questura of Milan also my passport was issued.

Translation of the following page. (image 2)

QUESTURA OF MILAN
POLICE OFFICE OF "GRECO TURRO"
Via Perotti n. 02 - MILANO
Tel 02.6943451 - Fax 02.69434541

OBJECT: Notification report for : BENATTI Luca, born in Poggio Rusco (MI), il 09.07.1963, res. in Milano in via F. Morandi n.7; ordinary passport n. 604296Z, issued date 28.09.2001, by the Questore of Milan. Tel.02.26113128 (home) 347.9688360 (mobile) - - - - -

Today 12/03/2002, at 16.42, in the offices of the Police Station "GRECO TURRO", in Milan Via Perotti n.02; in front of the undersigned Officer of Judiciary Police BATTISTIN Renato, Inspector of State Police, the person in object is present to collect the information, and copy was given to him. - - - - - - -

Of what was drafted above was issued a minute, re-read, confirmed and subscribed - - - -

Person in Object Police Inspector

QUESTURA DI MILANO
COMMISSARIATO DI P. S. "GRECO TURRO"
Via Perotti n.02 - M I L A N O -
Tel.02.6943451 - Fax.02.69434541

OGGETTO: Relata di notifica a carico di: BENATTI Luca, nato a Poggio Rusco (MI), il 09.07.1963, res. a Milano in Via F. Morandi n.7; passaporto ordinario n.604296Z, ril. il 28.09.2001, dal Questore di Milano. Tel.02.26113128 (Casa) 347.9688360 (Cell) -

Il 12/03/2002, alle ore 16.42, negli Uffici del Commissariato di P. S. "Greco Turro", in Milano Via Perotti n.02; innanzi al Sottoscritto Ufficiale di Polizia Giudiziaria BATTISTIN Renato, Ispettore della Polizia di Stato, è presente la persona in oggetto indicata alla quale, mediante consegna di una copia, viene notificato l'atto retro scritto. --
Di quanto sopra è stato redatto il presente verbale che viene riletto, confermato e sottoscritto. ------------------------------------

La Parte

Il Verbalizzante

I complained to the President of the Italian Republic for the reasons I explained in this book, especially concerning education and research, and in 2002 I had the following reply. Please note it was 26th March 2002.

Not long later I had a PhD offer in England, but by then I was not Luca anymore, and I had no Degree anymore. I found myself paperless in England looking like an impostor, with the best wishes of the Italian Public Administration.

Translation of the following page. (image 3)

Roma, 26 MAR 2002

GENERAL SECRETARY
OF THE PRESIDENCY OF THE REPUBLIC

OFFICE FOR JURIDIC AFFAIRS
AND CONSTITUTIONAL RELATIONS

UG
N.13406

Egregious dr. Benatti ,
in relation to Your letter, addressed to the Head of the State, I can reassure You that this Office has submitted Your concern for the attention of the Minister for Education, university and scientific research for examination.

In fact, the President of the Republic, once explicated his constitutional prerogatives, has no faculty of intervention on matters that are competence of other bodies of the State.

Best Regards - p. Director of the Office

As you can see the reply was sent to the address on my passport, again, my property where I was living, but obviously it is just a letter; it is not a Police inspector witnessing in person and confirming re-read information.

SEGRETARIATO GENERALE
DELLA PRESIDENZA DELLA REPUBBLICA

UFFICIO PER GLI AFFARI GIURIDICI
E LE RELAZIONI COSTITUZIONALI

UG
N. 13406

Roma, 26 MAR. 2002

Egregio dr. Benatti,

in relazione alla Sua lettera, indirizzata al Capo dello Stato, posso darLe assicurazione che questo Ufficio ha sottoposto quanto da Lei rappresentato all'attenzione del Ministero dell'istruzione, dell'università e della ricerca scientifica, per l'esame di competenza.

Il Presidente della Repubblica, infatti, attese le sue prerogative costituzionali, non ha facoltà d'~~intervento su~~ materie ~~attinenti alla sfera di attribuzioni di~~ altri organi dello Stato.

Con i migliori saluti.

p. Il Direttore dell'Ufficio
(prof. Marcello Romei)

dr. Luca Benatti
Via F. Morandi, 7
20100 MILANO

In the next page is copy of the Report of the theft of the passport. (image 4)

The theft happened on Sunday, and the next day I asked what to do. The Consulate told me to prepare a few documents and then to contact the Honorary Consul in Belfast to complete the procedure, and so I did. I went to the Police for the report of the theft, and with the photographs I filed the request with the Honorary Consul. He said the new passport would come in a matter of days.

It was the 10th November 2002

POLICE SERVICE OF NORTHERN IRELAND

SOUTH BELFAST DCU
CRIMINAL JUSTICE UNIT
DONEGALL PASS BELFAST NORTHERN IRELAND BT7 1BS

Telephone: Belfast (028) 90650222 Exts:26523/26587
Fax: (028) 90259740

Mr Luca Benatti C/o Linen House Hostel 20 Kent Street BELFAST BT1 2JA	Please reply to:	Inspector, CJU
	Your reference:	AR02/1251/10
	Our reference:	C & C 1142 10.11.02
	Date:	19 November 2002

Dear Sir

We can confirm that you reported your passport stolen.

I hope this is of assistance.

Yours faithfully

M.T

p/p. R TINSLEY
Office Manager
Criminal Justice Unit

After I filed the request for new passport, the Consulate replied 09/06/2003 (1).

Put the case you had your passport stolen, abroad. Would that be tolerable to you if the Consulate were to reply after 9 months? And what about if the Consulate, after 9 months, was to inform you that you were to exceed 12 months period abroad, and decided for you that you were better to relocate? And what if the Consulate, after 9 months, was to write you a letter asking your address, like it wasn't on the letter they just sent.

After I received the following letter, I informed the Consulate my address was on the letter they sent, and my reasons to be in the U.K. were temporary, personal matters concerning a University Course, and I would have already moved if I only had the passport.

This is the rendering of the letter you see in the next page, which is the reply I received from the Consulate after the request for new passport filed 9 months before (image 5).

09/06/2003 (1)

Dear Mr. Benatti ,

following your request for a new passport – you subscribed in presence of the Honorary Consul in Belfast – I am honored to inform you that the competent Italian Authorities have notified this office that your name "HAS BEEN CANCELLED FROM THE GENERAL REGISTRY OF THE RESIDENTS IN THE TOWN OF MILAN because of YOU WERE UNREACHABLE".

In the light of what is explained above, I ask you to notice that before we could proceed to the issue of a new passport in your name, this General Consulate has to ask you to register to the A.I.R.E. (Registry of the Italian resident abroad) of the town of Milan. For these reasons I consider it useful to inform you that, under the law n. 470/1988, the citizen who relocate his residence abroad for a period exceeding 12 months HAS to ask to register to the A.I.R.E. of the town of last residence in Italy.

Therefore, in order to proceed as you asked, I would be pleased if you could fill in, subscribe and return the attached form to this office. Waiting for your reply, with Best Regards

p. il Console Generale

Simonetta Corti

Consolato Generale d'Italia
Edimburgo

32 Melville Street
Edinburgh EH3 7HA
Tel: 0131-226 3631 Passport Visa Office
0131-220 3695 Secretary's Office
Fax: 0131-226 6260

03876
09 JUN 2003

Pos. 10038/sc

Egregio Signor Benatti,

a seguito della Sua richiesta di rilascio di nuovo passaporto – da Lei sottoscritta alla presenza del Console onorario d'Italia in Belfast –, mi pregio informarLa che le competenti Autorita' italiane hanno qui reso noto che il Suo nominativo "E' STATO CANCELLATO DALL'ANAGRAFE DELLA POPOLAZIONE RESIDENTE DEL COMUNE DI MILANO per Sua IRREPERIBILITA' ".

Alla luce di quanto sopra esposto La prego di voler notare che prima di poter procedere ad un rilascio di passaporto a Suo nome, questo Consolato Generale dovra' prima richiedere la Sua iscrizione all'A.I.R.E. (Anagrafe degli Italiani Residenti all'Estero) del suddetto Comune di Milano. A tale proposito ritengo utile renderLe noto che, ai sensi della legge n. 470/1988, il cittadino che trasferisce la propria residenza all'estero per un periodo superiore ai dodici mesi DEVE richiedere la propria iscrizione all'A.I.R.E. del Comune di ultima residenza in Italia.
Al fine, pertanto, di procedere a quanto sopra Le saro' grata se vorra' compilare, sottoscrivere e restituire a questo Ufficio l'allegato formulario.

Certa di un Suo sollecito riscontro.
Coridali saluti,

p. Il Console Generale
(Simonetta Corti)

Allegati: vari

Signor Luca Benatti
18 University Street
Belfast
BT7 1FZ
N. IRELAND

The Consulate replied informing me it had asked again for the mandate to issue new passport. It was 24/07/2003 (2)

This is the translation of the letter on the next page (image 6)

24/07/2003 (2)

Dear Mr Benatti

Following Your request for the issue of a new passport, I inform You that this General Consulate has sent a new request to the Central Police in Milan (for a mandate) to authorize the issue of the new passport, and this office will contact you as soon a reply is received.

Best Regards
p. THE CONSUL GENERAL OF ITALY
(P. Il Console Generale)
(The Officer)
Francesca Rinaldi

Consolato Generale d'Italia
Edimburgo

32 Melville Street
Edinburgh EH3 7HA
Tel: 0131-226 3631 Passport Visa Office
0131-220 3695 Secretary's Office
Fax: 0131-226 6260

Pos.10038/fr

05032

Sig. Luca BENATTI
18 University Street
BELFAST
BT7 1PZ

24 luglio 2003.

Gentile Sig. BENATTI,

A seguito della Sua richiesta di rilascio passaporto, La informo che questo Consolato Generale ha inviato una nuova richiesta di nulla osta e delega alla Questura di Milano e questo Ufficio si metterà in contatto con Lei non appena riceve la relativa risposta.

Distinti saluti.

p. THE CONSUL GENERAL OF ITALY

p. Il Console Generale
L'Impiegata
(Francesca Rinaldi)

The Consulate again replied 24/11/2003 (3)

This is the translation of the letter on the next page (image 7)

> 24/11/2003 (3)
>
> Dear Mr Benatti
>
> Concerning your request for a new passport I am to inform you that:
>
> 1 – The Central Police Station informed us that you have been cancelled from the General Registry of the population resident in Milan, because you were unreachable at the census 2001
>
> 2 – This Consulate can issue a passport to you only if
>
> a - You are resident in the consular district of Scotland and Northern Ireland
>
> b - After mandate authorization from the competent territorial authority where you reside, if you reside outside this consular district.
>
> Therefore we renew the request to inform us of your current residence, I inform you that under the art. 6 of the law 27.10.1988, the citizen moving his residence abroad from a town in Italy, has to declare to the consular office within 90 days from moving. I will be pleased if you could inform us if you intend to remain in this consular circumscription for a period longer than 12 months.
>
> We wait to receive as requested above.
>
> Best Regards
>
> THE CONSUL GENERAL
>
> Andrea Macchioni

32 Melville Street
Edinburgh EH3 7HA
Tel: 0131-226 3631 Passport Visa Office
0131-220 3695 Secretary's Office
Fax: 0131-226 6260

Pos.10038/AA

07921

24 NOV 2003

Oggetto: Passaporto

Gentile Signor Benatti,

In riferimento alla Sua richiesta di rilascio passaporto Le comunico quanto segue:

1) La Questura di Milano ha reso noto allo scrivente che Lei è stato cancellato dall'Anagrafe della Popolazione residente del Comune di Milano per irreperibilità al censimento del 2001;
2) Questo Consolato Generale può rilasciarLe un passaporto soltanto nei seguenti casi:

a) Lei risulta risiedere nella circoscrizione consolare della Scozia e Irlanda del Nord;
b) su delega dell'autorità competente per residenza qualora quest'ultima sia al di fuori di questa circoscrizione consolare.

Nel rinnovarLe pertanto la richiesta di comunicarci la Sua attuale residenza anagrafica, Le faccio presente che, ai sensi dell'art.6 Legge 27.10.1988, n.470, il cittadino italiano che trasferisce la propria residenza da un Comune italiano all'estero deve farne dichiarazione all'ufficio consolare entro novanta giorni dalla data di espatrio. Le sarò quindi grato se potrà comunicare stesso mezzo se Lei intende rimanere in questa circoscrizione consolare per un periodo superiore a dodici mesi.

Nell'attesa di ricevere quanto sopra richiesto porgo distinti saluti,

IL CONSOLE GENERALE
Andrea Macchioni

Sig. Luca BENATTI
2 Ulsterville Gardens
BELFAST
BT9 7BA
N. Ireland

A few months after I received the last letter from the Consulate, in January 2004 I decided to move to Leeds without a passport. In fact, after informing the Consulate I had my passport stolen, after I paid various fees almost one year before, I never had any replacement, not even a temporary one, but only the suggestion to relocate.

After contacting the University in Leeds, as suggested by the professor in Belfast, I had a PhD offer, so I had to return to the Consulate for the legal translation of my University Degree, but later the Professors in the picture of my degree ceremony didn't confirm the degree they issued, with their signature, stamps and photographs, and made me into an impostor.

So I had to return again to the Consulate, to complain about the vanishing of my degree, but the Consulate refused to report my legal suit to the competent offices in Italy, and as a consequence I sent it to the European Union, enquiring about my rights for traveling and my personal opportunities without my personal documents.

In the next page is the black and white version of the photograph of my graduation ceremony at the Verona University. You can see the full commission, but later, as I said, the same professors you see in the photograph didn't confirm the Degree they have issued, and made me into an impostor, a counterfeiter. (image 8)

I was living in my property in Milan.

The Questura Office of Milan (Head Police office) issued my passport, and sometime later the details of that Passport were reported by the Police Inspector of the same Questura on more documents.

Meanwhile, after the Passport, my University Degree also went missing, preventing me from fulfilling the opportunity I organized in autonomy.

Would you tolerate the Public Administration making you paperless, for years?

Would you tolerate a solicitor suggesting you conform to the will of the Consul and be the impostor, the traditional dodgy Italian, just to cover-up the Italian Mafia and the Public Administration blackmailing people for documents people have rights to, immediately and for free?

On the following page is the image 9

Henry Hyams

SOLICITORS

Mr L Benatti
[illegible]
LEEDS
LS2 9AU address

Our Ref: RES/KL/31214.1.6
Your Ref:
Date: 10 March 2004

Dear Mr Benatti

Nationality

I have spoken with the Italian Consulate in Edinburgh.

They stress that you have **never** lost your nationality. You remain an Italian National.

When you reported your passport lost to the Italian Consulate they had to, under Italian law make checks with the police where you said you were resident. You instructed them that you were resident in Milan. The police in Milan reported that whilst they have no objection to you obtaining a replacement passport they could not authorise the Consulate to issue one as you were no longer resident in Milan. Rather you were resident in Northern Ireland.

The Italian Consulate advised that you must therefore register with them in order to obtain a replacement passport. I understand from my telephone conversation that you refused to do so.

In all the circumstances I strongly advise you now, given that you are living in Leeds to register with the Italian Consulate in Manchester. Once you have done so you will be able to obtain a replacement passport.

I have to advise that in the event that you do not wish to register with the Italian Consulate in Manchester then there is nothing else I can do to assist you. It seems that there is a very simply solution to obtaining a replacement passport and I would therefore advise you to contact the Manchester Consulate immediately.

I will keep my file open for seven days in the event that you require any further advice arising out of the contents of this letter. In the event that I do not hear from you within this time then I will take steps to close your file.

Yours sincerely

Robert Sparks

7 South Parade, Leeds LS1 5QE · Telephone 0113 2432288 · Fax 0113 2460283 · DX 12028 LEEDS 1

Individual Solicitors are Members of the Law Society Criminal Duty Solicitor Panel, Children Panel, Personal Injury Panel, Mental Health Panel, Immigration Law Panel and Solicitors Family Law Association. Regulated by the Law Society.
Email: info@henryhyams.com Website: www.henryhyams.com

Partners: Neville Bush, Lloyd Bergen, Derek Hallam, Clive Bergen, Graham Parkin, Laurence Saffer, Dominic Nurse, Michael Bush, Jane Cooper.
Assistant Solicitors: Martin Morrow, Timothy Jacobs, Kate Rayfield, Graham Neil, Robert Sparks, Michael Walsh, Gemma Manning, Catrina Solan, Ruth Shedlow, Marcus Farrar, Simon Connolly, Shila Whitehead.
Consultant: Ian Vellins

I do repeat, would you tolerate a solicitor suggesting you to conform to the will of the Consul and be the impostor, the traditional dodgy Italian, just to cover-up the Italian Mafia and the Public Administration blackmailing people for documents people have rights to, immediately and for free?

How long are people supposed to wait for a passport replacement, until the after-life?

Meanwhile, was I free to travel and fulfill the opportunities I organized in autonomy? And what about my Rights as EU Citizen? But probably as paperless, with no papers, I was not an EU Citizen anymore, was I?

I underline the Italian Consulate not only failed to issue the passport replacement in reasonable time but also refused to help with any kind of temporary Passport to let me return to Italy and resolve their problems with their forgeries concerning my address and my University Degree. In all this time and with all the problems they caused since the time I paid cash for my passport replacement and later my lost University Degree, the Consulate never provided any help, nothing more than what you can see, and the Consul never showed up to explain who was the impostor.

On the following page is the image 10

Henry Hyams

SOLICITORS

Mr L Benatti	Our Ref:	RES/KL/31214.1.6
[illegible]	Your Ref:	
LEEDS	Date:	18 March 2004
LS2 9AU		

Dear Mr Benatti

I enclose a copy of the letter I sent you on the 10 March 2004. The Italian Consulate gave clear advice as to how you go about obtaining a replacement passport and I strongly advise you once again to follow their advice, contained in my letter of the 10 March 2004 and report to the Italian Consulate in Manchester.

You mentioned in my telephone conversation with you on the 16 March 2004 that you have a property dispute in Milan. I unfortunately cannot advise as to Italian property law and would recommend that in those circumstances you seek advice from an Italian lawyer who specialises in property disputes.

I write to inform you that I am now closing the file of papers in respect of the above matter.

We are under a duty to inform you as to what happens to the file of papers when they are closed. We store the papers in our archive in Armley. Items stored by us will be destroyed in six years time.

We archive our files at the conclusion of the case and unless we receive specific instructions not to destroy a particular file, it will automatically be destroyed together with all the documents in it. If you wish to have items retrieved you should notify us as soon as possible. You will need to quote the reference number on this letter to enable the file to be located.

Yours sincerely

Robert Sparks

7 South Parade, Leeds LS1 5QE · Telephone 0113 2432288 · Fax 0113 2460283 · DX 12028 LEEDS 1

Individual Solicitors are Members of the Law Society Criminal Duty Solicitor Panel, Children Panel, Personal Injury Panel, Mental Health Panel, Immigration Law Panel and Solicitors Family Law Association. Regulated by the Law Society.
Email: info@henryhyams.com **Website:** www.henryhyams.com

Partners: Neville Bush, Lloyd Bergen, Derek Hallam, Clive Bergen, Graham Parkin, Laurence Saffer, Dominic Nurse, Michael Bush, Jane Cooper.
Assistant Solicitors: Martin Morrow, Timothy Jacobs, Kate Rayfield, Graham Neil, Robert Sparks, Michael Walsh, Gemma Manning, Catrina Solan, Ruth Shedlow, Marcus Farrar, Simon Connolly, Shila Whitehead, Katy Cowans.
Consultant: Ian Vellins

Dissatisfied with the Solicitor Hyams, and not willing to be the impostor, or scapegoat covering up for the Italian Culture and Tradition of Mafia's, bribery and blackmail, I went to the Emergency of the NHS to report that I was prevented from going back home and from registering the PhD offer I had, and since making people paperless is criminal I asked for the intervention of the Police. The Police told me to go to the Citizen Advice Bureau, and from there to the solicitor Hyams. As I know the Emergency department of Hospitals have an obligation to report to the Police the crimes they become aware of, and I wanted to report that I was paperless for a long time, and prevented from traveling without real justification.

The doctor at the Emergency could not believe my situation, because Italy is a democratic place within the EU, and does not make people paperless. Therefore I got arrested (sectioned) because the doctor believed his preconceptions and prejudices more than the photograph of my graduation Degree Ceremony, or the letters of the Consulate or the Solicitor.

Please note I was invited to Leeds University, and after disclosing my project I had my PhD offer but could not register because the professors in the photograph of my graduation ceremony at the Verona University did not confirm the degree they have issued and made me to be an impostor or liar.

But References should not go missing, as they are official documents of the Curriculum of every student; this is evident trough my Curriculum that I had the best marks from the Professors in the Photograph of my Graduation Ceremony but I became paperless as if I had never been there.

On the following page is the image 11.

Leeds Mental Health ***NHS***

Teaching NHS Trust

St Mary's House
St Mary's Road
LEEDS LS7 3JX
TEL: 2952300

Dr T Mahmood
Malham House
Hyde Terrace
LEEDS 2

Secretary: 2952317
Ref: CHB/LDR/VC6121
Date: 8 June 2004

Tariq

Dear Dr Mahmood

LUCA BENATTI D.O.B. [redacted] address

~~[redacted]~~**, LEEDS LS2 9AU**

First of all I would like to thank you for agreeing to see Luca in your outpatient clinic on the 16th June 2004 at 2:00pm. I felt it was important to write to you regarding the outcome of his period of assessment on ward 3 at the Becklin Centre.

Despite the fact that Luca remained an inpatient, under Section 2 of the Mental Health Act for a period of 3 weeks', the clinical team did not arrive at a definitive diagnosis. However, a differential diagnosis would include: -

1. No mental illness.
2. A personality that contained paranoid traits.
3. Paranoid illness.

At the time of discharge Luca was not on any medication.

For your information I have included a copy of Peter Scanlon's SW assessment, which was conducted on the 15th May 2004.

Certainly during Luca's 3-week assessment on the ward, there was little additional information gleaned regarding social and family circumstances, and also the circumstances leading to admission.

During Luca's time on the ward, he was agreeable to me discussing his case with Professor Stephen Westland, Professor at the School of Design at Leeds University.

Professor Westland confirmed that Luca had contacted him, initially via e-mail, and it transpired that Luca did have some interesting ideas regarding the Luscher test. Subsequently Professor Westland suggested that Luca apply to do a PhD in the department. However, in order to pursue this Postgraduate course he had to be able to supply adequate references. Unfortunately, when Professor Westland pursued

It is difficult to explain how my Passport and my University Degree vanished at the same time, and the Consulate could not provide assistance of any kind. This is why Br Buller used the word conspiracy. But in reality they made me paperless for real, no theories or opinions on this, despite the promises of the Consulate to me first, then to the Police, than to the CAB and the solicitor, and then the NHS as well. But I couldn't travel with the promise of a Passport, could I?

Is this the moment they reduced me to slavery? After I reported again and again I was still waiting for my Passport? After I was complained my EU Rights and Freedom to travel and fulfill the opportunity I organized in autonomy were prevented?

Please note that there was nothing wrong with me, other than that I was paperless, could not travel, could not register the PhD I was offered, and without a Passport couldn't hire a decent Lawyer, and was not willing to be the impostor to cover-up the Consul, or to be paperless from an EU country and within EU borders.

Concerning the “frustration”, I wonder how long dr Buller would have tolerated being paperless. I explained the situation, they verified and wrote it down, but apparently didn't understand the severity of the situation and that I was a victim. As if making people paperless, and as such reducing people into slavery, could possibly be legal or tolerable.

Please note I was trying to address the situation via “legal channels”, but I was rather left paperless for some time more.

On the following page is the image 12

-2-

these references one referee did not reply, whilst the other only stated that they were aware that Luca had previously studied at their University. It certainly appears to be the case that Luca viewed these inadequate references as further evidence of a conspiracy by the Italian government, and a hidden agenda to prevent him developing any improvements in the Luscher test. It is important to note that the word (conspiracy) is my term not Luca's. Mr Scanlan's report also makes reference to the issue of Luca's lost passport. It is my understanding that the Italian authorities will issue him an Italian passport, but will provide him with one of the variety that is issued to Italians who are resident in the country. More specifically, Luca wants it clear on the passport that he is a citizen of Milan. However, that is clearly not the case at the present time, but Luca feels that they are being unreasonable. He was also not aware that he would require a passport to travel within the EU.

Clearly Luca feels that some injustice has been done and has been seeking redress via legal channels. He has also e-mailed a host of people regarding the above issues. However, he denied any plans to retaliate against those in authority, and accepted that it would be tantamount to harassment to be constantly e-mailing or sending letters to the same person regarding his frustrations.

Throughout Luca's time on the ward he presented as very pleasant and at no point became irritable or hostile. Although frustrated with aspects of his current circumstances, he denied any active plans to end his life. Luca always presented casually but smartly dressed and denied any significant disturbance in his mood, appetite or sleeping pattern. It is also relevant that there was no evidence of any hallucinatory phenomena, ideas of reference, disorders of thought possession or passivity phenomena.

Throughout his admission Luca was unwilling to consider a trial of antipsychotic medication. Although my differential diagnosis included a paranoid illness, it was both my opinion and the opinion of the clinical team that Luca did not suffer from a mental illness, which was of a nature or degree, which warranted enforced treatment. Certainly there were no issues of risk apparent. Although frustrated with his situation Luca never appeared significantly distressed by it.

It is also worth noting that at one point we organised the presence of an Italian interpreter. In fact, they confirmed some aspects of Luca's story regarding patent laws in Italy.

In the 8 to 10 days prior to discharge, Luca went on brief periods of leave, which appeared to go quite well. When I reviewed him in the ward round on the 7th June he appeared settled in his mood and I therefore rescinded the Section 2. Luca is agreeable to attend outpatients appointments with yourself, and given that he resides in your catchment area it seems sensible to organise at least some initial aftercare.

You should receive a copy of the discharge summary in due course, but I felt it was important that you receive some information regarding Luca prior to seeing him in clinic.

-3-

Kind Regards

Yours sincerely

Chris Buller

DR C H BULLER
CONSULTANT PSYCHIATRIST

16 June 2004 the European Court for Human Rights replied concerning my rights and freedoms. As you can see my request was denied as “inadmissible”.

On the following page is the image 13

COUR EUROPEENNE
DES
DROITS DE L'HOMME

CONSEIL DE L'EUROPE
STRASBOURG

EUROPEAN COURT
OF
HUMAN RIGHTS

COUNCIL OF EUROPE
STRASBOURG

Mr Luca BENATTI
[redacted] private address

FIRST SECTION

ECHR-LE11.0R(CD1)
EBA/chk

16 JUIN 2004

Application no. 4926/04
BENATTI v. Italy

Dear Sir,

I write to inform you that on 11 June 2004 the European Court of Human Rights, sitting as a Committee of three judges (N. Vajić, *President*, P. Lorenzen and V. Zagrebelsky) pursuant to Article 27 of the Convention, decided under Article 28 of the Convention to declare the above application inadmissible because it did not comply with the requirements set out in Articles 34 and 35 of the Convention.

In the light of all the material in its possession, and in so far as the matters complained of were within its competence, the Court found that they did not disclose any appearance of a violation of the rights and freedoms set out in the Convention or its Protocols.

This decision is final and not subject to any appeal to either the Court, including its Grand Chamber, or any other body. You will therefore appreciate that the Registry will be unable to provide any further details about the Committee's deliberations or to conduct further correspondence relating to its decision in this case. You will receive no further documents from the Court concerning this case and, in accordance with the Court's instructions, the file will be destroyed one year after the dispatch of this letter.

The present communication is made pursuant to Rule 53 § 2 of the Rules of Court.

Yours faithfully,
For the Committee

Santiago Quesada
Deputy Section Registrar

ADRESSE POSTALE / POSTAL ADDRESS: CONSEIL DE L'EUROPE / COUNCIL OF EUROPE F - 67075 STRASBOURG CEDEX | TELEPHONE: (0)3 88 41 20 18 | INTERNET: http://www.echr.coe.int | TELECOPIEUR/FAX: (0)3 88 41 27 30

On the following page is a letter from the European Office OLAF (image 14)

In July 2005 the OLAF office of the European Commission sent my legal claim to the Court in Milan, in fact without a passport I was clearly prevented from traveling, and with the vanishing of my degree I was also prevented from fulfilling the opportunities for the PhD I organized. But the Prosecutor in Milan, Corrado Carnevali, swept the claim under the carpet, like I didn't have any rights to my personal documents, or worst, like my only right was to conform to the High Moral Values of the National System of Corruption.

COMMISSIONE EUROPEA
UFFICIO EUROPEO PER LA LOTTA ANTIFRODE (OLAF)

Il Direttore Generale

D/05920 25.07.05
Bruxelles,
04 D (2005) 5524 MV/mp

Alla Cortese attenzione del Sig.
Luca BENATTI

)
ITALIA

Oggetto: **Lettera-esposto a firma Luca Benatti pervenuta via Fax in data 24/05/2005**

Egregio signor Benatti,

In data 20/06/205 i miei uffici Le hanno comunicato informalmente a mezzo posta elettronica che l'esame dettagliato del suo esposto era in corso d'esame.

La informo ora che tale esame é terminato e che la conclusione già anticipataLe in via informale non può che essere confermata in questa sede.

Infatti, ciò che Lei ha segnalato riguarda comportamenti che risultano da un lato di stretta pertinenza delle Autorità nazionali italiane (amministrative e/o giudiziarie), e dall'altro eventi che non rientrano nelle competenze dell'OLAF, la cui missione é strettamente legata alla tutela degli interessi finanziari della Commissione Europea (Regolamento CE 1073/99).

Potendo tuttavia i medesimi fatti rientrare nelle eventuali competenze della Direzione generale della Concorrenza, con la presente lettera si provvede a trasmettere copia del suo esposto alla Direzione COMP, per quanto di eventuale pertinenza di quest'ultima.

Riteniamo inoltre doveroso trasmettere copia del suo stesso esposto alla competente autorità giudiziaria italiana (Sig. Procuratore della Repubblica di MILANO), per quanto di eventuale competenza di tale autorità, in ordine ai fatti di presunti abusi ed illegalità da Lei subiti e denunciati nella sua lunga e dettagliata missiva del 24/05/2005.

Nel caso Ella ravvisi ulteriori e diversi elementi che possano rientrare nelle specifiche competenze dell'OLAF, si resta a sua disposizione per quanto Ella vorrà eventualmente comunicare a questo ufficio.

Distinti saluti,

F.-H. Brüner

Commission européenne, B-1049 Bruxelles / Europese Commissie, B-1049 Brussel - Belgio. Telefono: (32-2) 299 11 11.
Ufficio: 08/42. Telefono: linea diretta (32-2) 2991560. Fax: (32-2) 2998104.

E-mail: mario.vaudano@cec.eu.int

EU Office OLAF - Page 2 (image 15)

For acknowledgement copy was sent to the Prosecutor in Milan, Corrado Carnevali.

(quote from pag. 85)

The following year, in October 2006 I decided to write to the MP for High Education Bill Rammell, to report the situation to the European Offices for a solution."

"And what happened?" he asked curious, like if I said something he also would have tried.

"The reply said there was nothing he could have done, and suggested to contact a solicitor in Italy. Then, a few days later I was arrested, because someone had the insolence to pretend I could have been deluded and organized revenge, and turn into a terrorist, and plot mass murders as consequence of the situation I was reporting and complaining as unjust and illegal. (quote from pag. 85)

(quote from pag 68)

So, I was forced into silence, in the confine of their lies, to make real their pretence I was not Luca, was not Degree at Verona University, and never had any reason or rights to claim. They can make your documents vanish, and then pretend the problem is you, not conforming to their will, the will of the Institutions; they can design you like a character from a novel, and you will never be able to complain. (quote from pag 68)

Copia conoscenza a:

- José Manuel Barroso – Presidente della Commissione Europea
- Philip Lowe - Direttore generale della DG Concorrenza della Commissione Europea
- Corrado Carnevali – Procuratore della Repubblica di Milano

Allegati:

- Lettera del Sig.Luca Benatti al Presidente della Commissione Europea
- Lettera del Sig. Luca Benatti al dott. Mario Vaudano
- E-mail del dott. Mario Vaudano al Sig. Luca Benatti
- Traduzione italiana della lettera del Sig. Luca Benatti al dott. Mario Vaudano per l'A. G. italiana

Commission européenne, B-1049 Bruxelles / Europese Commissie, B-1049 Brussel - Belgium. Telephone: (32-2) 299 11 11.
Office. 08/42. Telephone: direct line (32-2) 2991560. Fax: (32-2) 2988104

E-mail: mario.vaudano@cec.eu.int

On the following page is copy of a letter from the Minister for Higher Education MP Bill Rammell. (image 16)

After trying the emergency department of the Hospital I wrote to MP Bill Rammell, asking him to help me to resolve the problem with the Italian Consulate, in respect of EU Laws concerning the freedom of traveling and opportunities.

Mr MP Bill Rammell was Minister for Higher Education in the Government of PM Tony Blair.

As you can see the letter doesn't say a word about making people paperless within EU borders.

It doesn't say anything about the Ambassador or any Italian Consul, as I would have liked a clear plain explanation from them for what they were doing, the honorable and reliable Italians of the Public Administration.

On the other hand it mention that I was claiming my Rights as an EU citizen, my right to travel and fulfill the opportunity I organized in autonomy, and as such suggested to look for legal advice in Italy. But I wasn't free to travel to Italy to do this, and probably was more important to cover-up the Consulate.

department for

education and skills

creating opportunity, releasing potential, achieving excellence

Castle View House
P.O. Box 12, Runcorn
Cheshire, WA7 2GJ

tel: 0870 000 2288
fax: 01928 794248
info@dfes.gsi.gov.uk
www.dfes.gov.uk

Dott. Luca Benatti
address

Our ref: 2006/0320918

20 October 2006

Dear Dott. Benatti

Thank you for your letter of 5 October, addressed to Bill Rammell MP, about admissions to the University of Leeds. I hope you understand that the Minister receives a large number of letters and emails and is unfortunately unable to reply to them all individually. Therefore, I have been asked to reply.

Firstly may I say I am sorry to read of the difficulties you have experienced since first trying to enrol at the University of Leeds as a PhD student. However, I should explain that UK universities are autonomous bodies responsible for their own admissions policies and procedures. This autonomy is enshrined in law and the Government does not have any power to direct universities in admissions procedures. The criteria adopted by universities when considering PhD applications are a matter for the individual institutions concerned. I am afraid it would therefore be inappropriate for Mr Rammell to meet with you to discuss your situation when he visits the University of Leeds on 29 November.

In addition, I am sorry to tell you that the failure of your previous place of study in Italy to verify your qualifications in a timely way, and in doing so enable you to enrol at the University of Leeds, is a matter which this Department can not advise you on. You may wish to consider taking legal advice in Italy on your position regarding this and the difficulties you experienced with the Italian Consulate.

If you would like to discuss your current situation with an impartial adviser the Council for International Education, UKCOSA, offers information about other sources of support which might be available to you as an international student. UKCOSA's advice line number is 0207 107 9922 and is open Mondays to Fridays between 1pm and 4pm. Alternatively you may wish to visit their website at www.ukcosa.org.uk.

Finally I note that the University of Leeds recently invited you to register your interest again as a prospective PhD student. I hope you are able to resume your studies either at the University of Leeds or another institution in the near future.

I realise this reply may not be as helpful as you would have wished. Nevertheless I hope I have clarified the Department's position.

Yours sincerely

Jan Purdy

Jan Purdy
On behalf of the Head of the Public Communications Unit

INVESTOR IN PEOPLE

On the following pages are two letters from the same solicitor (image 17).

The RMO (Resident Medical Officer) indicated it wouldn't be in the Public Interest for the Police to pursue this matter.

Flannigan, the RMO, made up false accusations of all kinds, and despite the Police not finding anything to be investigated, she (RMO) had the insolence to pretend to be honest, that I didn't want to be discharged as she said to the solicitor, and later more false accusations when I was handed over to the Forensic Psychiatrist Dissanayaka. As if she ever had any reason to section me, before or after the Police dismissed her accusations as unsubstantiated.

I asked a solicitor to legally acknowledged and witness my situation, that my documents had vanished and the false accusations made against me.

Your ref:

Our ref: ANB.HSS

When calling, please ask for – **Alastair Bateman**

17 January 2007

Dear Lucas

I write further to my recent discussions with you on the 12th January 2007. I raised this matter with the Mental Health Review Tribunal and it would seem that they have mislaid your application. They have now formally acknowledged that your have applied to the Mental Health Review Tribunal and have promised me that they will endeavour to list the Mental Health Review Tribunal as a matter of urgency.

In the meantime I also confirm that I am going to press the Mental Health Act Administrator to arrange a Managers Meeting.

Yours Faithfully

Alastair Bateman
ALASTAIR BATEMAN & CO

TEL. (01274) 73 99 73 FAX. (01274) 74 55 04
34-36 SUNBRIDGE ROAD, BRADFORD, WEST YORKSHIRE, BD1 2AA
EMERGENCY NUMBERS. (07770) 785 651 & (07957) 280 202

PRINCIPAL:Alastair N Bateman LL.B PARTNER:Kamaldeep S Dhesi LL.B ASSISTAT SOLICITOR Helen Moyle LLB LEGAL EXECUTIVE:Susan K Allen F.Inst.L.Ex

But out of mislaid applications, misleading reports, the lack of progress he mentions, and the false accusations dismissed every time by the Police, the manipulation and plagiarism of the RMO, the solicitor was happy to be paid anyway.
As matter of fact, as you can see, this kind of solicitor doesn't even need to spell my name correctly to be paid.

Flannigan, after stalking me and making false accusations to the Police, repeatedly, also made false statements to the solicitor pretending I was happy to be there, and later to the Forensic Psychiatrist Dr Dissanayaka, pretending I was the problem, the terrorist.

On the following page is the image 18.

Your ref:
Our ref: ANB.HSS

When calling, please ask for – **Alastair Bateman**

25 January 2007

Dear Lucas

I write to confirm my advice to you on the 20th January 2007.

I write to confirm that the police are not going to interview you in connection with an allegation of threats to kill due to the fact that the RMO indicated that it would not be in the public interest for the police to pursue this matter.

If the police however take the view that they should interview please do not hesitate to contact me and I will make sure that I am present at all police interviews.

Please note that I have applied for a Hospital Managers Meeting and a Mental Health Review Tribunal, I am continuing to press for an early date and I am somewhat concerned about the total lack of progress in terms of listing a hearing in your case.

You did also raise the with me the issue that you are likely to be discharged within the next 7 days by your RMO and you did not want this to take place.

I confirm my advice: -

1. If the RMO decides that you should be discharged from hospital then you will have little choice in the matter – you can not remain on a section through your own choice
2. Please also note that I do not believe that if you were taken off section it would affect any civil action you may or may not wish to take against the hospital in due course.

Please however keep me fully informed if you are taken off section in due course.

Yours Faithfully

Alastair Bateman
ALASTAIR BATEMAN & CO

Lucas Bretani
Ward 3
Becklin Centre
St James Hospital
Leeds
West Yorkshire

Criminal Defence Service

TEL. (01274) 739973 FAX. (01274) 745504
34-36 SUNBRIDGE ROAD, BRADFORD, WEST YORKSHIRE, BDI 2AA
EMERGENCY NUMBERS. (07770) 785 651 & (07957) 280 202
*PRINCIPAL.:Alastair N Bateman LL.B *+* *PARTNER:Kamaldeep S Dhesi LL.B* *LEGAL EXECUTIVE: Susan K Allen FInst.L.Ex*
* Solicitor-Advocate (Higher Courts Criminal) +Member of Mental Health Panel

On the following page is another letter from another solicitor (image 19).

Again the Police couldn't find anything to prosecute, despite the evidence of more false accusations, slander, defamation, and the stalking of a paperless person prevented from appropriate legal representation.

But the solicitor was more compromising and tolerant, as if he was to be paid anyway and I was to be paperless anyway.

David Ake LLB*
Theresa Clark* Mark Pritchard* Jayne Dodson*
Falk House, Westgate, Leeds LS1 2RA
Telephone: 0113 2448808 Fax: 0113 2468303 DX: 718022 Leeds Park Square
Out of Hours / Emergency: 07850 356856 & 07860 304413

13th May 2010
Our Ref: KK/PW 71944 N.S.
Please ask for Karen Kidd

Mr L Benatti
address

Dear Mr Benatti

RE: Your Property (Computer)

Further to your message on the 11th March where you asked us to help you recover the computers which were seized by the police in October 2008, we can inform you that we have on the 15th 16th and 29th March, and also on the 1st, 27th and 28th April tried in vain to effect the release of your computers.

Unfortunately despite our enquiries and having an e-mail sent to the officer in this case's supervisor we have yet to receive a satisfactory response from the police.

To this end we now recommend you contact Mr Simon Purchase at Ison Harrison solicitors, on Leeds 0113 2845000 as we understand Mr Purchase is well versed in the field of making claims against the police.

For your information the officer involved in this matter is DC 4167 Hare, you were originally arrested on the 3rd December 2008, although you were not interviewed regarding these offences until the 8th December 2008 and your custody reference number was C00184583.

Whilst writing we would also confirm that we have tried to contact you on your home telephone number as supplied but unfortunately have not received an answer to this line.

We wish you well in your endeavours to retrieve your property.

Yours sincerely

DAVID AKE & Co

Web Site: www.davidake.co.uk e-mail: dja@davidake.co.uk Assistant Solicitors: Christina O'Connell & Ian Cook
Accredited PACE Representative: Karen Kidd
**Denotes Equity Partner*
Regulated by the Solicitors Regulation Authority

On the following page is a letter from Dr Dissanayaka (image 20).

I wonder why the false accusations of Flannigan have never been investigated. She accused me of being a terrorist and a murderer in order to get me arrested by the Police, and when the Police dismissed the case, she and her colleagues had not been investigated for false accusations.

So they went further with their insolence and I was section by Flannigan on the ground of the false accusation she made up and the Police could not accept, not even with the backup of all her best professional friends.

Every time Flannigan organized new accusations I had a new solicitor, not because I chose it but because without a passport I couldn't hire one; and every time a different solicitor told me that the false accusations were to be dismissed as unsubstantiated, as if the repeating of false accusations was not evidence of substantiated stalking, harassing, slander, defamation, and false information provided to mislead the Police.

I have been repeatedly accused of the most pervert and vicious scums Ms Flannigan could organize, anonymously, but the Police could never find anything to investigate, nothing more than the false accusations of Flannigan, the Police always dismissed as unsubstantiated.

What about the insolence of Flannigan, pretending all of this never happened. As if I didn't voice the rights for my passport replacement long before she arrived, and she was not to cover-up the good relations of the Italian Embassy at my expenses, during the government of Tony Blair, just before his conversion to the Catholic Church.

Leeds Partnerships NHS
NHS Foundation Trust

Assertive Outreach Service
Sycamore House
St Mary's Hospital
Greenhill Road
Leeds LS12 3QE
Secretary's Tel No: 0113 3055301
Fax No: 0113 3055326
Email: Carol.Hudson@leedspft.nhs.uk

Dr Lee
Address

21 May 2010
ND/CH/VC6121

Dear Dr Lee

Re: Luca Benatti – DOB Address
NHS NO:

Thank you for your letter of the 14th May 2010.

I am afraid that I am not in a position to see Luca again without a referral from secondary psychiatric services as my service, the Assertive Outreach Team is a tertiary service which takes on patients who require particular specialist input.

I have enclosed some correspondence from both me and Luca's previous care co-ordinator which briefly detail his time with us.

Given his likelihood of not seeing psychiatric services other than ours we did discharge him directly back to primary care but if his needs have changed and he is asking for help with symptoms including anxiety then if specialist input is required he should be referred to your local CMHT in the usual way. I do know that he had some difficulties with his previous CMHT and I am not sure as to whether he would go to the same service today following the recent resectorisation.

Either way he did not fit the criteria for our service for most of his time with us as he was very easily engaged in the community and did not require any specific interventions around his mental health needs, risk management being maintained on a low frequency of visits. If there is an issue with him returning to the same community team then this is a matter for the consultants in your area to resolve amongst themselves in order that alternative arrangements can be made.

I am very sympathetic to Luca's situation and indeed developed a good working relationship with him but our interactions had little to do with trying to modify his beliefs, most of which he gave quite compelling arguments for casting doubt on whether they were all delusional as previously stated. Towards the latter end of my contact with him his main need was for me to be supporting him in trying to sort out this terrible mess in which he is as you say "paperless".

1

On the following page is the second page of the letter from Dr Dissanayaka (image 21).

You can see also the Forensic Psychiatrist Dr Dissanayaka mentions legal claims I should have reported to Italy. As if all of this didn't happen in England, as if they had no obligation to report crimes to the EU Police from the start. As if anything of this could have possibly ever been in my best interest, at any time, to be paperless from EU Country and within EU Borders, and I didn't report appropriately from the start.

It was clear since the time of Dr Buller that it was a legal matter, and that I was not the problem but the victim, despite the superior understanding of Flannigan, far above the average.

Dear Dissanayaka, could you tell why the Catholic Syllabus never mention the Racial Laws? Could you tell how the Catholic Heresies have become Catholic Legacy, or is the subject not in your background?

To hear this from his own mouth visit the Audio recording of Dissanayaka [A10]

Note to this document:

Please, visit the video [A10] with the audio tape recording and hear the true voice of DR N. Dissanayaka "It is an intolerable way to have to live"

https://youtu.be/dpFJ2kHr9kg

"It is an intolerable way to have to live" [A10]

Sadly I do not have any authority in this area and as much as we would have liked to have helped him the most appropriate manner for this to be handled is via a good solicitor perhaps with the use of an advocate as Luca does tend to speak quite passionately which sometimes gets in the way of him getting his message across clearly.

I do wish him well and I am happy for the contents of this letter to be shared with him.

Yours sincerely

DR N DISSANAYAKA
CONSULTANT PSYCHIATRIST

2

Youtube Video: “Anonymous e non, al capo della Polizia (lettera aperta)”

https://www.youtube.com/watch?v=HZVIX85qj5o

The English rendering of the title would be: “Not Anonymous only, open letter to the head Police”

It is a video [A28], banned on the Italian territory because of the government censorship, filtering out from the Internet the lawsuit the Courts of Justice sweep into the afterlife.

In the next page is the image 22

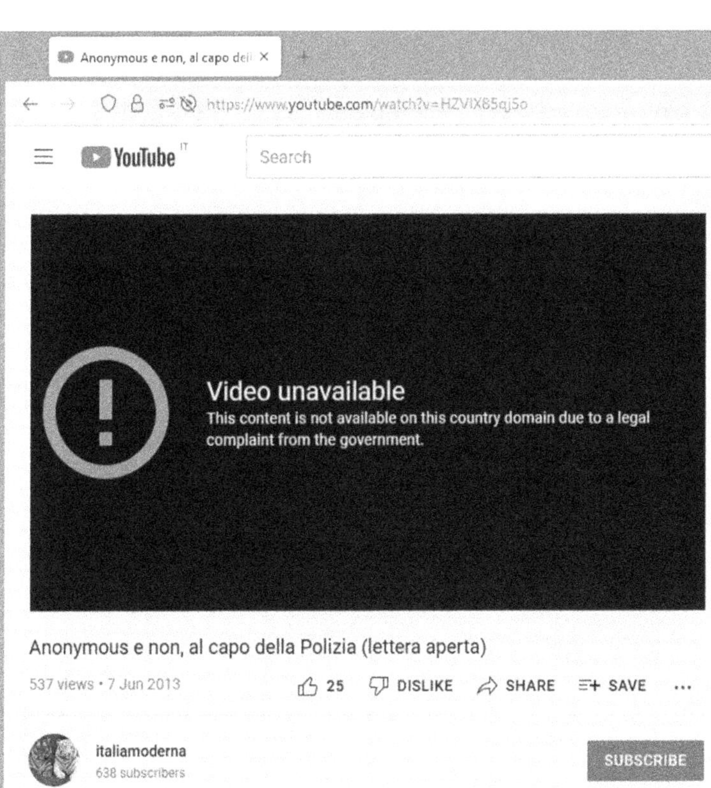
Anonymous e non, al capo del
https://www.youtube.com/watch?v=HZVIX85qj5o
YouTube
Search
Video unavailable
This content is not available on this country domain due to a legal complaint from the government.
Anonymous e non, al capo della Polizia (lettera aperta)
537 views • 7 Jun 2013
25
DISLIKE
SHARE
SAVE
italiamoderna
638 subscribers
SUBSCRIBE
Gentile Alessandro Pansa, Capo della Polizia e della pubblica sicurezza. Anzitutto le voglio dare il benvenuto su Internet. Inoltre le voglio confermare che sottoscrivo e concordo al 100% con Anonymous, con la sola eccezione per l'anonimato.
Quindi le dico subito il mio nome, mi chiamo Luca Benatti, e ci tengo a dirle apertamente, in pubblico che lei e' un pezzo di merda, un imbecille, ma soprattutto falso e codardo, un verme privo di qualsiasi percezione morale.
Gentile Alessandro Pansa, Capo della Polizia e della sicurezza pubica.

Recently I contacted a solicitor, and he replied:

«Whilst, we do appreciate your situation and the injustices you have faced, we have to comply with these obligations. Unfortunately, all solicitors in the UK are bound by the same obligations and accordingly, you might struggle to find someone to act for you without identification documents unless they know you personally.»

Apparently, to make people paperless, is tolerated and promoted with systematic indifference.

On the following page is Image 23.

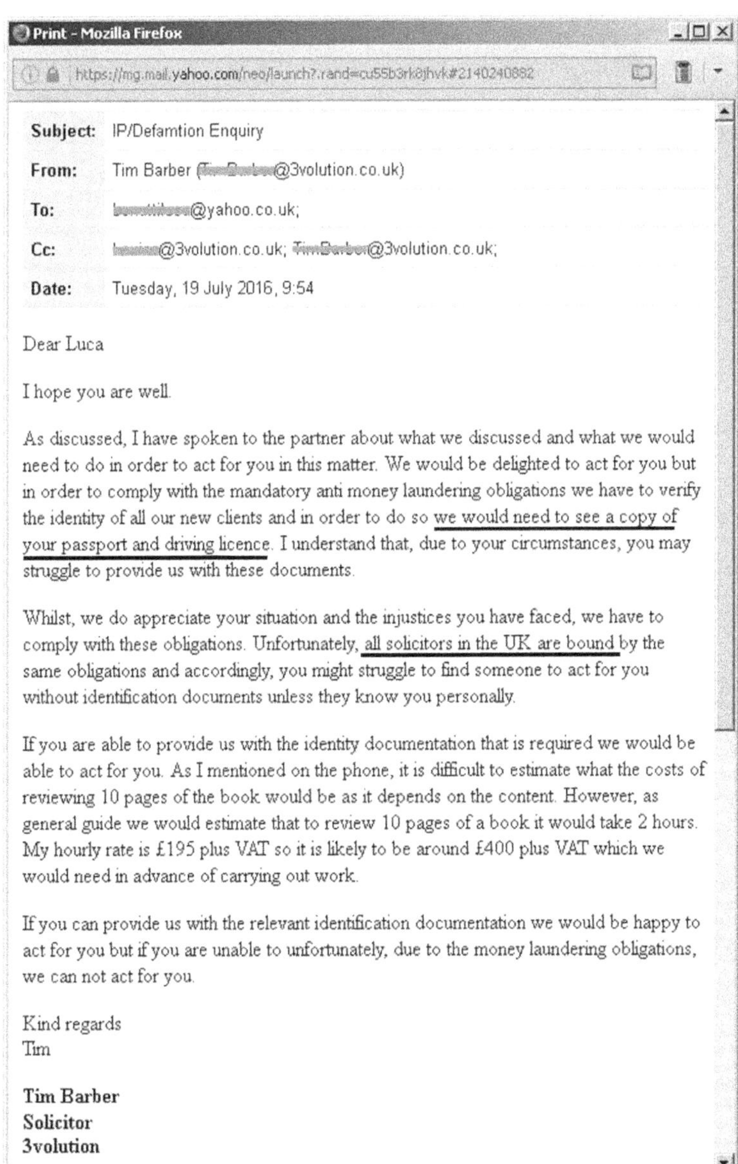
Print - Mozilla Firefox

https://mg.mail.yahoo.com/neo/launch?.rand=cu55b3rk8jhvk#2140240882

Subject: IP/Defamtion Enquiry

From: Tim Barber (████@3volution.co.uk)

To: ████@yahoo.co.uk;

Cc: ████@3volution.co.uk; ████@3volution.co.uk;

Date: Tuesday, 19 July 2016, 9:54

Dear Luca

I hope you are well.

As discussed, I have spoken to the partner about what we discussed and what we would need to do in order to act for you in this matter. We would be delighted to act for you but in order to comply with the mandatory anti money laundering obligations we have to verify the identity of all our new clients and in order to do so we would need to see a copy of your passport and driving licence. I understand that, due to your circumstances, you may struggle to provide us with these documents.

Whilst, we do appreciate your situation and the injustices you have faced, we have to comply with these obligations. Unfortunately, all solicitors in the UK are bound by the same obligations and accordingly, you might struggle to find someone to act for you without identification documents unless they know you personally.

If you are able to provide us with the identity documentation that is required we would be able to act for you. As I mentioned on the phone, it is difficult to estimate what the costs of reviewing 10 pages of the book would be as it depends on the content. However, as general guide we would estimate that to review 10 pages of a book it would take 2 hours. My hourly rate is £195 plus VAT so it is likely to be around £400 plus VAT which we would need in advance of carrying out work.

If you can provide us with the relevant identification documentation we would be happy to act for you but if you are unable to unfortunately, due to the money laundering obligations, we can not act for you.

Kind regards
Tim

Tim Barber
Solicitor
3volution

Some time later I contacted the Office of the President of the European Commission Jean-Claude Juncker, but this is the only European Union provided and probably I should understand that making people paperless is not discriminating or targeting anybody in particular and it is perfectly legal, the recommended solution; no gas no tears.

On the following page is Image 24.

Ref. Ares(2018)3022875 - 08/06/2018

EUROPEAN COMMISSION
DIRECTORATE-GENERAL JUSTICE AND CONSUMERS

Directorate D:Equality and Union Citizenship
Unit D.3: Union citizenship rights and free movement
Deputy Head of Unit

Brussels,
JUST.D.3/JS/mb(2018)s3278651

Mr Luca Benatti
E-mail: [redacted]

Subject: Your e-mail of 21 March 2018

Dear Mr Benatti,

I write in relation to your e-mail of 21 March 2018 addressed to President Juncker, which concerns a number of issues you faced following the theft of your passport and which was registered under reference number Ares(2018)2060765(*please quote this reference in any further correspondence)*. I have been asked to reply to your correspondence on the President's behalf. Please accept our apologies for the delay in replying to your complaint.

It appears from the documents that you have sent us that the Italian authorities were unable to issue you a new passport as you had been removed from the Italian residency register following your absence during the 2001 Italian census. The Italian consular authorities asked you to register in the Registry of Italians Residing Abroad (*Anagrafe degli Italiani Residenti all'Estero - AIRE*)[1], which is a registry for Italian citizens who reside outside Italy for a period of at least 12 months. It is unclear, from the documents you have sent, whether you have ever registered in AIRE.

We do not know the current status of your passport application. We would suggest contacting the Italian consulate responsible for you[2] to inquire about the status of your application as well as about any documents or formalities that prevent that a passport is issued to you. These formalities might include having to register in AIRE.

I hope you find this information useful.

Yours sincerely,

Monika MOSSHAMMER

[1] https://www.esteri.it/mae/en/italiani_nel_mondo/serviziconsolari/

[2] A list of all Italian diplomatic-consular missions in the world and their phone numbers/addresses are available here: https://www.esteri.it/mae/en/ministero/laretediplomatica?ricerca=ris

Commission européenne/Europese Commissie, 1049 Bruxelles/Brussel, BELGIQUE/BELGIË — Tel. +32 22991111
Office: LX40 02/044 — Tel. direct line +32 229 53843

- -

email from Ares: 8th June 2018

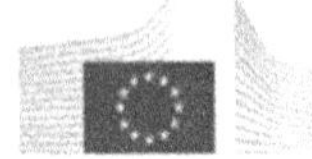

Ref. Ares(2019)7282540 - 26/11/2019

EUROPEAN COMMISSION
DIRECTORATE-GENERAL JUSTICE AND CONSUMERS

Directorate D:Equality and Union Citizenship
Unit D.3: Union citizenship rights and free movement
Deputy Head of Unit

Brussels,
JUST.D.3/JS/md (2019) 8001537s

Mr Luca Benatti
E-mail: [redacted]

Subject: Your e-mail of 19 November 2019

Dear Mr Benatti,

I write in relation to your e-mail of 19 November, registered under *Ares(2019)7143699*.

In your e-mail, you essentially repeat statements on which we have already responded on 8 June 2018 (*Ares(2018)3022875*) on 13 December 2018 (*Ares(2018)6415905*).

I regret to inform you that we have nothing to add to our previous correspondence. In particular, we do not know why the Italian consular authorities in the United Kingdom are refusing to issue you a new passport.

I would like to inform you that, in accordance with the Code of good administrative behaviour, the European Commission reserves itself the right to cease any exchange of correspondence in the case of repetitive correspondence.

Thank you for your understanding.

Yours sincerely,

(e-signed)

Monika MOSSHAMMER

Contact: Mr Jan Stadler, e-mail: just-citizenship@ec.europa.eu

Commission européenne/Europese Commissie, 1049 Bruxelles/Brussel, BELGIQUE/BELGIË
just-citizenship@ec.europa.eu

Electronically signed on 22/11/2019 17:11 (UTC+01) in accordance with article 4.2 (Validity of electronic documents) of Commission Decision 2004/563

- -

email from Ares: 26th Nov 2019 (Image 25)

Ref. Ares(2019)7579854 - 10/12/2019

EUROPEAN COMMISSION
DIRECTORATE-GENERAL JUSTICE AND CONSUMERS

Directorate D: Equality and Union Citizenship
Unit D.3: Union citizenship rights and free movement
Deputy Head of Unit

Brussels,
JUST.D.3/NF/md (2019) 8460508s

Mr Luca Benatti
E-mail: [redacted]

Dear Mr Benatti,

I refer to your e-mail of 19 November 2019, address to President Juncker, concerning the problems you have faced following the theft of your passport in the United Kingdom.

Your letter was registered under the reference number Ares(2019)7175584 *(please quote this reference in any further correspondence).*

As my Unit is responsible for Union citizenship, I was asked to reply to you.

As previously stated in my letter of 8 June 2018 (reference number Ares(2018)302287), we do not have any knowledge of the status of your passport application, nor do we know what could possibly have gone wrong in the application process.

As Italy is competent to decide on the procedure for the issuing of an Italian passport, including the requirement for Italians living outside of Italy to register, in certain circumstances, in the Registry of Italians Residing Abroad (*Anagrafe degli Italiani Residenti all'Estero -AIRE*), we advise you to address any related questions to the Italian authorities. Only they can give you information on the status of your application and provide you with advice on the steps to take to eventually be issued with a new Italian passport.

Regarding your mention of a lawsuit, we are not aware of any EU-level (legal) proceedings on the matters covered by your e-mail.

For your information, OLAF, the European Anti-Fraud Office, investigates fraud against the EU budget, corruption and serious misconduct within the European institutions. It does not conduct any investigations related to the issuing of passports by the Member States to its own nationals.

I hope that you will find this information useful.

Yours sincerely,

Monika MOSSHAMMER
(e-signed)
Deputy Head of Unit

Contact: *Ms Nastasja Fuxa, e-mail: just-citizenship@ec.europa.eu*

Commission européenne/Europese Commissie, 1049 Bruxelles/Brussel, BELGIQUE/BELGIË - Tel. +32 22991111
Office: LU40 2/42 - Tel. direct line +32 2 29-74457, Email: JUST-CITIZENSHIP@ec.europa.eu

Electronically signed on 09/12/2019 19:01 (UTC+01) in accordance with article 4.2 (Validity of electronic documents) of Commission Decision 2004/563

- -

email from Ares: 10th Dec 2019 (Image 26)

With the consent of the Police I recorded the meeting and provided copy of this book to resume the original documentation I also provided.

Case Reference Number 0962, 09 October 2020.

The photograph is from the meeting that took place 13 October 2020 at 10.00

In the next Page, Image 27

2020 October 13 - 09:58:56:19

Then I wrote to the Prime Minister Boris Johnson, to send copy of the book with the appendix and the DVD with the report to the Police.

In the next page, Image 28

Leeds, 16th October 2020

Sender
Luca Benatti
[redacted]
[redacted]

FOR THE PERSONAL ATTENTION

The Rt Hon Boris Johnson MP
Prime Minister
10 Downing Street
London
SW1A 2AA

Object: Acknowledgement

Dear Prime Minister,

I am writing to you because I believe "the law of the land" is an essential value for civil society, but it is also one of the best Catholic Heresies persecuted in History.

I am originally from Italy, and I arrived in England because I had a PhD offer, but the next day I was paperless like an illegal immigrant. Both passport and university degree have vanished in the Italian Offices, and there was no way to have an answer from the Consul, for years. That because it was God will, sure not the law of the land.

As you can see I have sent COPY of this LEGAL CLAIM to few EU Member State Embassies, as it is my believe the EU needs to be concerned of this situation.
In fact the EU knows from the start, as they sent lawsuit to Italy before false accusations and torture I had to suffer as part of the cover up here in England.

Dear Prime Minister, I am not a communist or an anarchist. I am a democrat demanding his rights, but as I said the law of the land is one of the best heresies. It is for this reason I am sending my invitation to you, to send this matter concerning "the law of the land" to the EU.

Yours Faithful
Luca Benatti

The reply

In the next page, Image 29

10 DOWNING STREET
LONDON SW1A 2AA
www.gov.uk/Number10

From the Direct Communications Unit

19 November 2020

Mr Luca Benatti

Dear Mr Benatti

I am writing on behalf of the Prime Minister to thank you for your correspondence of 16 October 2020.

As the Home Office has responsibility for the matters you raise, I am forwarding your letter to them so that they are made aware of your views.

Thank you, once again, for writing.

Yours sincerely

Correspondence Officer

For information on how we use your personal data, and your rights, please visit:
https://www.gov.uk/government/organisations/cabinet-office/about/personal-information-charter

Then I complained to the Metropolitan Police

In the next page, Image 30

Provide more information to be added to a crime report

Date: **04 December 2020**
Time: **11:18**
This form has been sent to the Metropolitan Police via the Single Online Home reporting service.

CIN-51668-20-0100-000

First name
Luca

Surname
Benatti

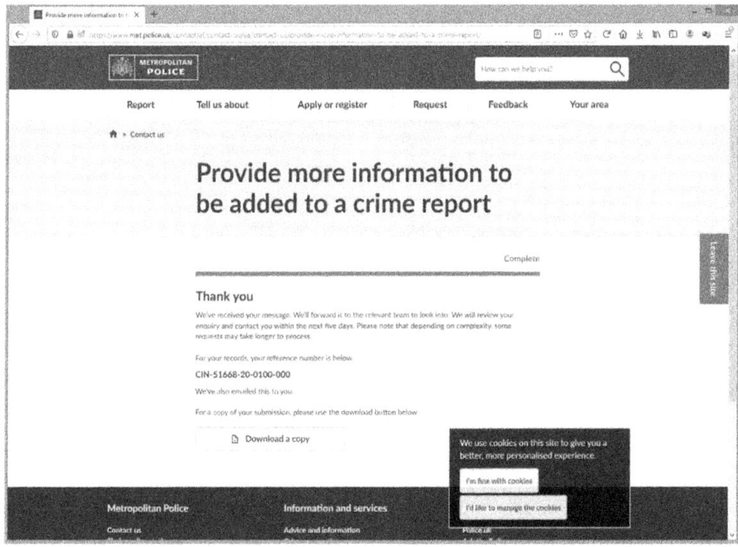

I have received request to apply the EUSS

After meeting in person with DWP and offering copy of the book with the appendix, I have replied in writing sending the book with the appendix via post mail.

I also sent copy of the letter from Boris Johnson, the DVD with the report to the Police, and the letter of the EUSS solicitor that follow.

In the next page the letter from DWP, Image 31

Then in the following 4 pages is the letter of the EUSS Solicitor, (images 32-35)

To complete is my reply to DWP, images 36 and 37

LUCA BENATTI

00038
007598\334

www.gov.uk/eusettlementscheme

09 August 2021

The EU Settlement Scheme deadline has now passed – you must take urgent action to secure your rights

Dear LUCA BENATTI

Now that the UK has left the European Union (EU), anyone who is a EU, European Economic Area (EEA) or Swiss national and their family members need a valid UK immigration status to continue living in the UK (for example, valid leave to enter or remain or indefinite leave to enter or remain, including leave granted under the EU Settlement Scheme (EUSS)).

Our records indicate you are an EU, EEA, or Swiss citizen living in the UK and you:

- may not have valid UK immigration status; and
- have not applied to the EUSS.

What this means for you

If you applied to the EUSS before the 30 June deadline, including using a paper application form, and are awaiting a decision, you do not need to take any further action at this point.

If you have not applied to the EUSS and do not have another valid immigration status, you need to make a late application to the scheme within 28 days of the date of this letter. If you do not make a late application, you will not be able to work or access public services and any benefits you receive will stop. For more information and to apply to the scheme visit: www.gov.uk/settled-status-eu-citizens-families.

If you are a British or Irish citizen, or believe you already have a valid UK immigration status and have got this letter in error, please contact 0300 1050 888 (lines will be open 09:30-4:30pm Monday – Friday) within 28 days of the date of this letter so we can update our records.

Page **1** of **6**

OFFICIAL

Kirklees Citizens Advice and Law Centre

Units 11 - 12, Empire House, Dewsbury WF12 8DJ

www.kcalc.org.uk

Mr Luca Benatti

Date: 2 September 2021
Our Ref: JM/R-390

Dear Mr Benatti

Further to our recent telephone meeting I am writing to confirm the instructions that you gave me. I am a solicitor and EU Settlement Advice Worker and will be advising on your case. This area of work is managed by Harry Pratt, who is my line manager. Overall professional supervision of the Practice is by Joe Power, our Supervising Solicitor.

Should you wish to speak with me regarding your case you can telephone me directly on 07908 078831. I will normally be available from 10am to 4pm, Monday to Friday. I am often dealing with other clients or in meetings so if I do not answer please leave a voicemail and I will get back to you.

Our services are free

Your Instructions

During our telephone meeting on 1 September 2021 we discussed your instructions, requirements and objectives, which I have summarised below.

You explained that you are an Italian national and you have been living in the UK for approximately 20 years.

Your Italian passport was either lost or stolen around 2001-2002 and your reported this at the time. You have since been unable to obtain a new passport. You were told by the Italian authorities that they could not issue a new passport for you while you were in Northern Island. You then moved to Leeds and were advised to obtain one from the Italian consulate in Manchester. You have so far not been able to obtain a new passport.

EUSS Solicitor, page 1 of 4, Images 32

You do not have an alternative ID document. You believe your brother may have your original birth certificate in Italy, but you do not believe you will be able to obtain a new passport.

Your main objective is to understand the requirements for an EU Settlement Scheme application and whether you are eligible to apply.

Advice and options available

I advised you that the main requirement for any EU Settlement application is proof of ID. Usually the Home Office expects you to provide a valid passport, but you are also permitted to submit an expired passport, a national ID card, or some other form of ID such as a birth certificate.

I advised that you currently are not eligible to apply because you do not have any ID document.

However, you do have a large quantity of evidence about the difficulties you have faced in attempting to obtain a new Italian passport. I am not confident that you would be successful in obtaining EU Settled Status as there is no evidence in your documents you have attempted to renew your passport at the Manchester consulate. However, if you feel you can provide the evidence that you have tried to renew your passport at the consulate, as well as from the authorities in Italy, then you could present all of this evidence to the Home Office using a paper application form.

I have provided a blank paper application form along with this letter for you to complete if you wish. If you are able to find some form of ID, such as a renewed passport or your original birth certificate then I will be able to assist you with this application. At the moment, with no ID available, I am afraid I am not able to help you submit the application.

Further, you do not need to worry about your status printed in an expired passport, but you should make sure you have both your old passport and your valid passport when you travel.

This letter and the advice I provided over the phone is the extent of the work we can do on your case. Do contact me if you need any help with an application in the future, for example if you are able to obtain new ID document. Do also contact me if you have any follow up questions.

I hope that you are satisfied with the service we provide. If you wish to make a comment on this at any time, I hope very much you will feel able to do so, either to me or to another person at the Kirklees Citizens Advice and Law Centre (KCALC).

- -

EUSS Solicitor, page 2 of 4, Images 33

Complaints procedure

If you are unhappy with any part of the service we provide then we have an internal complaints procedure where you can discuss your concerns with our Complaints Officer, Nick Whittingham and if you are still unhappy, you may raise the matter with: The Legal Ombudsman, PO Box 6806, Wolverhampton WV1 9WJ.

Terminating your case

In some circumstances you may consider that the Kirklees Citizens Advice and Law Centre ought to stop acting for you, for example, if clear or proper instructions on how KCALC is to proceed with your case cannot be given or if you lose confidence in the KCALC's ability to carry out your instructions. You may terminate your instructions to the KCALC in writing at any time.

On the other hand the KCALC may only decide to stop acting for you if it has good reason. For example, if your case no longer justifies the merits test could be a good reason. If the KCALC decides to terminate your case it must write to you and give you reasonable notice so that you can find other legal advice.

We are registered with the Information Commissioner's Office under Z9821213 and will process your personal data in accordance with the General Data Protection Regulation and Data Protection Act 2018. We are therefore required and have obtained your consent to hold your personal information in paper form and electronically on our case management system.

You are entitled to examine your files at any time, and request a copy of your personal information. Your personal information will be stored securely and will not be shared with any third party.

In addition you have given consent for your case records including personal information being audited by external authorities for quality and regulator purposes.

The KCALC will not tolerate clients who use racist, sexist, homophobic, abusive or oppressive language. Clients who use such language will be warned of their conduct, in writing if necessary, and warned that future incidents will lead to the KCALC refusing to advise them or take on their case or continue with their case.

Closing your case

I will now close your file as there is no further work to be done on this matter. I have checked the file and given you back your original documents there are no original documents on your file.

- -

EUSS Solicitor, page 3 of 4, Images 34

Closed files are retained for 6 years thereafter they may be destroyed.

If you need our help in the future please contact us on the above number.

Yours sincerely

Jamie McLean
EU Settlement Advice Worker / Solicitor
Kirklees Law Centre

- -
EUSS Solicitor, page 4 of 4, Images 35

21 November 2021

Luca Benatti
[redacted]
[redacted]
[redacted]

For the attention of

EUSS Paper Forms
EU Settlement Scheme
PO Box 2076
Liverpool
L69 3PG

Dear Office,
I am writing to your office after contacting the solicitor for the settlement scheme.

As you can see last week I received the letter from the doctor, for the solicitor of the EU Settlement scheme, but the solicitor closed the case in September.
As you can see the solicitor had no problem to refuse assistance, as consequence of the fact that I have no passport. Nevertheless I believe he was paid anyway for the legal advice, and I have lost many more rights he didn't mention because of his professionalism.

As you can see from the letter of barrister Paul Diamond (pag 225), making people paperless (without personal ID) means reducing people into SLAVERY. This is also clear from the letter of the solicitor Tim Barber (pag 219), informing that without a passport I have no rights to hire an independent lawyer. As you can see the solicitors I was assigned "by the office" never had any problem to advise and impose on me to conform to the will of the Consul and be the impostor, the counterfeiter, despite I am not the impostor.

As matter of facts I arrived in England because I had a PhD offer, but the professors in the photograph of my graduation ceremony at the Verona University did not confirm my true academic career and made me do the impression of the impostor. In the same period of time I had my passport stolen, and never had any passport replacement, not even temporary to travel back to resolve the problems they were causing in the offices.

Now you ask me again for a passport, again, after I have been humiliated and forced to be be paperless, against my rights and my complaints. I have been treated like an impostor despite I am not, and I have been coerced with violence to be the scapegoat to cover up the Italian mafia.

In evidence some people like Kyenge and Regeni, they can have the recommendations of the bishop for diplomas and degrees they never had, and be honest with it also after confessing the scam, while some other cannot have confirmation of their true academic career from Italian state universities and will be forced with coercion to be paperless, like impostors.

As you can see from the letter of MP Bill Rammell (pag 207) the govern was informed

- -

My reply to DWP, page 1 of 2, Images 36

at the time of the happening, but decided that EU Citizens paperless within EU border was not a problem, or a threat for the victims. That happened after the EU OLAF sent my lawsuit to Italy, and the prosecutor had the insolence to pretend it was never happened.

I hope you understand this situation is humiliating, stressful and oppressive, as there is nothing I could do against this regime of corruption and mafia I have reported from the start. Sincerely I am not willing to be the impostor, the scapegoat to cover up the mafia that did this to me, and I report this situation of SLAVERY imposed on me, with violence and coercion, with the consequences you can see.

Concerning this situation I wrote a book, and the appendix of documents in attachment was carved from it. These are scans of real documents, step by step all the legal assistance I had to become paperless within EU borders, and then the impostor, the potential terrorist, and whatever recommendations they liked to provide as institutions, but not my passport or my degree. Because of the Appendix I offered copy of the book to the DWP Staff during their home visit, but they said was not necessary, despite it is documenting that becoming paperless was against my rights, against my will, and against my best interest.

With best regards
Luca Benatti

My website with the Appendix and the Excerpt may be found here
http://www.lbblacksmith.org/

In Attachment

Appendix with 27 documents
Form EU Settlement Scheme
Letter from Solicitor EUSS Scheme
Letter from GP for the Solicitor EUSS Scheme

DVD – Police Report RN 0962 – 9th October 2020 (recorded with police permission)
DVD – Dissanayaka audio (Appendix pag 215-217)

Page 2 of 2

- -

My reply to DWP, page 2 of 2, Images 37

Appendix: In conclusion

By the law I have no rights to hire a layer because I am paperless, like an illegal immigrant, and only have the rights to be tortured by the same people who made me paperless. In evidence to make people paperless is a crime, it is against the law, and for sure I had the rights to my personal documents since long before they arrived with their fabrications, insults, blackmails, and nothing may change this fact. There is no chance to make people paperless without breaking the law, and there are no people paperless to talk about, but only people made paperless, in the offices, illegally, and kept paperless with the criminal intent to prevent them from their rights and from Justice.

Depriving people of personal ID documents is criminal because reduces people to slavery, and this is exactly what they did to me. So, since I am sure only a bunch of criminals may find all of this as tolerable, or legal, I decided to write this publication, to inform you concerning education, rights and freedoms that have been lost.

With Best Regards
L.B.

In the following page is copy of an email from Barrister Paul Diamond.

Please note the date is June 2008 (image 38).

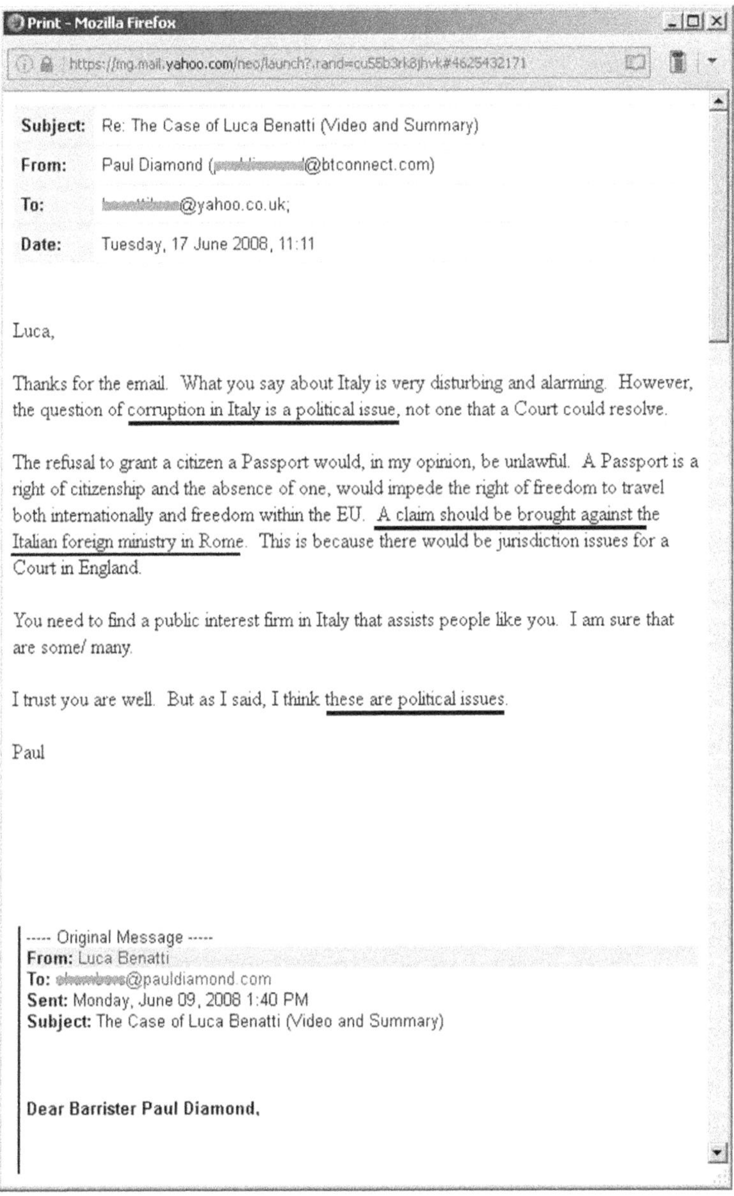

Print - Mozilla Firefox

https://mg.mail.yahoo.com/neo/launch?.rand=cu55b3rk8jhvk#4625432171

Subject: Re: The Case of Luca Benatti (Video and Summary)

From: Paul Diamond (@btconnect.com)

To: @yahoo.co.uk;

Date: Tuesday, 17 June 2008, 11:11

Luca,

Thanks for the email. What you say about Italy is very disturbing and alarming. However, the question of corruption in Italy is a political issue, not one that a Court could resolve.

The refusal to grant a citizen a Passport would, in my opinion, be unlawful. A Passport is a right of citizenship and the absence of one, would impede the right of freedom to travel both internationally and freedom within the EU. A claim should be brought against the Italian foreign ministry in Rome. This is because there would be jurisdiction issues for a Court in England.

You need to find a public interest firm in Italy that assists people like you. I am sure that are some/ many.

I trust you are well. But as I said, I think these are political issues.

Paul

----- Original Message -----
From: Luca Benatti
To: @pauldiamond.com
Sent: Monday, June 09, 2008 1:40 PM
Subject: The Case of Luca Benatti (Video and Summary)

Dear Barrister Paul Diamond,

Wikipedia doesn't offer appropriate rendering of the Decree against Communism, so here I have one.

By now you should know the problem was not with Communism but the Fundamental Values of Democracy, the Freedom of Choice and the Secular Value of Justice historically persecuted as Heresies for Heretics, Anarchists, and more recently Apostates of the Faith.

The leaflets were on display and distributed at the entrance of the Churches; just after the Nuremberg Trials it resumes the Cultural Principles of the Concordat at the origin of the Racial Laws of Mussolini, persecuting the democrats as Apostates of the Faith.

CURIA OF THE BISHOP OF PIACENZA

- ♦ -

AFTER THE DECREE OF THE HOLY OFFICE

- ♦ -

NOTICE

It is severe sin to:

1 Register as member of the Communist Party
2 Support in any way or to Vote to the Communist Party
3 Read Communist Publications
4 Distribute Communist Publications

Therefore one cannot receive absolution without repentance and firm disposition not to repeat

♦

Whoever, registered or not to the Communist Party, who acknowledges the Marxist doctrine, Atheist and anti-Christian and propaganda such ideals, is

APOSTATES OF THE FAITH AND EXCOMMUNICATED

and can be absolved only by the Holy See

♦

What said for the Communist Party is extended to the other parties making common cause with it

May God enlighten and have mercy of those sinners about so serious matter, because the eternal life is at risk

CURIA VESCOVILE DI PIACENZA

DOPO IL DECRETO DEL SANTO UFFIZIO

AVVISO

E' peccato grave:

1° Iscriversi al Partito Comunista.
2° Favorirlo in qualsiasi modo, **specie col voto.**
3° Leggere la stampa comunista.
4° Propagare la stampa comunista.

Quindi non si può ricevere l'assoluzione se non si è pentiti e fermamente disposti a non commetterlo più.

●

Chi, iscritto o no al Partito Comunista, ne ammette la dottrina marxista, atea ed anticristiana e ne fa propaganda, è

APOSTATA DALLA FEDE E SCOMUNICATO

e non può essere assolto che dalla Santa Sede.

●

Quanto si è detto per il Partito Comunista deve estendersi agli altri Partiti che fanno causa comune con esso.

Il Signore illumini e conceda ai colpevoli in materia tanto grave, il pieno ravvedimento, poichè è in pericolo la stessa salvezza dell'eternita

Photograph from Piacenza, Italy, 1949. From Wikipedia [W71]. English graphics on pag 5 (Prologue). (image 39)

Overtime

From the Second Edition: Foreword

Dear President of the European Commission Jean-Claude Juncker,

since the first edition was published BREXIT has happened, and this letter is just a reminder for people's rights.

As you can see from the letter of the solicitor Tim Barber, in appendix, I cannot hire a lawyer because I have no Passport. In fact I had my passport stolen in 2002, 15 years ago, and despite I paid immediately for the replacement in the hands of the Italian Consul, I never had the new ID.

In 2005, the EU OLAF office sent my lawsuit to the Court in Milan but with no success, in fact the Prosecutor in Italy had the insolence to pretend that "It didn't happen" and flushed the case down the drain.

Dear Mr Juncker, at the time of the happenings I made some audio tape recordings and you can hear that from their voices, admitting they never had any evidence but only false accusations, but what was the point of this?

Important is that Ms Federica Mogherini, vice president of the European Commission, and Katya Adler BBC Presenter ("After Brexit: The Battle for Europe")[A5] have the opportunity to talk about well known Human Rights violations perpetrated in Europe, and to squeeze at least one more coffee from the lives of the victims.

So, in conclusion, the solicitor said that I have no rights for legal representation because I have no passport, and the only positive action I could do was to write a book about this factual story, and publish original documents, photographs, and the audio tape recordings.

Just a reminder of people's rights that they have actually lost with the advent of the European Union as we know it. Thank you for your time and attention.

Best Regards

L.B.

From the Second Edition: Farewell

Few days ago the President of the European Commission Jean-Claude Juncker was disappointed with the Italian Prime Minister Matteo Renzi [A30]

Dear Jean-Claude Juncker, I am also disappointed with Mr Renzi. Next time you see him, could you please ask him about my passport, or my degree, or about the prosecutors sweeping the legal suits under the carpet?

But overall, concerning Mr Renzi, I would like to know from the European Union if the Italian High Moral Values above the Law are to be considered as mafia to be prosecuted, or culture and tradition to be honoured and preserved as symbol of the Ancient Values under which Europe was recently Re-United.

Dear Jean-Claude Juncker, it is recently the news that the Italian Government published the content of the 'Armoire of Shame' [W11][A27], a double door closet filled with 695 folders of records of massacres perpetrated in Italy by Fascists and Nazis during and after 1943, when the war was almost over. The closet was probably waiting for the attention of the Court for war crimes but never got there, and its disappearance was to set the standard for the democracy to come with the Republic.

I wonder, from the rights of the victims, what probability do we really have for Justice, since the High Moral Values inspiring the Fascist holocaust, have became raison d'etre of the European Union?

Dear Jean-Claude Juncker, in Europe today people vanish the same as it was at the time of Mussolini, exactly for the same reasons, and there is no chance for Justice by the Law, because the Legal Suit are swept under the carpets. Eventually be aware the System of Corruption and these High Moral Values above the law, which transform Criminals into Saints, are exactly the same reasons at the origin of the divisions of Europe since the end of the Dark Ages.

with best regards

L. B.

Foreword to the third edition

Dear President of the European Commission, Ms Ursula von der Leyen,

the Nuremberg Trials have never prosecuted any Fascist for the persecutions and intellectual cleansing perpetrated in Italy during the Fascist Regime, why?

The Nuremberg Trials absolved the Fascist Regime as Culture and Tradition; is this the very same reason the Racial Laws have been enacted again in 1949, by Decree of the Holy Sight? On the other hand, it was not Mussolini who invented the Roman Supremacy, was it?

Concerning Democracy, the documentation in the School Syllabus, is for believers. As a matter of fact the Freedom of Choice has never been a Catholic Value but a Catholic Heresy, persecuted on the stake throughout history, and the same is for the Secular Value of Justice.

Dear President of the European Commission, Ms Ursula von der Leyen, the foundations of Democracy, the Democratic Values, are in the index of the Catholic Inquisition, and if people cannot really claim the rights they are supposed to have it is only because still today the Racial Laws are celebrated as Culture and Tradition.

I wouldn't sound impolite or uneducated, but would you call yourself Racist, the same as Mussolini was, exactly for the same reasons? Nevertheless this is exactly what the European Union is doing, and you represent it.

Please, would you ask Mr Michel Barnier about my passport?

Best Regards
L.B.

Cambridge's deception and Giulio Regeni

For the Attention of

Rt Hon David John Sainsbury, Baron Sainsbury of Turville, Chancellor
Cambridge University

Prof Jude Browne Head of Department
Department of Politics and International Studies

Prof Ms Maha Abdelrahman
PhD Tutor of Giulio Regeni

Prof Anne Alexander
Academic Referee of Giulio Regeni

Dear Professor Maha, Anne and Jude, of the Department of Politics of Cambridge University [A36].

From the start Giulio Regeni in Italy never graduated any further diploma or university degree, but completed only the compulsory education at the age of 13 like everyone. Then, after 2 years in the college-oratory of the bishop in new Mexico he registered Oxford with the recommendations of the bishop for diplomas and degrees he never had, and then Cambridge, consulting the Think Tank and Oxford Analytica with the big data professor Anne.

A similar story is from Cecile Kyenge, confessing during a television interview that she knew she didn't have the rights for the documents she was asking for, the passport and the funding to register the University, but thanks to the network of friends of the bishop in the public offices she had all the documents she needed, and later she was also elected member of parliament and appointed minister for integration and equal opportunities.

But my point here is to address the system of corruption, and not the individuals; Cecile Kyenge and Giulio Regeni are just two EXAMPLES of the several thousands students they represent, superior students above the average from the colleges-oratory of the bishops, with the recommendations for diplomas and degrees they never had. Honest and trustable people with the rights to feel honest also after the confession of their frauds and scams is public knowledge in the news.

I am doing this because on the other hand, the other students are blackmailed for the confirmation of their true academic career from state universities and become impostors and paperless within EU borders, and are coerced with violence to be the scapegoat, and are prevented from their rights in order to cover up that "alternative system of values", the system of value of the recommendation, bribery and blackmail. The alternative system of values you professor Maha you promote in the classrooms as democracy for the high standards of your selected students above the average.

The Cambridge Prize

Dear Maha, Anne and Jude, you are the PhD professors of Giulio Regeni in Politics. Maybe I am not obedient like Giulio Regeni, but I have better reasons, and my documented and objective question for you is this.

On the 3rd of January 1925 Mussolini said that "the democratic values have to be found in the Catholic tradition", then he dismissed the parliament, imposed the Religion of State and persecuted the opposition as "apostates of the faith" and "enemies of the state".

I wonder if someone was to ask you to state one democratic value that has ever been a Catholic value in history, would you be able to answer, or you are better to admit you mislead, brainwash and discriminate the students, in favour of an alternative system of value?

Surely, if your superior students, such a Regeni, really want to graduate with Cambridge honours then they should be able to state one democratic value that has ever been a Catholic value in history.

I ask because the democratic values are the result of the emancipation from the absolute power of the church, and the democratic values, especially the freedom of choice and the secular value of justice, have been persecuted throughout history as Catholic heresies undermining the absolute power of the church, in the quest for absolute obedience.

There is absolutely no way any democratic value has ever been a Catholic value, until Mussolini said so, closed the parliament and persecuted "the oppositions" as apostates of the faith and enemies of the state, anticipating the words his spiritual leader repeated after WWII, in the excommunication of the democratic values and all those making common cause with it.

Complaint

Dear Chancellor Rt Hon David John Sainsbury, Baron Sainsbury of Turville, could you state one democratic value that has ever been a Catholic value in History?

I wonder if someone pretending the democratic values are Catholic legacy, may be able to distinguish good and evil at all.

As matter of facts, only a fascist or an idiot would pretend the democratic values are Catholic legacy, and the reconstitution of the fascist party is a crime. Could you state one democratic value that has ever been a Catholic value in History, or this is just a plain reconstitution of the fascist party, Mr Chancellor?

So I like to ask the PhD professors of Giulio Regeni, if they could state one democratic value that has ever been a Catholic value in history, or they could only quote the speech of Mussolini for this explanation, pretending the democratic value have be found within the Catholic tradition, with the recommendations of the bishop.

I am impressed the PhD tutor of Giulio Regeni Maha Abdelrahman Department of Politics and International

Studies of Cambridge University cannot explain in what way the democratic value have become Catholic legacy, but if you spend a moment you understand without the tutor from Cambridge that the democratic values are the result of the emancipation from the absolute power of the church, and only a fascist or an idiot would pretend the democratic values have ever been Catholic values.

Also the reformation of the Churches was about rights and freedoms more than religion, but considering the education as £12.000 per year and more, it is a good business and even better propaganda at geopolitical scale. In fact after the students have paid all that money they feel to be intelligent and superiorly educated.

I wonder if the academic referee of Giulio Regeni, Anne Alexander, or the Head of Department Professor Jude Browne could rank themselves and Giulio Regeni above the average against every standard, or only against the standard they represent, the standard of the recommendation of the bishop.

I also wonder about the right wing's manipulations, from the schoolbooks to the big data/statistics...

I wonder about Regeni as consultant for the Think Tank and Oxford Analytica, with the recommendations of the bishop for diplomas and degree he never had, with the big data professor as assistant, and Cambridge Analityca 'ancilla fidei'.

I wonder about the honesty of such good professors and politicians concerning people's rights, and the system of recommendation they represent.

Furthermore, concerning professor Anne feeling compelled to ride and campaign against Al-Sisi as the responsible for civil rights violations [A37], I like to inform concerning civil rights violations and abuses against EU Citizens that actually happen in England, reducing the victims into slavery with violence and coercion.

Going personal

This is a true story, and you can find the documents in the appendix of my book.

As you can see I am from Italy and I arrived in England because I organised a PhD opportunity in autonomy. I had a PhD offer but the professors in the photograph of my graduation ceremony at the Verona University did not confirm my academic career to Leeds University (also in my book's appendix), consequentially making me do the impression of an impostor and counterfeiter. I highlight that the Italian Consulate never provided any assistance, nothing more than imposing on me to be a paperless impostor. In fact the Italian Consulate never provided any passport replacement after it's theft which prevented me from the rights to hire a lawyer.

As you can see in appendix, the police headquarters in Milan issued my passport, sometime later confirmed my address and my presence in person with the signature of police inspector. To the same address I also received a letter from the president of the Italian republic concerning the subject in discussion. So I had my PhD offer but I had become paperless, an impostor and a counterfeiter in the UK.

The EU sent my lawsuit to Italy convening my rights for travelling and fulfil the opportunities I organised in autonomy but the prosecutor in Italy (2005) stated that "it never happened".

This letter is from your prime minister Tony Blair (2006) before his conversion to Catholic, but after the EU sent my lawsuit to Italy. I like to address the false accusations, coercion and violence I had with the reply, the retaliation and the political cover up.

This is from the barrister Paul Diamond, informing that a lawsuit should be brought against the Italian foreign office, for the assistance provided by the consul in making me paperless and looking like I am the impostor, for preventing me from fulfilling the PhD offer I had, for preventing me from the rights to hire a lawyer and from travelling. It is also concerning civil rights and reducing people into slavery, with violence and coercion in order to cover up complaint and evidences, and to make a scapegoat out of the victims.

In addition to this perjury of public officers, they also go on to accuse victims of having reasons to become terrorists and plot mass murders, and gives them excuses to warrant their arrest in the name of national security and public order.

On the other hand, the tradition of bribery and blackmail, with the holy cross in the Italian courtrooms transforming the forgery and the perjury of public officers into acts of devotion and career opportunities. This is the Catholic culture and tradition, and the supposed divine rights they claim to perpetrate whatever crime and abuses in the name of their religion.

MP Sajid Javid and the holocaust

Dear MP Rt Hon Sajid Javid, my name is Luca, I am from Italy, and the best way to explain it to you is with quote from my book reading that «Only a fascist or an idiot would pretend the democratic values are Catholic legacy, without being able to tell any of these democratic values of Catholic origin».

This is why Mussolini made it religion of state, with secret Police, inquisition, and intellectual cleansing to persecute the oppositions as apostates of the faith, as it was a true religious war against heretics.

So, I am here to address your approximate and patchy education oratory-like, with a few questions for you and the best professors you can find at Oxford and Cambridge. If they feel they can help you ...

Dear Mr Rt Hon Javid, the 3 January 1925 Mussolini said that "the democratic values have to be found in the Catholic tradition", then he dismissed the parliament and persecuted the opposition as "apostates of the faith" and "enemy of the state".

What do you know about the intellectual cleansing of

Mussolini, what do you know about the fascist persecution of the democrats as apostates of the faith and enemy of the state? Do you believe it didn't happen because it is not in your Catholic schoolbooks?

Mussolini closed the parliament in 1925, 14 years before he enacted the racial laws in December 1938. Why don't you ask the senator for life Liliana Segre [W74], she was there she can tell you the holocaust for the democrats started 14 years before, and still today has not ended yet.

In fact after WWII the holocaust for the senator for life Liliana Segre was ended, but for the democrats, the excommunication of the democratic values was to renew the principles inspiring the fascist regime, as stated in the concordat, and still today the democratic values have to be found in the fascist regime of Mussolini.

How do you believe some people may have recommendations for diplomas and degrees they never had, while others cannot have confirmation of their true academic career from state university, become paperless, and coerced to be the impostor to cover up the administrative horrors of your holy democracy...

Concerning the excommunication of the democratic value, the reason is that the clergy never liked to be treated as commoners; they don't like to be subject to the common laws, and as consequence they had a campaign against communism, with the excommunication of the communists and those making common cause with them, demanding the secular value of justice not to be postponed into the afterlife. The matter in discussion were not the values of the communist party but the values of the common laws, and the secular values of justice to limit their pretence of absolute power and tyranny.

In fact the clergy loves to be above the laws and revels in this immunity, selling passports and recommendations for diplomas and degrees to their devoted customers, like indulgences for every abuse and every idiot they can exploit, knowing that the holy cross in the courtrooms will transform the perjury of public officers into acts of devotion and career opportunities, reinterpreting their good intentions.

Dear Mr Rt Hon Sajid Javid, only and idiot or a fascist would pretend the democratic values are Catholic legacy. Can you find a professor good enough to tell how the Catholic heresies have become Catholic legacy?

Why don't you ask the Italian ambassador about the assistance they provided, after they vanished my degree and made me look like an impostor, after they made me paperless, preventing me from the rights to hire a lawyer?

Why don't you ask the prime minister Tony Blair about this?

This letter is from his office when he was in office, and was dealing with Dr David Kelly, do you remember Dr David Kelly?

Why don't you ask the police about my report?

Why don't you ask the Italian Newspaper "la Repubblica"? They have a competition for the best professor in Italy, ask them to tell you one democratic value that has ever been a Catholic value in history.

Ask them how the democratic values have become Catholic legacy...

Ask them what system of value is transforming the perjury of public officers into acts of devotion and career opportunities. There are more than 9.000.000 backlogged legal cases, but the most significant cases are not in that list, because they pretend they never happened.

Concerning the democratic values and the holocaust, you should apologize to Mr Corbyn for your incompetence, but I understand you are functional, instrumental to cover up the racist tradition of your colleagues [A38][A42][W73].

MP Nusrat Ghani and the definition of islamophobia

Dear MP Rt Hon Ms Nusrat Ghani, could you tell one democratic value that has ever been a Catholic value in history? Can you see the average where it is, from where you are? You studied Politics, ask Oxford and Cambridge to help you to find an answer.

Concerning the definition of Islamophobia, I see you are

dedicated to alternative systems of values, and the democratic values are not of your concern, but eventually to prevaricate the rule of the law with some more alternative system of values based on high moral grounds.

From the moral point of view, you can pretend the democratic values are Catholic legacy, but recommend the necessity for a definition of Islamophobia.

Can you see how functional and instrumental and poorly educated you are.

Why don't you ask someone like you, someone spiritual, expert with multiple systems of values, honest in conscience and with faith in God like you ... Ask the bishop, how the democratic values have become Catholic legacy.

In the words of the ancient Romans, the pre-Christian, the people of faith and morality like the Christians, with their alternative systems of values, were just uncivilized barbarians. Sociopaths disrespecting the laws and other people rights.

How do you believe to be different, with your alternative system of value compared to the alternative system of value of someone else? And what about my true rights not to be the impostor, and the official system of values you don't care, bigot above the average with your multi system of values.

The democrats don't have the rights for a definition of democracy since the 3 January 1925, and you ask the definition of Islamophobia? Can you see you are instrumental to cover up the racist tradition of the most racist right wing? How do you pretend to have rights the native democrats cannot have, because of religious dogmas and mafia that are above the law? [A39]

MP Nadhim Zahawi

Dear MP Rt Hon Nadhim Zahawi, Education Secretary.

I feel confident you can provide an answer for my questions, will you?

MP Kwasi Kwarteng

Dear MP Rt Hon Kwasi Kwarteng Secretary of State for Business, Energy and Industrial Strategy.

I see you have been in all the places a student would dream of, from Eton to Harvard and Cambridge.

What a misery you cannot tell one democratic value that has ever been a Catholic value in history, despite of the level of tuition you have had.

Since you are a businessman, my question for you would be about Brexit.

I would like you to find one professor of yours from Harvard, to confirm that cutting 20% of the biggest spenders from the market could improve the economy.

The Opposition

Lets try with the opposition...

Dear MP Rt Hon Mr Keir Starmer, concerning your complaint to Boris Johnson for parroting fascists [A40], I have become paperless in your country Mr Starmer, and your public officers couldn't find anything better than imposing it on me, to prevent me from the rights to hire a lawyer and cover up the Italian Mafia.

So they made it, with recommendations, that I would be an impostor, a counterfeiter, and after the EU sent lawsuit to Italy and the prosecutor swept the case into the afterlife for justice, I have been tortured in your country Mr Starmer, to cover up your alternative system of values.

Since you claim you fought the fascists, ask Tony Blair what he would do concerning EU Citizens paperless like illegal immigrants, claiming their rights not to be the impostor just to cover up the good tradition of bribery and blackmail.

This is from the office of Tony Blair, after the EU sent lawsuit to Italy (pag 209).

This is from your PM Boris Johnson (pag 231)...

This is from the President of the Italian Republic (183).

And this is from secret police (pag 221), making territorial bans on YouTube videos repeating on the internet the lawsuit the courts of justice sweep into the afterlife [A28].

What kind of labour are you, a new labour Mr Starmer?

Also Mussolini was a new socialist like you. And the reformation of the churches was more about rights and freedoms than religion.

What about my rights not to be the impostor in order to cover up the Administrative horrors of this alternative system of values, the moral foundation of fascism that still today vanishes people into thin air, paperless like illegal immigrants within the EU border?

I have no rights to hire a lawyer because I have no passport, and the solicitor provided by the Citizen Advice Bureau told me to conform to the will of the Consul and be paperless...

What a bigotry Mr Starmer, what a bigotry!

And what a misery no professor, no member of parliament are able to tell one democratic value that has ever been a Catholic value in History, and still believe to be democrats and well educated [A41][W62].

But I am not the impostor, and making people paperless is criminal [A45]. So I report racist motivated hate crimes, violence and coercion against the victims, EU Citizens you have made paperless, victims refusing to be the scapegoat of your alternative system of values. I like to report the torture, the entrapment you force against the victims with coercion and violence to cover up the administrative horrors you organise, and the incitement to commit a crime as the only way out. This is slavery and torture as it was stated by barrister Paul Diamond, and what Tony Blair did was to cover the administrative horrors with more recommendations, violence and coercion. Ask the Italian Ambassador why they never complained about this situation of political and religious convenience?

With best regards
Luca

List of Images in Appendix

n.	description	date (y/m/d)
1	Passport details (photocopy)	2001/09/23
2	Questura (passport details)	2002/03/12
3	Letter from Italian President	2002/03/26
4	N.I. Police theft report	2002/11/19
5	Italian Consulate doc 1	2003/06/09
6	Italian Consulate doc 2	2003/07/24
7	Italian Consulate doc 3	2003/11/24
8	Verona University Graduation C.	1990
9	Solicitor H. Hyam doc 1	2004/03/10
10	Solicitor H. Hyam doc 2	2004/03/18
11(2)	NHS - C.H. Buller 2 pag	2004/05/15
13	EU – CHR	2004/06/16
14(2)	EU - OLAF 2 pag	2005/07/25
16	M.P. B. Rammell	2006/10/20
17	Solicitor A. Bateman doc1	2007/01/17
18	Solicitor A. Bateman doc2	2007/01/25
19	Solicitor D. Ake	2010/05/13
20(2)	NHS - N. Dissanayaka 2 pag	2010/05/21
22	Government censorship on YouTube	2013
23	Law Firm 3Volution	2016/07/19
24	EU - Ares 1	2018/06/08
25	EU - Ares 2	2019/11/26
26	EU - Ares 3	2019/12/10
27	Police Interview	2020/10/09
28	PM Boris Johnson, my letter	2020/11/16
29	PM Boris Johnson	2020/11/19
30	Police Online Scotland Yard	2020/12/04
31	DWP EUSS	2021/08/09
32(4)	EUSS Solicitor 4 pag	2021/09/02
36(2)	DWP EUSS my letter	2021/11/21
38	Barrister P. Diamond	2008/06/17
39	Holy Decree against Apostates (Italian) [W71]	1949/07/01
40	Holy Decree against Apostates (English)	1949/07/01

Index of names

Abdelrahman Maha....253
Adler Katya....249
Alexander Anne....253
Allesina Stefano....112, 114, 121
Aragona Pasquale....56
Benatti Luca....68, 78, 134, 180, 182, 186, 188, 190
Blair Tony....74, 135
Browne Jude....253
Buller C. H....84
Carnevali Corrado....34, 56, 76, 78, 85, 114, 154, 155, 204, 206
Colville Rupert....142
De Bernardi Bianca....78, 114, 154
Dissanayaka Newan....79, 81, 83, 85, 87, 90, 134, 136, 218
Flannigan Claire....86, 134
Frassoni Monica....88
Galli Paolo....56
Ghani Nusrat....260
Gherush92....165, 170
Hyams Henry....84
Javid Sajid....258
Juncker Jean-Claude....249, 250
Kyenge Cecile....17, 38, 69, 71, 74, 87, 110, 140, 142, 146, 149
Malmström Cecilia....142, 143
Massoni Serafino....169, 170
Matteotti Giacomo....16, 35, 37
Mogherini Federica....249
Pansa Alessandro....76
Papalia Guido....76, 114, 154
Rammell Bill....85, 206
Regeni Giulio....17, 38, 69, 70, 74, 87, 110
Renzi Matteo....250
Salvia Lorenzo....112
Segre Liliana....35, 37, 148, 149
Severino Paola....76
Starmer Keir....262
Tiberi Emilio....78, 114, 154
Tosti Luigi....37, 149
Vettori Andrea....88
Von der Leyen Ursula....251
Zimmermann Augusto....163, 164

Bibliography and further reading

Notes "A"

[A1] Rushdie, Salman. *The satanic verses.* New York, N.Y. : Viking, 1988

[A2] C.T. McIntire, *England against the Papacy*, Cambridge University Press, 2008

[A3] Michael A. Cremo and Richard L. Thompson, "*Forbidden Archeology: The Hidden History of the Human Race*", BBT Science Books, 1996

[A4] Bill Cote, *The mysterious origin of Man*, BC Video, 1996 Documentary. Host Charlton Heston, with Michael A. Cremo and Richard L. Thompson (see [A3]) http://www.imdb.com/title/tt0323339/

Quotes from Dr. Michael Cremo and Dr. Richard Thompson interview:
4.1 "Cover up as much as dug out" (Time 5:45)
4.2 "Knowledge filter, a fundamental feature of science. It is also a fundamental feature of human nature. People tends to filter out what don't make sense in term of their paradigm and their way of thinking." (Time 5:55)
4.3 "Is not a deliberate conspiracy, in the sense of some people getting together in a smoky room and saying we are going to deceive people" (Time 8:50)

[A5] "After Brexit: The battle for Europe", Katya Adler, "This world", 19 Feb 2017, BBC 2 http://www.bbc.co.uk/programmes/b08dx4lz

[A6] Augusto Zimmermann, Ph.D., LLB, LLM. "*A Law above the Law: Christian Roots of the English Common Law*", in "A Journal of the University of the Nations.", [S.l.], v. 1, n. 1, p. 85-98, November 2013
http://gc.uofn.edu/index.php/gc/article/view/24
Download: http://gc.uofn.edu/index.php/gc/article/view/24/71
(also in Glocal Conversations Vol 1(1) November 2013)

[A7] Gates B (2005) '*Faith schools and colleges of education since 1800*' in R Gardner, J Cairns and D Lawton (eds) (2005) Faith schools: consensus or conflict? Abingdon: RoutledgeFalmer 14-35

[A8] Gillard D., "The History of Education in England" http://www.educationengland.org.uk

8.1. Education Act 1944 http://www.educationengland.org.uk/history/chapter05.html

8.2. Education Act 1902 http://www.educationengland.org.uk/history/chapter04.html

[A9] "*Verona's answer to the brain drain: the case of Luca Benatti*", Domenico Pacitti, 17 Dec 2004, Just Response

http://www.humnet.unipi.it/~pacitti/Archive20049.htm

[A10] "It is an intolerable way to have to live", 7 July 2016, Youtube
https://youtu.be/dpFJ2kHr9kg (Meeting with Dissanaiaka)
https://youtu.be/FJi2CVqeaZY (Interview with "Aisling")

[A11] "*Measuring Nepotism through Shared Last Names: The Case of Italian Academia.*", Stefano Allesina , 3 August 2011, PLoS ONE 6(8): e21160. doi:10.1371/journal.pone.0021160 http://journals.plos.org/plosone/article?id=10.1371/journal.pone.0021160

[A12] "*Nepotism? Or Newmanism?*", John Kass, 4 August 2011, Chicago Tribune. http://articles.chicagotribune.com/2011-08-04/news/ct-met-kass-0804-20110804_1_nepotism-chicago-way-assistant-professor (Only Archive)

[A13] "*La formula che scova il nepotismo nelle università italiane*", Lorenzo Salvia, 4 August 2011, Corriere della Sera. http://www.corriere.it/cronache/11_agosto_04/formula-scova-nepotismo-universita-salvia_e49824c8-be59-11e0-aa43-16a8e9a1d0c7.shtml

(In English see [A11][A12])

[A14] FEMEN
http://femen.org/

[A15] "Cecile Kyenge", Lucia Annunziata, 5 May 2013, *"In ½ ora"*, RAI3, http://www.rai.tv/dl/RaiTV/programmi/media/ContentItem-f7830543-375f-4844-aa20-7bc48685e163.html

[A16] Cecile Kyenge, concerning Bananas

"Bananas thrown at Italy's first black minister Cecile Kyenge", Holly Yan, Lauren Russell and Boriana Milanova, 29 July 2013, CNN:
http://edition.cnn.com/2013/07/28/world/europe/italy-politics-racism

"Black Italian minister Kyenge suffers banana insult", 27 July 2013 , BBC
http://www.bbc.co.uk/news/world-europe-23480489

"Fury after banana thrown at Italy's first black minister Cecile Kyenge in latest racist attack", Rob Williams, 28 July 2013, The Independent
http://www.independent.co.uk/news/world/europe/fury-after-banana-thrown-at-italys-first-black-minister-cecile-kyenge-in-latest-racist-attack-8735282.html

"Bananas thrown at Italy's first black minister Cécile Kyenge", Hollie Clemence, 27 July 2013, The Times - Europe
http://www.thetimes.co.uk/tto/news/world/europe/article3827499.ece

[A17] "In my country", John Boorman, Columbia TriStar, 2004

https://www.imdb.com/title/tt0349260/
https://en.wikipedia.org/wiki/In_My_Country

[A18] "Giustizia, Severino in Parlamento: La lentezza ci costa un punto di Pil", 17 January 2012, la Repubblica.
http://www.repubblica.it/politica/2012/01/17/news/severino_giustizia-28281135/
(Minister for Justice, Paola Severino, reporting 9.000.000 cases backlog to the Govern)

[A19] From the Italian News, concerning "Faking Degrees"

"Giannino? Ma quale master se non ha nemmeno la laurea!", Vittorio Feltri - 19 Febbraio 2013, Panorama http://www.panorama.it/news/politica/oscar-giannino-master-chicago-dimissioni/

"Crosetto e la finta laurea: sono stato uno sciocco", Fabrizio Roncone, 3 marzo 2013, Corriere della Sera http://www.corriere.it/politica/13_marzo_03/crosetto-e-la-finta-laurea-sono-stato-uno-sciocco-fabrizio-roncone_5893b686-83c4-11e2-9582-bc92fde137a8.shtml

"Laurea falsa, lo sfogo di Pezzoni «Non fate come me, dite la verità»", Riccardo Nisoli, 24 Sept 2015, Corriere della Sera http://bergamo.corriere.it/notizie/cronaca/15_settembre_24/non-fate-mio-errore-bugie-hanno-gambe-corte-f42aa224-6285-11e5-95fc-7c4133631b69.shtml

"Insegnava all'Università ma non aveva mai preso la laurea", Giuliana Ubbiali, 13 ottobre 2012, Corriere della Sera http://bergamo.corriere.it/bergamo/notizie/cronaca/12_ottobre_13/professore-lauree-universita-inchiesta-truffa-faletti-bergamoministero-2112236670254.shtml

"Copia ma non perde il concorso", Gian Antonio Stella - 1 Feb 2016, Corriere della Sera http://www.corriere.it/cronache/16_febbraio_01/testi-copiati-esame-prof-84e09d94-c8b3-11e5-8532-9fbac1d67c73.shtml

[A20] "Francesco: La fine di un papa e' la tomba", 29 Giugno 2014, la Repubblica (The end of a Pope is the Tomb), http://www.repubblica.it/esteri/2014/06/29/news/francesco_la_fine_di_un_papa_la_tomba-90281165/

[A21] Alejandro Amenábar, 'Agora'. Mod Producciones et al., 2009.
http://www.imdb.com/title/tt1186830/

[A22] Dante Alighieri and Gherush92

"Divine Comedy is 'offensive and discriminatory', says Italian NGO", Alison Flood, 14 March 2012, The Guardian
http://www.theguardian.com/books/2012/mar/14/the-divine-comedy-offensive-discriminatory

"Dante's Divine Comedy 'offensive and should be banned'", Nick Squires, 13 Mar 2012, The Telegraph
http://www.telegraph.co.uk/culture/culturenews/9140869/Dantes-Divine-Comedy-offensive-and-should-be-banned.html

"Dante's Divine Comedy too hot for school use", Michael Day, 14 March 2012, The Independent
http://www.independent.co.uk/news/world/europe/dantes-divine-comedy-too-hot-for-school-use-7565667.html

"Via la Divina Commedia dalle Scuole (ovvero razzismo istituzionale mascherato da arte)", 6 Jan 2012, Gherush92, gherush92.com
http://www.gherush92.com/news_it.asp?tipo=A&id=2985

"Una risposta ai lettori della Divina Commedia", 29 Jan 2012, Gherush92, gherush92.com
http://www.gherush92.com/news_it.asp?tipo=A&id=2986

[A23] The Doors – "When The Music's Over", in "Strange days", Analogue Productions, 1967

[A24] Woywod Stanislaus, 1918, "*The new canon law: a commentary and summary of the new code of canon law*", New York, N.Y. : J.F. Wagner

TITLE XII, "*Catholic Schools*" (PP. 283-284)
https://openlibrary.org/books/OL7132132M/The_new_canon_law
https://archive.org/details/newcanonlaw00woywuoft

Latin original Text
Pietro Card. Gasparri, "*CODEX IURIS CANONICI*", Typis polyglottis Vaticanis, Romae, 1917
http://www.internetsv.info/Text/CIC1917.pdf

[A25] "*Dante e la poesia della lode*", Corso di Letteratura Italiana, Lezione 11, Prof. Marco Santagata, UniNettuno http://www.uninettunouniversity.net/it/cyberspaziomateria.aspx?faculty=°ree=151&planid=213&courseid=4067 http://www.consorzionettuno.it/it/cyberspaziomateria.aspx?faculty=°ree=12&planid=24&courseid=522&lf=it

[A26] "*Ancient Babylonian astronomers calculated Jupiter's position from the area under a time-velocity graph*", Mathieu Ossendrijver, Science, 29 Jan 2016: Vol. 351, Issue 6272, pp. 482-484
http://science.sciencemag.org/content/351/6272/482

"Signs of Modern Astronomy Seen in Ancient Babylon", Kenneth Chang, 28 Jan 2016, New York Times
http://www.nytimes.com/2016/01/29/science/babylonians-clay-tablets-geometry-astronomy-jupiter.html?_r=0

[A27] Armoire of Shame (Armadio della Vergogna).
From Italian news. In English please see [W11]
"*Stragi nazifasciste: online i documenti dell'Armadio della Vergogna",* Alberto Custodero, la Repubblica, 16 Feb 2016
http://www.repubblica.it/politica/2016/02/16/news/stragi_nazifasciste_online_archivio_vergogna_-133585481/

"*Stragi nazifasciste, «l'Armadio della vergogna» adesso consultabile online",* Pier Vittorio Buffa, L'Espresso , 13 Feb 2016
http://espresso.repubblica.it/attualita/2016/02/15/news/stragi-nazifasciste-l-armadio-della-vergogna-adesso-consultabile-online-1.250535

"*«L'armadio della vergogna»: ante chiuse verso la parete per nascondere i dossier",* Alessandro Fulloni, 17 Feb 2016, Corriere Della Sera
http://www.corriere.it/cronache/cards/armadio-vergogna-ante-chiuse-la-parete-nascondere-dossier/dalla-strage-cefalonia-all-uccisione-buozzi_principale.shtml

[A28] "Anonymous e non, al capo della Polizia (lettera aperta)", Youtube, 7th June 2013; also pag 221
("Not Anonymous only. Open letter to the head Police")
https://www.youtube.com/watch?v=HZVlX85qj5o

[A29] From Italian news concerning Abortion
"Aborto, fino a 800 km per un ospedale. Prima le donne o gli obiettori?", Riccardo Iacona, Elena Stramentinoli, 16 Jan 2016, Corriere della Sera
http://27esimaora.corriere.it/articolo/aborto-fino-a-800-km-per-un-ospedale-prima-le-donne-o-gli-obiettori/

"Aborto, diritto negato", sempre più medici obiettori: appello alla Regione", Antonello Cassano, 30 giugno 2014, La Repubblica,
http://bari.repubblica.it/cronaca/2014/06/30/news/legge_194-90232863/

[A30] "Giulio Regeni, dal liceo al Collegio del New Mexico", 1 Feb 2016, Il Piccolo
http://ilpiccolo.gelocal.it/trieste/cronaca/2016/02/01/news/giulio-regeni-dal-liceo-al-collegio-del-new-mexico-1.12878429

"Chi era Giulio Regeni, morto al Cairo, che scriveva articoli di denuncia", 4 Feb 2016, Panorama
http://www.panorama.it/news/cronaca/serio-e-appassionato-chi-era-giulio-regeni-lo-studente-morto-al-cairo/

"Regeni: Renzi, è il momento che inglesi dicano verità" Ansa 12 June 2020
https://www.ansa.it/sito/notizie/topnews/2020/06/12/regeni-renzi-e-il-momento-che-inglesi-dicano-verita_bd115e8b-921e-4d7b-a950-5dac80cd38d8.html

"Caso Regeni, Renzi: Adesso gli inglesi dicano la verità" la Repubblica 12 June 2020
https://video.repubblica.it/dossier/caso-regeni/caso-regeni-renzi-adesso-gli-inglesi-dicano-la-verita/362124/362678

English News

"Renzi blasts Cambridge University for failing to co-operate with investigation into murdered Italian student", Andrea Vogt, The Telegraph 01 Ago 2016
https://www.telegraph.co.uk/news/2016/08/01/renzi-blasts-cambridge-university-for-failing-to-co-operate-with/

... more ...

"Cambridge 'is blocking Guilio Regeni murder inquiry' says Matteo Renzi", Philip Willan, The Sunday Times 02 Nov 2017 https://www.thetimes.co.uk/article/cambridge-is-blocking-guilio-regeni-murder-inquiry-says-matteo-renzi-sqr8fglf9

"Giulio Regeni: hopes rest on Italian inquiry on fourth anniversary of death", R. Michaelson L. Tondo, The Guardian 03 Feb 2020
https://www.theguardian.com/world/2020/feb/03/giulio-regeni-hopes-rest-on-italian-inquiry-on-fourth-anniversary-of-death

"Family of Giulio Regeni 'betrayed' by Italian PM over arms sale to Egypt", R. Michaelson L. Tondo, The Guardian 16 June 2020
https://www.theguardian.com/world/2020/jun/16/family-giulio-regeni-betrayed-italian-pm-arms-sale-egypt

[A31] Joseph Rossi, "National Consciousness in Italian Literature", The Bulletin of the Rocky Mountain Modern Language Association, Vol. 27, No. 3 (Sep., 1973), pp. 159-166, Rocky Mountain Modern Language Association. http://www.jstor.org/stable/1346655

[A32] "Doctors claim cover-up over death of weapons expert Dr David Kelly", Sam Lister, 17th July 2013, Belfast Telegraph,

https://www.belfasttelegraph.co.uk/news/uk/doctors-claim-coverup-over-death-of-weapons-expert-dr-david-kelly-29426678.html

[A33] Judge Luigi Tosti has been disbar as Judge and Lawyer for suggesting to remove the crucifix from the Courts of Justice. A few links to introduce in Italian and English. https://www.repubblica.it/2007/05/sezioni/cronaca/crocifisso-appello/crocifisso-appello/crocifisso-appello.html https://www.uaar.it/uaar/campagne/scrocifiggiamo/35.html/

Links in English
https://humanists.international/2006/02/call-acquittal-judge-tosti/
http://news.bbc.co.uk/1/hi/world/europe/4676300.stm

[A34] 3 January 1925 - Mussolini speech.
See also [W73]
https://www.britannica.com/event/Matteotti-Crisis
[A35] Lateran Treaty 1929 - Mussolini re-establish Vatican City
https://www.britannica.com/biography/Pius-XI
See also W3

[A36] Giulio Regeni PhD at Cambridge. Department of Politics
Professor dr Maha Abdelrahman, Department of Politics and International Studies. Tutor of Giulio Regeni.
https://www.polis.cam.ac.uk/Staff_and_Students/dr-maha-abdelrahman

Director Anne Alexander, ethics of big data, activist media in the Middle East and the political economy of the Internet. Academic Referee for Giulio Regeni.
https://www.crassh.cam.ac.uk/about/people/anne-alexander/

Head of Department Jude Browne,
https://www.polis.cam.ac.uk/Staff_and_Students/head-of-department
https://www.polis.cam.ac.uk/

[A37] More news concerning the death of Giulio Regeni

"A murdered Cambridge student, and an international blame game. Why is there still no truth for Giulio Regeni?" by Patrick Wernham, 29 Apr 2018, Varsity (the independent student newspaper for the University of Cambridge).
https://www.varsity.co.uk/news/15229

"Regeni, la sua docente arringava la folla contro Al Sisi" - Video, 25 Feb 2016, Panorama
https://www.panorama.it/news/omicidio-regeni-tutor-contro-al-sisi

"Regeni, università di Cambridge: 'Contro la Abdelrahman campagna vergognosa'", 17 Jan 2018, Il Fatto Quotidiano.
https://www.ilfattoquotidiano.it/2018/01/17/regeni-universita-di-cambridge-contro-la-abdelrahman-campagna-vergognosa/4098657/

... more ...

"Giulio Regeni, 250 accademici firmano una lettera di supporto alla sua tutor: 'L'articolo di Repubblica è fuorviante', 28 Novembre 2017, Il Fatto Quotidiano.
https://www.ilfattoquotidiano.it/2017/11/28/giulio-regeni-250-accademici-firmano-una-lettera-di-supporto-alla-sua-tutor-larticolo-di-repubblica-e-fuorviante/4005965/

"Chi era Giulio Regeni, il ricercatore ucciso in Egitto nel 2016" 18 lug 2018, Sky tg24
https://tg24.sky.it/mondo/2018/07/18/giulio-regeni-chi-era

[A38] Rt Hon MP Sajid Javid and the Holocaust
"Sajid Javid backtracks on Jeremy Corbyn 'Holocaust denier' tweet following backlash", 21 July 2018, Independent.
https://www.independent.co.uk/news/uk/politics/sajid-javid-jeremy-corbyn-holocaust-denier-twitter-backlash-a8457706.html

"Sajid Javid backtracks after Jeremy Corbyn threatens legal action for linking him with Holocaust denial", 21 July 2018, Independent.
https://www.dailymail.co.uk/news/article-5978179/Sajid-Javid-backtracks-Corbyn-threatens-legal-action-linking-Holocaust-denial.html

"UK Home Secretary implies Jeremy Corbyn promotes holocaust denial", 19 July 2018, The National
https://www.thenational.scot/news/16364917.uk-home-secretary-implies-jeremy-corbyn-promotes-holocaust-denial/

[A39] Rt Hon MP Nusrat Ghani, the definition of Islamophobia
"Tory MP says she was sacked as minister because her Muslim faith 'made colleagues uncomfortable'", 23 January 2022, Independent
https://www.independent.co.uk/news/uk/politics/nusrat-ghani-tory-mp-muslim-b1998749.html

"Nusrat Ghani: PM urged to launch inquiry as MP says government failed to take Islamophobia complaints 'seriously'", 23 January 2022, Independent.
https://www.independent.co.uk/news/uk/politics/nusrat-ghani-muslim-mp-boris-johnson-b1998889.html
… more …

Boris Johnson launches inquiry into Nusrat Ghani's claim she was sacked because of her 'Muslimness', 24 January 2022, Independent.
https://www.independent.co.uk/news/uk/politics/boris-johnson-nusrat-ghani-inquiry-b1999207.html

"Nusrat Ghani row: Imam appointed to define Islamophobia has had 'no meaningful engagement' from ministers", 24 January 2022, Independent.
https://www.independent.co.uk/news/uk/politics/tory-islamophobia-nusrat-ghani-definition-b1999584.html

[A40] MP Starmer and PM Boris Johnson parroting fascists

"Boris Johnson refuses to retract Savile smear after Starmer accuses him of 'parroting fascists'", 2 Feb 2022, Independent
https://www.independent.co.uk/news/uk/politics/keir-starmer-boris-johnson-savile-pmqs-b2005931.html

"Keir Starmer accuses Boris Johnson of 'parroting conspiracy theories'", 2 Feb 2022, The Guardian
https://www.theguardian.com/politics/2022/feb/02/boris-johnson-nothing-apologise-jimmy-savile-comments-keir-starmer-gove

"Boris Johnson should sack 'woke crowd' and 'neo-socialists' at No 10, says Lord Frost", 27 Jan 2022, Independent
https://www.independent.co.uk/news/uk/politics/boris-johnson-sack-woke-frost-b2002257.html

"Elections watchdog tells government to drop power-grab with 'no precedent' in western democracies", Rob Merrick, 21 Feb 2022, Independent
https://www.independent.co.uk/news/uk/politics/electoral-commission-elections-bill-gove-b2019611.html

"UK election watchdog warns new law could impact its independence", William James, Elizabeth Piper, 21 Feb 2022, Reuters
https://www.reuters.com/world/uk/uk-election-watchdog-warns-new-law-could-impacts-it-independence-2022-02-21/

[A41] Human Rights Act 1998, interview with Tony Blair

"Reflecting On The Human Rights Act 1998 And 'Bringing Rights Home'", 9 November 2018
https://eachother.org.uk/on-the-human-rights-act-1998-and-bringing-rights-home/
See also [W62]

"Tony Blair's approach to EU helped cause Brexit, says Jean-Claude Juncker", Jon Stone, 4 November 2019, Independent
https://www.independent.co.uk/news/uk/politics/brexit-tony-blair-juncker-interview-referendum-remain-a9184781.html

[A42] Antisemitism from the fascist point of view

"We can't fight antisemitism in Britain until we truly understand what we're dealing with", David Feldman, 18 Feb 2022, The Guardian
https://www.theguardian.com/commentisfree/2022/feb/18/antisemitism-britain-anti-jewish-hate-incidents

[A43] Racism: no one is safe

"UK police chiefs consider public admission of institutional racism", Vikram Dodd, 12 Dec 2021, The Guardian
https://www.theguardian.com/uk-news/2021/dec/12/uk-police-leaders-debate-public-admission-institutional-racism

"If the police accept the idea of structural racism, no one is safe", Nick Timothy, 23 May 2021, The Telegraph
https://www.telegraph.co.uk/news/2021/05/23/police-accept-idea-ofstructural-racism-no-one-safe/

[A44] Corruption, legal study

"Corruption as a Violation of International Human Rights", Anne Peters, European Journal of International Law, Volume 29, Issue 4, November 2018, Pages 1251–1287
https://doi.org/10.1093/ejil/chy070
https://academic.oup.com/ejil/article/29/4/1251/5320164#

[A45] The criminal justice system is in tatters

"The criminal justice system is in tatters – and it will lead to the collapse of the rule of law unless something is done", Christina Blacklaws, 15 June 2019, Independent
https://www.independent.co.uk/voices/legal-aid-cuts-criminal-justice-system-rule-of-law-collapse-austerity-a8959886.html

"Former Met police chief calls for focus on 'very tattered' justice system", Owen Bowcott, 22 Nov 2019, The Guardian
https://www.theguardian.com/uk-news/2019/nov/22/former-met-police-chief-ian-blair-calls-for-focus-on-very-tattered-justice-system

[A46] The United World College (UWC)
The United World College (UWC) is a chain of schools and colleges around the world, teaching that the democratic values are catholic legacy. It was the high school of Giulio Regeni.
www.uwcad.it
www.uwc.org

Notes “B”

[B1] Matthew, 16:17-19 «And Jesus said to Simon, “You are Peter, and upon this rock I will build my Church.»

[B2] Genesis, 1:27 «God made man at his own image»

[B3] Acts, 5:29 «But Peter and the apostles answered, “We must obey God rather than men!”»

[B4] Mark, 12:17 «Then Jesus said to them, “Give back to Caesar what is Caesar’s and to God what is God’s.»

[B5] Luke, 20:25 «So Jesus told them, "Give to Caesar what is Caesar's, and to God what is God's."»

[B6] Matthew, 22:21 «"Caesar's," they answered. So Jesus told them, "Give to Caesar what is Caesar's, and to God what is God's."»

Notes "W"

[W1] Bible Text (See also [W7], [W37])
https://en.wikipedia.org/wiki/Modern_English_Bible_translations
New Testament apocrypha
https://en.wikipedia.org/wiki/New_Testament_apocrypha
- Development of the New Testament canon
https://en.wikipedia.org/wiki/Development_of_the_New_Testament_canon
[W2] Papal Infallibility (First Vatican Council, 1869-70)
https://en.wikipedia.org/wiki/Papal_infallibility
[W3] Lateran Treaty and the Concordat
In 1929 Mussolini re-establish Vatican City, and endorsed the system of values of the Church against the system of values of the State. He also imposed the Catholic Religion as the only religion of State, and introduced secret police to enforce the intellectual cleansing he organised against the opposition. See also [A34][A35][W73]
https://en.wikipedia.org/wiki/Lateran_Treaty
https://en.wikipedia.org/wiki/Concordat
[W4] Ptolemy
https://en.wikipedia.org/wiki/Ptolemy
[W5] Eusebius (260-340 AD)
https://en.wikipedia.org/wiki/Eusebius

[W6] 50 Bibles of Constantine (331 AD) (Eusebius)
https://en.wikipedia.org/wiki/Fifty_Bibles_of_Constantine
[W7] Bible (The Books of)
https://en.wikipedia.org/wiki/Bible;
https://en.wikipedia.org/wiki/Development_of_the_Christian_biblical_canon
[W8] Canon Law
https://en.wikipedia.org/wiki/Canon_law
https://en.wikipedia.org/wiki/Canon_law_(Catholic_Church)
[W9] Papal Conclave
https://en.wikipedia.org/wiki/Papal_conclave,_January_1276
https://en.wikipedia.org/wiki/Papal_conclave

[W10] Pontifical Yearbook (Annuario Pontificio)
https://en.wikipedia.org/wiki/List_of_popes
https://en.wikipedia.org/wiki/Annuario_Pontificio

[W11] Armoire of Shame (Armadio della vergogna)
https://en.wikipedia.org/wiki/Armadio_della_vergogna
[W12] Gnostic Gospels
https://en.wikipedia.org/wiki/Gnostic_Gospels
[W13] Lost Gospels
https://en.wikipedia.org/wiki/List_of_Gospels
[W14] Gospel of Peter
https://en.wikipedia.org/wiki/Gospel_of_Peter
[W15] Saint Peter
https://en.wikipedia.org/wiki/Saint_Peter
[W16] Docetism
https://en.wikipedia.org/wiki/Docetism
[W17] Forbidden Archeology
https://en.wikipedia.org/wiki/Forbidden_Archeology
[W18] Galileo: Dialogue concerning the two chief world systems
https://en.wikipedia.org/wiki/Dialogue_Concerning_the_Two_Chief_World_Systems
https://it.wikipedia.org/wiki/Dialogo_sopra_i_due_massimi_sistemi_del_mondo
[W19] Sistine Chapel (Michelangelo, Braghettone, and Cardinal Carafa)
https://en.wikipedia.org/wiki/Sistine_Chapel

[W20] Daniele da Volterra, alias Braghettone
https://en.wikipedia.org/wiki/Daniele_da_Volterra
[W21] Fig Leaf Movement
https://en.wikipedia.org/wiki/Fig_leaf
[W22] The Ninety-Five Theses of Martin Luther against indulgences
https://en.wikipedia.org/wiki/The_Ninety-Five_Theses
[W23] Indulgence
https://en.wikipedia.org/wiki/Indulgence
[W24] Simony
https://en.wikipedia.org/wiki/Simony
[W25] Congress of Vienna (1814-15)
https://en.wikipedia.org/wiki/Congress_of_Vienna
[W26] Klemens von Metternich: «Italy is a geographic expression»
https://en.wikipedia.org/wiki/Italian_unification#cite_note-10
https://en.wikipedia.org/wiki/Klemens_von_Metternich
[W27] Origin of the name “Italy”
https://en.wikipedia.org/wiki/Name_of_Italy

[W28] Galileo Galilei (1564 – 1642)
https://en.wikipedia.org/wiki/Galileo_Galilei
[W29] Eratosthenes (276 - 194 BC)
https://en.wikipedia.org/wiki/Eratosthenes

[W30] Aristarchus of Samos (310 BC – 230 BC)
https://en.wikipedia.org/wiki/Aristarchus_of_Samos
[W31] Giordano Bruno (1548 – 17 February 1600)
https://en.wikipedia.org/wiki/Giordano_Bruno
[W32] Council of Trent (1545 - 1563)
https://en.wikipedia.org/wiki/Council_of_Trent
[W33] Hypatia (Born 350~370 AD, died 415 AD)
https://en.wikipedia.org/wiki/Hypatia
[W34] Declaration of the Rights of Man (1789)
https://en.wikipedia.org/wiki/Declaration_of_the_Rights_of_Man_and_of_the_Citizen

[W35] Henry VIII (1491 – 1547)
https://en.wikipedia.org/wiki/Henry_VIII_of_England
[W36] Act of Supremacy (1534 AD)
https://en.wikipedia.org/wiki/Acts_of_Supremacy
[W37] List of Christian heresies (also [W40])
https://en.wikipedia.org/wiki/List_of_Christian_heresies
[W38] François-Marie Arouet alias "Voltaire" (1694 –1778 AD)
https://en.wikipedia.org/wiki/Voltaire
[W39] First Council of Nicaea (325 AD)
https://en.wikipedia.org/wiki/First_Council_of_Nicaea

[W40] Heresy
https://en.wikipedia.org/wiki/Heresy
[W41] Niccolò Machiavelli (1469 –1527 AD)
https://en.wikipedia.org/wiki/Niccolò_Machiavelli
[W42] Absolute Power of the Church
The leader of the Catholic Church is a deity with the rights of a deity. Concerning the infallibility of the Pope see [W2]
https://en.wikipedia.org/wiki/Temporal_power_of_the_Holy_See
https://en.wikipedia.org/wiki/Papal_supremacy
[W43] Gnosticism
https://en.wikipedia.org/wiki/Gnosticism
[W44] Catharism
https://en.wikipedia.org/wiki/Catharism

[W45] Waldensians
https://en.wikipedia.org/wiki/Waldensians
[W46] Map of Piri Reis
https://en.wikipedia.org/wiki/Piri_Reis_map
[W47] Women in the French Revolution
https://en.wikipedia.org/wiki/Women_in_the_French_Revolution
[W48] Cecile Kyenge
I wonder why the English and Italian pages are so different. The English page doesn't even mention the Interview [A15]
https://en.wikipedia.org/wiki/Cécile_Kyenge
https://it.wikipedia.org/wiki/Cécile_Kyenge
[W49] Magdalene Asylum, alias, the Magdalene laundries
https://en.wikipedia.org/wiki/Magdalene_asylum
https://en.wikipedia.org/wiki/Magdalene_laundries_in_Ireland
"The Magdalene Sisters" (2002) by Peter Mullan.
https://en.wikipedia.org/wiki/The_Magdalene_Sisters

[W50] South Africa – Truth and Reconciliation Commission
https://en.wikipedia.org/wiki/Truth_and_Reconciliation_Commission_(South_Africa)
[W51] Canon Law 1374 (1917)
https://en.wikipedia.org/wiki/1917_Code_of_Canon_Law
See also [A24]
[W52] Racial Laws of Mussolini (1938)
https://en.wikipedia.org/wiki/Manifesto_of_Race
https://en.wikipedia.org/wiki/Italian_Racial_Laws
[W53] Operation Gladio
https://en.wikipedia.org/wiki/Operation_Gladio
[W54] Mussolini, 25 ottobre 1932, Milano "L'Europa sarà fascista o fascistizzata!" (Europe will be fascist, or fascist like)
https://it.wikipedia.org/wiki/Cronologia_dell'Italia_fascista

[W55] David Kelly (weapons expert)
https://en.wikipedia.org/wiki/David_Kelly_(weapons_expert)
[W56] Natural Law (Diritto Naturale – Giusnaturalismo)
https://en.wikipedia.org/wiki/Natural_law
[W57] Positive Law (Diritto Positivo)
https://en.wikipedia.org/wiki/Positive_law

[W58] "Questione della lingua", (Matters of the language)
https://it.wikipedia.org/wiki/Questione_della_lingua

Bembo: Prose della volgar lingua
https://it.wikipedia.org/wiki/Prose_nelle_quali_si_ragiona_della_volgar_lingua
Dante: De Vulgari Eloquentia
https://en.wikipedia.org/wiki/De_vulgari_eloquentia
[W59] The legend of the "Capitoline Wolf"
https://en.wikipedia.org/wiki/Capitoline_Wolf

[W60] Primacy of the Bishop of Rome
https://en.wikipedia.org/wiki/Primacy_of_the_Bishop_of_Rome
W61] Astronomy in the medieval Islamic world
https://en.wikipedia.org/wiki/Astronomy_in_the_medieval_Islamic_world
[W62] Tony Blair and the New Labour
https://en.wikipedia.org/wiki/New_Labour
See also [A41]
[W63] Nuremberg trials
https://en.wikipedia.org/wiki/Nuremberg_trials
[W64] Giulio Regeni
https://en.wikipedia.org/wiki/Murder_of_Giulio_Regeni
[W65] Render unto Caesar
https://en.wikipedia.org/wiki/Render_unto_Caesar

[W66] Donations of Constantine and Pipin
https://en.wikipedia.org/wiki/Donation_of_Constantine
https://en.wikipedia.org/wiki/Donation_of_Pepin
[W67] President of the EU Commission Mr Jean-Claude Juncker
https://en.wikipedia.org/wiki/Jean-Claude_Juncker
[W68] Tony Blair
https://en.wikipedia.org/wiki/Tony_Blair
[W69] Iraq Inquiry
https://en.wikipedia.org/wiki/Iraq_Inquiry

[W70] Hutton Inquiry
https://en.wikipedia.org/wiki/Hutton_Inquiry
(See also [A32], [W55], [W69])

[W71] Vatican, The Decree against Communism, 1 July 1949

After WWII and the Nuremberg Trials, this Decree resumes and re-establishes the Cultural principles of the Concordat at the origin of the Racial Laws of Mussolini, persecuting the Democrats as Apostates of the Faith.

https://it.wikipedia.org/wiki/Scomunica_ai_comunisti
https://en.wikipedia.org/wiki/Decree_against_Communism

From the Italian page of Wikipedia you can see a photograph of the original leaflets that were on display and distributed at the entrance of the Churches at the time, just after the Nuremberg Trials.

[W72] Apostates
The Freedom of Choice and the Secular Values of Justice are Catholic Heresies, but during the time the Heretics supporting such ideas have had their nickname changed, from Heretics to Anarchists and Apostates

Ita https://it.wikipedia.org/wiki/Apostasia
Eng https://en.wikipedia.org/wiki/Apostasy

[W73] Rt Hon MP Sajid Javid and the Holocaust
https://en.wikipedia.org/wiki/Sajid_Javid
https://en.wikipedia.org/wiki/Sajid_Javid#Campaign_against_anti-Semitism

[W74] Holocaust survivor, Senator for life Liliana Segre
https://en.wikipedia.org/wiki/Liliana_Segre

www.ingramcontent.com/pod-product-compliance
Lightning Source LLC
Chambersburg PA
CBHW030004290326
41934CB00005B/215

* 9 7 8 0 9 9 3 5 4 1 7 4 2 *